MW00849862

THE SEVEN MOUNTAIN
RENAISSANCE

Vision and Strategy through 2050

JOHNNY ENLOW

WHITAKER
HOUSE

Unless otherwise indicated, all Scripture quotations are taken from the *New King James Version*, © 1979, 1980, 1982 by Thomas Nelson, Inc. Used by permission. All rights reserved. Scripture quotations marked (KJV) are taken from the King James Version of the Holy Bible. Scripture quotations marked (NIV) are taken from the *Holy Bible, New International Version*®, NIV®, © 1973, 1978, 1984 by the International Bible Society. Used by permission of Zondervan. All rights reserved. Scripture quotations marked (HCSB) are taken from the *Holman Christian Standard Bible*®, © 1999, 2000, 2002, 2003 by Holman Bible Publishers. Used by permission.

Boldface type in the Scripture quotations indicates the author's emphasis.

THE SEVEN MOUNTAIN RENAISSANCE:
Vision and Strategy Through 2050

Johnny Enlow
www.johnnyandelizabeth.com

ISBN: 978-1-62911-556-6
eBook ISBN: 978-1-62911-578-8
Printed in the United States of America
© 2015 by Johnny Enlow

Whitaker House
1030 Hunt Valley Circle
New Kensington, PA 15068
www.whitakerhouse.com

No part of this book may be reproduced or transmitted in any form or by any means, electronic or mechanical—including photocopying, recording, or by any information storage and retrieval system—without permission in writing from the publisher. Please direct your inquiries to permissionseditor@whitakerhouse.com.

1 2 3 4 5 6 7 8 9 10 11 ⒲ 22 21 20 19 18 17 16 15

CONTENTS

ACKNOWLEDGMENTS

I would like to acknowledge the invaluable support and input of my amazing wife, Elizabeth. She is my best friend, confidante, and ministry partner and carried a vital role in every stage of this book coming to print. From assuring I had uninterrupted time for research and writing to her first edit of the manuscript, her assistance was constant and thorough from start to finish. We have become so one in all we do that every book project is clearly coauthored by her, as well, whether her name is on it or not.

Thank you to the following, who each made valuable contributions to this book project: my son-in-law, Ross Lapin, for your first read-through and encouraging perspective; Amanda Hastings, for your faithful assistance; Henry Hastings, for your editorial input; the Whitaker House team—Christine Whitaker, Don Milam, and Lois Puglisi for your superb editing; my daughter Promise Lapin, for the cover design; and Shan Wallace, for your graphic design expertise.

Finally, I would like to acknowledge the wonderful help of the Holy Spirit at every stage of this book—from initial inspiration and revelation to the right connections and input. Truly, without Him, I can do nothing; but with Him, all things are possible. May a multitude of hearts be stirred to believe in Him in an upgraded manner for all that He is about to do in this unprecedented age of the kingdom of God. He will be the Great Orchestrator of this Era of Renaissance we have just stepped into. May we eagerly advance with all that He releases.

—Johnny Enlow

FOREWORD

I love to hear my husband preach. I guess it's not only because I'm his wife but also because of his unique perspective on just about everything. Even when I don't agree with him, I appreciate the way he makes me think and understand the origins of my thinking—which I've learned are just as important as the conclusions I reach. Ever since Johnny began his research on the subject of societal reformation for this book, he and I have had many hours and even days of conversations about the way our generation of Christians tends to think and where that way of thinking has come from—the motivation behind our conclusions. As Johnny will clearly communicate in *The Seven*

Mountain Renaissance, he found a strong correlation between the prevailing mind-sets of the Christian founding fathers of America and the current beliefs that many present-day Christians hold concerning the latest hot topics and issues of our time. I've learned more from these conversations and the pages of this book than I have from a lifetime of hearing and reading the words of other Christian and secular speakers, authors, and political analysts.

What Are Our Options?

Regarding the behavior of the world and how "bad" it's getting, it seems we've basically been offered two options by our Christian leaders: (1) enter the fight to go back to our supposed godly roots and hope there's still a chance for that to happen or (2) keep to ourselves, hunker down when necessary, and hope "they" don't steal too many of our rights. Could there be another option? You're about to hear Johnny answer that question with a resounding "Yes!" Be prepared to hear a perspective that's truly fresh and authentically hopeful, one that will make you exclaim, "I never knew that!" Personally, after being exposed to a new way of relating to God's heart for the issues of our day, I'm more convinced than ever that it's not time to go back to anything, nor is it time to roll over and disengage from society. I believe God has given us permission to love more radically and extravagantly than we've previously understood, as well as to position ourselves to demonstrate the goodness of our God for many generations to come. Just imagine how we could advance the kingdom of God (God's better way of doing everything) if we weren't afraid of misrepresenting Him by appearing to condone sin? What if we approached others as God approaches us, with no agenda but love—and without a need to "seal the deal" with an immediate conversion. What if we simplified everything to love and allowed the Holy Spirit to do what He has done for each of us—draw us closer with His kindness and grow us up into what life in and with Him looks like when we experience our Father's unconditional love?

Recently, I heard Johnny say something so profound that it changed me. Before I tell you what he said, let me explain an interesting dynamic between us. While Johnny has tended to be more innately in touch with the big picture and focused on discovering what God's kingdom looks like on earth, I've had a tendency to be more in touch with how I *feel* about something (or, actually, everything). I'd say I've been more of a student of God's *heart* toward us, individually and as a society. This has made the topic of societal reformation super interesting in our house because we come at it from both sides—externally, according to various spiritual, cultural, and historical markers in cultures across time; and internally, according to the communication between God's Spirit and the hearts of His children. Of course, both perspectives are important and relevant, and both easily coalesce into a more accurate picture of who God is and what He's all about.

One thing Johnny and I have become absolutely amazed by is the way God relates to the hearts of each one of us with such intimacy and intentionality, while also caring for the collective hearts of entire cities and nations. Somehow, in His deity, He is able to fully engage with us on both levels. So, how does this relate to reformation and simultaneously bringing God's solutions to our broken lives and our broken society? We find the answer by going back to what Johnny said that so inspired me: "Religious people were always trying to get Jesus to reveal His official stance on sin, while Jesus was always focused on revealing our Father's stance, or position, on our hearts."

Isn't that scenario still true today? Aren't we still stuck in the complicated web of religion while people in the world all around us desperately need to know what God thinks about them—how He truly cares for their hearts? What would it mean to you—and to society—if every single one of us knew that God cares about our hearts, about each one of us as individuals? What if you knew that you matter, I mean, *really matter*, to God? What if you were actually more important than you'd ever hoped or dared to believe you were? How would the world be different if every single human were fully convinced of their personal value and worth, as well as the worth of others? What if we believed and then lived from the belief that it wasn't Jesus alone who gave us our worth to God but that the Father sent Jesus as proof of our constant worth to Him? Wouldn't that translate into reformation on every level, personally and culturally? If we understood that the reason He is concerned about people's behavior and about sin is that He cares so much about us, wouldn't we do a better job of representing that message to others? Perhaps we would become known for love rather than for all the things that we (and God) are against. If we stepped forward with love, rather than always trying to convey truth, wouldn't the Truth be made manifest in all His glory?

At the core of every emotion, every pain, and every heart's cry, I believe there's one and only one question that is being asked: "Do I matter?" I also believe there is only One who can provide the answer to our heart's satisfaction. Think about this: Why does it hurt so badly when you lose a relationship, or when a person you love dies, or when you're diagnosed with a disease, or when your career and finances fall apart? I mean, above and beyond the obvious practical issues of grief, sickness, and lack, when we experience any of those things, what's the message that usually formulates in our hearts? It is this: "I don't matter." Our thinking goes something like this: "How this [insert your latest heartbreak] makes me feel right now must not be important, because I'm not important. If I truly were important, wouldn't God do something about it or at least clearly show me some greater reason why He didn't intervene in my situation?" Can there be any greater wound to the spirit, soul, or body than to believe that the One who can do something about your pain won't do anything about it?

Whether we're honest with ourselves about this or not, our hearts are wired to instinctively know that we were first envisioned and then created by the One who existed before we came into this world. Because He exists, we also instinctively know that He alone can assign us our value and worth. And if we don't have enough value in His eyes for Him to protect and rescue us, then do we really matter? For example, if my nation doesn't have enough value in His eyes for Him to fix its broken systems, which hold its citizens hostage to poverty, dysfunction, disease, and immorality, then do I (and everyone else who lives in this nation) really matter to God? If He doesn't care about my heart, about me and what I feel, then am I significant?

Not only must each one of us be able to address these questions, but we must also personally be so assured of the answers that we learn how to answer them for others. Throughout the following chapters, you'll find a dialogue that God Himself is inviting you into so you might discover all the limitless ways that a correct understanding of His character and of His heart toward us can be restored through the solutions He desires to reveal to us. We must each do our part to share and to apply these solutions to every problem that exists in every area of culture in every nation. Any approach less than this just wouldn't be a proper reflection of the God I've come to know. How about the God you know?

Paradigm Shift

I believe that, as a generation, we are in the midst of a huge paradigm shift. With regard to all the hot topics and debates in every area of culture, we hear many opinions and perspectives from Christians and non-Christians, yet it's difficult to find any that we actually agree with. I'd say most of us are fairly certain of what we simply *cannot* agree with, yet we haven't discovered the moving-forward convictions that we can agree with, that we can give our lives to and live wholeheartedly from. Of course, I'm not talking about the basics of our faith but rather what our faith looks and sounds like in this unique time in history, in the context of the pressure points of our current national and international issues. Should you choose to enter in, this book provides new and extremely relevant insights into the heated debates that are well underway on just about every front of the battle for societal reformation.

I think the one thing absolutely every human could agree on right now is that things must change, advance, and get better. But again, what that actually looks like is something we can't seem to find agreement on, even among those of us who share the same faith. Although none of you will agree with absolutely every idea Johnny puts forth in the pages of this book (I'm not even sure I do, as his number one fan!), you'll definitely find new options for thinking about the issues of our day. You'll not only be provoked to think from a hopeful perspective but also experience plenty of what I call "yes moments," where you'll say to yourself, "That makes so much sense! I knew the other way couldn't be right, but I just didn't know what other options we had—and this resonates so much with what I've been sensing but didn't know how to articulate!" As the subtitle of this book expresses, the ideas Johnny presents lay out "vision and strategy." So get ready! Get ready to be challenged to think in new ways, to think more long-term than you may previously have given yourself permission to think, and to look to the horizon with more excitement and hope than you've ever had.

One last thing. I probably shouldn't assume that you're completely sold on the idea of the reformation of society—that the Seven Mountains of culture (Religion, Education, Family, Government, Economy, Media, and Celebration/Arts) are intended to be the context in which the sons and daughters of God restore to the earth the truth about who He is and how He is. Christians have varying ideas about the kingdom of God, and that's okay. But let me encourage you, for the sake of getting the most out of the time you'll spend reading this book, to dare to believe that our God is up to something far more grand and victorious than any of us can presently envision. Dare to believe that He cares about you, about each of us, far more than we even hope He does. And because He cares about us, He cares about absolutely every detail of our lives and every system in culture that affects our personal and collective world. And what He cares about, He has solutions for—for you, for me, and for our world through us. And if He cares, shouldn't we? Shouldn't you? You're about to care, like never before, from a place of confidence and freedom. But first, let's set the stage for our own reformation by committing ourselves to journeying through these pages with our beautiful Papa God:

Father, I invite You into the way I personally experience this book. Holy Spirit, I ask for Your discernment and Your understanding. I give You permission, Jesus, to reveal more of Yourself to me as I read. Would You please give me a hunger that matches what You plan to feed me through the revelation that is meant for me here? Make me ready for whatever You want to propel me into, whatever new ways of thinking You may have for me, and grant me wisdom on how to follow through with the vision and strategies You "download" to my heart and mind. For the sake of Your kingdom, and in the name of Jesus Christ, the Savior of my heart and the Savior of my generation and all who will follow, amen!

—*Elizabeth Enlow*

Coauthor, *Rainbow God: The Seven Colors of Love*

One

THE SEVEN MOUNTAIN REVOLUTION AND THE "SHOT HEARD AROUND THE WORLD"

April 19, 2007: I was in Costa Rica, experiencing the most intense day of my life. It was a day when I felt such strong spiritual confrontation at all times that, whenever I wasn't preaching, I was speaking in tongues under my breath. I believe that, on that day, a "shot heard around the world" dynamic took place that marked a kickoff point for what I will call "The Seven Mountain Revolution." Let me explain.

I had preached about the Seven Mountains previously, but not beyond my local church in Atlanta, Georgia. I had never presented it in another country before. Furthermore, this message was going to be televised to over seventy nations. Although I already knew this was a paradigm-shifting message that had the potential to awaken Christians to the reality that we are called to manifest the kingdom of God in the seven primary spheres of society, I had no idea just how much God Himself would confirm it. As I landed in Costa Rica, I remember thinking that my briefcase, which contained a notebook filled with this new revelation God had given me, was like one of those attaché cases containing a nuclear bomb. However, despite my awareness of the historicity of the moment, I wasn't prepared for the phenomena that would accompany the sharing of this message.

> *God had shown me that the power outages in San Jose were a sign and wonder attached to the Seven Mountain message.*

I had multiple key meetings and speaking engagements in San Jose, Costa Rica, and everywhere I shared about the Seven Mountains, there would be this phenomena of a power outage in an entire neighborhood or even region of the city. My host noticed the trend after about the third outage and let me know that he had picked up on the seeming coincidence. This power outage sign and wonder occurred at a radio station when I began talking about the Seven Mountains, and then again at the Enlace TV station the instant I started speaking—declaring that God's better ways of doing things would begin to invade every area of society. It also happened throughout the Seven Mountain conference where I spoke at my host's church. For three days, every time I stood up to preach, the electrical power of the church and the neighborhood went out. My host brought a backup generator for day three of our conference and announced, "I am ready for you today." The next time I began to preach, the power went out, but the backup generator also blew! By day three of the conference, the power outages were so obvious that I decided to explain the phenomenon to those in attendance. I told them God had shown me that the power outages of the city were a sign and wonder attached to the Seven Mountain message. I explained that this revelation from God was short-circuiting the normal power grid because it was a message designed to manifest His rule over every other power on earth.

The power remained on during worship, but from the moment I began to speak at 8:00 PM, we lost power again. I attempted to preach by candlelight without a microphone. At 8:10, I stated that I wouldn't be surprised if the mere declaration of this message might blow the national power grid. As I spoke those very words, the national power grid of Costa Rica blew, and the entire nation went pitch-black for five hours. The next day, the newspaper simply stated that a "power surge" had occurred that had blown the Arenal Power Plant, creating a domino effect of sorts through the rest of the nation's power plants. To this day, exactly what caused the surge remains a mystery. Additionally, it was announced that a volcano that had been dormant for decades had just begun to smoke.

Of course, when the national power grid went out, there was significant pandemonium; it blew out the international airport's backup generator, and there was a report that it might be a week or more before the power could be restored. Even though I understood that this was a sign and wonder from God, I wasn't enjoying how eerie it felt. I could hear the sounds of car accidents, and an atmosphere of anxiety hung in the air. I told my host that I shouldn't speak anymore about the Seven Mountains because the power grid was saturated with the power of that revelation and couldn't handle any more. I closed out the conference by teaching about the prophetic in only a general way. I assured the attendees that the power would begin coming back sooner than expected because the outages had been caused by the declaration of this powerful prophetic message and not by any natural causes. Sure enough, the power started returning after five hours and gradually was completely restored over the course of a couple of days. The subsequent phenomenon was that whichever part of town I entered received power again. Once I was back in the United States, my host called and thanked me for my visit, adding, "Thank you even more for leaving! We have had no more power outages or fluctuations at all since you left!"

A couple of years later, when we met with President Oscar Arias of Costa Rica, we were able to refer back to that day when the national power grid went out. I gave him a copy of my first book, *The Seven Mountain Prophecy*, in Spanish. He remembered that very unusual situation in the nation, and I had the opportunity to explain to him that the very message in that book had caused the power surge.

The reason I am describing the events of that day in detail is that they directly connect to a sermon from May 2014 that my friend Lloyd Phillips sent me on CD. That particular sermon by Lloyd was a tribute to the prophet Bob Jones, who had passed away on Valentine's Day 2014. In his message, Lloyd shared many anecdotes from his interactions with Bob Jones. However, Lloyd had sent me the CD because he wanted me to hear the significant prophetic marker that connected something Bob Jones had said with my experience in Costa Rica. He shared that in 2007, he had been in an informal meeting with Bob in which the prophet had stated that if the church did not have a "shot heard around the world" within two years, we would basically be dead as a church and as a nation. The phrase "shot heard around the world" was coined by poet Ralph Waldo Emerson in his 1837 "Concord Hymn" describing the start of the American Revolution, with the historic shots fired against the British by the Americans at Concord, Massachusetts, on April 19, 1775.

Lloyd Phillips had gone home and pondered what Bob Jones had said. The words had intrigued him enough that he had further researched the "shot heard around the world" storyline. In the message Lloyd sent me, he spoke of a most interesting day he'd had a year or two after his time with Bob Jones. He shared how, on April 19—the same date as the battle—he had received a package in the mail with two items in it. One was the movie *Johnny Tremaine*, which chronicled the story of a young man who heard the "shot heard around the world" and signed up for revolutionary duty. The cover of the movie DVD included the word *Revolution* and the tagline "He Answered Freedom's Call." In the same package was a copy of my book *The Seven Mountain Prophecy*. Lloyd immediately noted how both items had the name *Johnny* and the word *revolution* on them. He began reading my book, starting with my wife's foreword, which tells some of the story of the supernatural phenomena of the power outages in Costa Rica.

In that foreword, my wife stated that the day the lights went out in Costa Rica was April 19, 2007! Though we had never made this connection before, Lloyd immediately recognized it as a significant prophetic marker. The power outage had actually occurred on the same date as the beginning of the American Revolution. Bob Jones had said that we needed another "shot heard around the world" to awaken the church from the limited inheritance she was walking in. For Lloyd, the coincidence that the movie and the book both had a key date of April 19 was too great to ignore. God essentially used Lloyd to lead me to an understanding of what that day represented—a marker in time when a new kind of revolution began that will ultimately release God's freedom into every sphere of society. I certainly didn't make it happen, but I felt honored just to have been allowed to be a participant in the process.

The Seven Mountain Revolution

Before I go any further, I want to acknowledge that I am not the first nor the only person to use the term "Seven Mountains." Early in 2007, I was preaching my very first series about the Seven Mountains in my local church. When I was on week four of the seven-week series, I was approached by my friend Os Hillman, who was a member of our church at that time but unable to attend regularly because of his travel schedule. Os is a speaker and author who also teaches about the Seven Mountains, as well as many other topics. He came up to me at the end of the service and asked, "Do you realize that there is a guy named

Lance Wallnau who has a message out called 'The Seven Mountain Strategy'?" I responded, "No way! Is it about the seven mountains of Jerusalem or of Rome?" Os replied, "No, it's the same Seven Mountains you're talking about."

I then asked him for Lance Wallnau's message on CD, which he gave me later that week. As I listened, to my increasing surprise, I discovered that Lance had actually heard the term from Bill Bright of Campus Crusade for Christ and Loren Cunningham of Youth With a Mission (YWAM), who had received an initial template of the Seven Mountains decades earlier. This was all news to me, as I had never heard anyone else talk about it. When I received the revelation, it came to me very personally and in various supernatural ways. Even while the Lord instructed me to write *The Seven Mountain Prophecy*, I was telling Him, "God, this revelation is so powerful that You should have given it to someone more famous so it could get out quicker." He just said, "You do your part, and I'll do My part." I have found Him to be true to His word.

> *Different people from around the world have come to me and said that years ago, they too had received some level of revelation on the Seven Mountains.*

I do want to acknowledge that Lance Wallnau, who is now a friend, was in fact preaching his version of the Seven Mountains years before I was. Bill Bright and Loren Cunningham also advanced the revelation, in the way they knew how to, years before that. In addition, different people from around the world have come to me and said that years ago, they too had received some level of revelation on the idea of the Seven Mountains.

I say all of this in an attempt to respond accurately to the frequent questions I am asked about who received what part of the message from whom. I received none of my material from anyone else; it was very personal for me, yet I was so glad to hear that others were advancing it in some way or another. The Holy Spirit gets the credit for giving out bits and pieces of the message to different individuals at different times. However, I do believe that the date of April 19, 2007, signifies a watershed day in history when this message reached a new level of power.

As usual, whatever the Holy Spirit is saying, He is saying to more than one person. Yet there can be a moment of synergistic spark when it all seems to coalesce and hit critical mass. Each of the various Seven Mountain messengers has had a different focus or light on it that has advanced the message, but it has all been on the central premise that these seven primary areas of society must be impacted by the influence of the kingdom of God operating through His sons and daughters. For me, the day I will never forget is that day in Costa Rica, the most intense day of my life, April 19, 2007.

Notable Seven-Mountain Advancements

It has been very satisfying for me to see how much attention this message has garnered in a relatively short time. I have been pleased and surprised at how so many people have heard and received the clarion call of this revolution and how it seemingly involves voices from every camp in Christianity.

For example, I had the privilege of meeting John Maxwell and traveling on a trip to Colombia with him. It was encouraging to find out that he has steered his entire five-million-strong Equip leadership team in over 170 nations to focusing on transformation using the Seven Mountain paradigm. John has coined the term "Seven Streams" for his network, but we are talking about the same seven areas of society.

Jerry Anderson of La Red Business Network and Global Priority Solutions has also greatly advanced his own values-and-principles-based resources through a strategic Seven Mountain template. He, too, is now a friend, and it has been amazing to see him advance this message of transformation in over seventy nations. Ché Ahn, the apostolic leader and pastor who oversees Harvest International Ministries (HIM), a network of apostolic networks that extends to over 50 nations representing more than 20,000 churches, also actively advances the Seven Mountain goals and focus.

The prestigious Wagner Leadership Institute (WLI), founded by Dr. Peter Wagner, whom I also claim as a friend, has over fifty branches around the world and uses Seven Mountain theology and ideas as some of its core curriculum. The Pinnacle Forum, an organization inspired by Dr. Bill Bright, recently ignited to another level under the leadership of Steve Fedyski. It, too, operates using a Seven Mountain paradigm and has a bold initial plan to impact 100 cities in America. Other significant ministries, prayer movements, universities, and training centers are currently advancing, as well, with Seven Mountain paradigms fully in place.

> *The Seven Mountains has clearly exploded as a new focal point on the horizon for the church.*

Although the message of the Seven Mountains still has not become as mainstream as it needs to, from any objective observation, it has clearly exploded as a new focal point on the horizon for the church. I have noted that no one who really understands it ever backs away from it, because it is truly foundational kingdom thinking as opposed to a passing, fancy doctrinal theme. It really doesn't matter whether it's called "Seven Mountains," "Seven Streams," "Seven Spheres," "Seven Gates," or anything else. I prefer to use "Seven Mountain" terminology because it is the only one that incorporates specific biblical wording. (See Revelation 17:9.) The important thing to understand is that the parameters of our kingdom assignment extend beyond the church and into the main cultural centers of society. The Seven Mountain Revolution is now fully engaged, and it has set the stage for the coming global Renaissance that will reshape the world as we know it.

Two

RENAISSANCE 2.0: THIS TIME, IT'S ALL ABOUT GOD

On December 10, 2012, I had a significant dream in which I was given the word *Renaissance*. I then began hearing many things from God on the subject and was instructed that we had entered into an extended "Era of Renaissance." This was interesting to me, as I had already received significant revelation from the Holy Spirit during the preceding Rosh Hashanah period in September 2012; I had been shown that "the age of the restoration of all things" spoken of in Scripture had in fact started at that time.

[Jesus Christ] *whom heaven must receive until **the times of restoration of all things**, which God has spoken by the mouth of all His
holy prophets since the world began.*   (Acts 3:21)

Now, in everything I share prophetically, I can only be faithful to
report on what I think I hear, and the rest is up to the Holy Spirit to
further confirm to the hearers. Acts 3:21 tells us that Jesus has been
received in the heavens ("held in the heavens" in other translations) until this "age of restoration" is fulfilled. I was being shown that this Era
of Renaissance was part of the "age of restoration" and that we would
finally experience the real Renaissance.

The First Renaissance:
The Brilliance of Man

As we begin to discuss what this new Renaissance means for us,
and how it compares to the first Renaissance, let us look at a definition
of the word *renaissance:*

A revival or rebirth, especially of culture and learning.

The first Renaissance was a period of rebirth and renewal that last-
ed from the fourteenth to the seventeenth century, interrupting the
late Middle Ages. This era was marked by people casting off restrictive
religious shackles and, in so doing, creating a contrasting spark of life
and creativity that reverberated into all areas of culture. This time period was also marked by the rebirth of the already failed ancient Greek
and Roman philosophies and values. These ideas took a while to advance, but by the sixteenth century, they seem to have impacted much
of the literature, art, music, philosophy, and politics of Europe. Even
Christianity became reinterpreted through the humanistic paradigm
that ruled then—and, honestly, it was a more interesting and creative
version of Christianity, though still mostly devoid of the Holy Spirit's
presence and power.

Why is this period of history so important to us today? Because humanism—the system of thought that puts humans, rather than God, as the center of everything—which was conceived during the Renaissance, has yet to lose its foothold in Western society. Humanism is still considered to be the most appealing enlightenment of culture in history.

What made room for humanism? The oppressive, restrictive, pharisaical, deadly Christianity of the times. As toxic as humanism might be, stale religiosity is worse. At that time, religious leaders had some of the worst God-views imaginable, and they, of course, spread them to the people. Finally, the suffocation from religion reached its die-or-break-loose stage—and people indeed began to break loose. The first Renaissance was birthed in concepts of human enlightenment and human intelligence; man's abilities were lauded and celebrated. The Christianity of the day was truly the "opium of the people," as Karl Marx would say, and getting off the drugs of religious narrowness and deadness was an accomplishment from that perspective, particularly because stale religiosity was insulting the character and deforming the image of the very One it claimed to reverence.

This Renaissance:
The Brilliance of God on Display

What will mark the new Era of Renaissance in which we are now living? There will be such an increase in the knowledge of God and His ways that life on earth will be changed forever. This reality is described in the book of Habakkuk:

> *For the [whole] earth will be filled with the knowledge of the glory of the LORD, as the waters cover the sea.* (Habakkuk 2:14)

Generally, when Christians think of this verse or of the reality of the knowledge of God covering the earth, they think of it in terms of people knowing that God saves. Though that is a most wonderful thing—God sent His only begotten Son, Jesus, to offer salvation to whosoever would repent and receive Him—it is clearly evident that this perspective restricts "knowledge of God" to only one aspect of who He is. The knowledge of God cannot be limited to only the knowledge that He saves. Part of the beauty of the Seven Mountain message is that it proclaims a God who not only saves (Mountain of Religion) but also governs (Mountain of Government), is creative (Mountain of Celebration/Arts), is a Communications Expert (Mountain of Media), is our Father, or "Papa" (Mountain of Family), is our Provider (Mountain of Economy), and is our Teacher (Mountain of Education).

Beyond these seven primary expressions of who God is lies an additional array of many hills of secondary aspects of His character that He desires to reveal to us. This Era of Renaissance that we have entered into will not be complete until the invisible God is made visible through the lives of His ambassadorial kids in every area of society.

This Era of Renaissance will not be complete until the invisible God is made visible through the lives of His ambassadorial kids in every area of society.

That's what the above verse means when it says *"as the waters cover the sea."* It will be a full saturation of knowledge that covers every nook and cranny of society. Jesus will not return until He has filled the whole earth with an understanding of God's amazing ways of doing everything.

Knowledge of the Glory

Notice that Habakkuk 2:14 doesn't just say that there will be "knowledge of God," as other Scripture passages also disclose to us. Here it speaks of "*knowledge of the glory of God.*" The word *glory* carries many definitions in the Hebrew language, and among those are the ideas of unusual presence, prosperity, and the goodness of God. For our purposes, the word *awesomeness* might best describe God's glory. The whole earth will be filled with people who know the awesomeness of God! In His awesomeness, there is great and unusual presence. In His awesomeness, there is great prosperity. In His awesomeness, there is great joy and great peace. These are all marks of His goodness. In Exodus 33:18–19, when Moses asked God if he could see His "*glory,*" God answered, in effect, "I will show you My '*goodness.*'" God identified His goodness with His glory. Speaking of something awesome, wouldn't it be something to actually visibly see and experience goodness? Well, that's going to happen before *this* Renaissance period is over. *Glory* will become a word that actually fits its description.

As we get further into this book, I will share some aspects of God's glory that will be made apparent in the Seven Mountains of society. For example, there is a glory to a properly run government. There is a glory to an educational system that functions well, and a glory to truly creative arts. There is a glory to families functioning in the way they were meant to, and to the news being reported correctly. There is a glory to supernatural provision, and to church meetings where God's presence is electric and powerful.

Chapter by chapter, we will unveil some of the advances in the knowledge of God that will be taking place. This time, the Renaissance will all be about God—but, amazingly enough, people will also be in awe as never before at the brilliance of those who follow Him. God will use many of His kids to make Himself famous in all the earth, and it will be our pleasure to cooperate with that assignment. There is almost no true societal knowledge of God at present; He is regarded by most people as a distant, invisible Deity who has a niche only in religion or in religious houses of worship. That is all going to dramatically change, as this Era of Renaissance is a period when He has chosen to disclose Himself as never before. Knowledge of the nuances of the goodness of God and how He thinks and what He does will fill the whole earth. Most people will respond to this knowledge in a loving and responsive way. As the Renaissance matures, only that which is rooted in a core evil will resist God. All else and all others will be smitten by His beauty and by His revealed awesomeness.

It is the greatest privilege in history to live in such a day as this.

The original Renaissance carried sparks of God but also a distorted narrative that didn't acknowledge His connecting role. The coming 2.0 Renaissance will carry an unprecedented manifestation of the brilliance and beauty of God connected to a proper storyline. It is the greatest privilege in history to live in such a day as this.

Three

CALEB-VISION: TREASURE HUNTING VERSUS TROUBLESHOOTING

When I was a full-time pastor, I was somewhat known for inventing new words. The people in my church called them "Johnny-isms." Similarly, I want to start this chapter by introducing a new word into the English language. That word is *Caleb-vision*. As we advance in the "age of the restoration of all things" and in the Era of Renaissance, it will be those who are blessed with the ability to have Caleb-vision who will be the greatest at moving forward into every area of society with heavenly reform and transformation. Renaissance is about people of hope and vision bringing into the culture that which their spiritual eyes can see. Caleb-vision is the ability to see the good things that God wants us to see without being derailed from our assignment by the obstacles before us.

You are probably familiar with the biblical story of Caleb from the Old Testament book of Numbers. Caleb was one of the twelve spies sent out by Moses to scope out the land that God had predestined for the Israelites. Remember that the Israelites had been slaves to the Egyptians for a staggering 400 years. Then God called to Moses from the midst of a burning bush and told him that He had seen the oppression of His people Israel and was calling Moses to lead them into a delightful Promised Land. God described this land as a place *"flowing with milk and honey"* (Exodus 3:8). He told Moses that this was a place of plenty and fruitfulness, watered by God Himself. It was a land where they would be *"the head and not the tail"* (Deuteronomy 28:13), as they had been the tail for many generations.

God also told Moses that this Promised Land of amazing potential was filled with enemies. In the land He had given them as their inheritance, there were seven enemy nations—the Hittites, Jebusites, Girgashites, Canaanites, Amorites, Perizzites, and Hivites. God informed Moses that these nations were greater and mightier than Israel, but that the Israelites should not say they were greater and mightier, because God was in their midst, and He would fight for them. They were to remember how He had parted the Red Sea and moved heaven and earth for them when He had taken out the Egyptians who had enslaved them. That same God would continue to help them with any and every enemy in the land He had promised to give them.

Thus representatives from all twelve tribes of Israel, including Caleb, were sent on the assignment of spying out the land in preparation for entering it. As the biblical account says, ten of the spies came back and gave a bad report of the land. They told of all the abortions taking place; all the corruption in government; all the homosexual agendas; all the sexual immorality; all the humanists, adulterers, blasphemers, and so forth. Okay, they didn't actually say that, but perhaps they did say the equivalent for that day. They acknowledged that the land did seem fruitful; that yes, in theory, it would make a good place in which to live—but there were *giants* in the land!

All of these "ites" (Jebusites, Hittites, and so on) were giants. Ten of the spies, believing that they were giving a helpful report to the people, said, "*We were like grasshoppers in our own sight, and so were we in their sight*" (Numbers 13:33). To them, this seemed like truthful reporting, and they proudly expressed their views, as if they were saving the people from catastrophic losses through misplaced high hopes and presumptuousness. Those ten men felt like they were providing the needed reality check for Israel.

> *We in the church have developed greatly as professional reality-checkers while chasing off the Caleb voices of hope and assurance.*

Now, before we start pointing fingers too quickly, I should mention that the ten-spy paradigm is rampant in the body of Christ today and is, in fact, more the rule than the exception. We have developed greatly as professional reality-checkers while chasing off the Caleb voices of hope and assurance.

The two remaining spies, Caleb and Joshua—who was Moses' personal assistant—not only gave a good report of the land, but they also had two men bring one huge bunch of oversized grapes back as evidence. They didn't want to just tell of the land's potential—they wanted the people to see it. You can just imagine all the extra work involved in carrying those grapes, perhaps for days, just so the people could see them. They knew the power of a testimony—they thought—yet the ten "spy-theologians" were so convincing in their negativity that the people of Israel were on board with them and against Joshua and Caleb and their report. The people began to scream and holler, *"If only we had died in the land of Egypt!"* (Numbers 14:1). God forbid they try to do something difficult.

Joshua and Caleb tried to calm the people so that they could again make their case. They said, in effect, "The land is an exceedingly good land, and it really does flow with milk and honey, as God told us. Furthermore, the Lord is with us, and our enemies' protection has departed from them." Caleb also told the people a most courageous statement about the giants; he claimed that they would be the Israelites' *"bread."* (See Numbers 14:6–9.) He was essentially saying that the Israelites would get stronger by "eating" these giants. Wow, what a perspective! You have to have Caleb-vision to be able to see things that way. Unfortunately, the rest of the Israelites remained stuck in the normal human tendency of "worm-vision" and were not able to make the shift into seeing properly for another forty years!

The Bible tells us that God Himself said of Caleb that he had *"a different spirit"* (Numbers 14:24). Only in our inner self-talk is it easy for us to believe that we would have responded as Caleb did under the circumstances. We all may fantasize about being a Caleb, but there really is a good reason why Caleb and Joshua were the only two who could see things through a proper lens. That good reason is that it really is hard for humans to see things God's way. Instead, we tend toward worm-vision. Seeing things God's way requires viewing the world from a different vantage point. It requires seeing with a different set of eyes. It takes sight-correcting lenses. It takes Caleb-vision.

Fruit Focus Versus Giant Focus

The Promised Land had two competing elements, fruit and giants—oversized grapes and oversized enemies. Our Promised Land today is comprised of the Seven Mountains of our cities and nations, and it has the same two conflicting elements. Today's "fruit" is the potential that could become a reality in our culture if we showed up in the land. Today's "giants" are the demons, the evil principalities, and the other tremendous challenges that rule in that land of promised inheritance. Therefore, if we were to view Hollywood as a promised land, the fruit we would reap might be the oversized grape that a faith-based movie has succeeded in mainstream America, thus influencing millions. As an example, the recent movie *Heaven Is for Real* has done very well in terms of both attendance and revenue. It has been effective at spreading a message that heaven is real and so is Jesus Christ—and it has made a good profit while doing so. This has been truly exciting for people of goodwill. It conditions us to dream and imagine what Hollywood might be like if people of nobility, morality, and integrity produced the movies. It is invigorating to use the possibility thinking that comes with Caleb-vision.

My wife and I currently live twenty-five miles from Hollywood, and we've had the opportunity to hear reports from many Christians about the difficulty of working in the entertainment business and of trying to bring influence into Hollywood. So, once we take the story out of the Bible and apply it to real life, it suddenly becomes quite challenging and revealing. Caleb-vision sounds good when you read about it in the book of Numbers, but it is really hard to have when you are actually contending for the Promised Land.

If it is that hard to develop Caleb-vision, how do we do it? Is it simply about ignoring the giants in the land? Is it about pretending there aren't any great obstacles? Let's learn the answer from Caleb himself.

Caleb-vision Starts with God's Narrative

Caleb did not pretend there were no giants in the land. It's just that the giants were beside the point. Caleb's *"different spirit"* allowed him to be inspired by God's narrative and to see everything in that light. God had said, repeatedly and with detail, that this Land of Promise was for the Israelites. He had also said that He would fight for them if they would just show up with courage. With those two matters taken care of, Caleb could live from a God-view. Yes, maybe the giants dwarfed the Israelites and their abilities, but compared to God, those giants were measurable only as pieces of bread to be eaten. The Israelites would gain strength by taking out these giants because, as God's representatives in the land, they would grow up to be God-size. Caleb knew that participating in God's storyline with His interests in mind put him in a place of privilege that defied common sense. Caleb's boldness was birthed from his understanding of the storyline, or narrative, that God was inviting the Israelites to join in, and then making the choice to believe it. Caleb-vision starts with knowing God's promises and then choosing to believe them above anything else. It's not easy. It's just necessary.

Years ago, noting my love for researching strongholds, principalities, and things of the devil, the Lord warned me not to become an expert in such things. He told me that those who overstudy the "giants" will always lose resolve, and

Once the dynamic of God's presence is known, there is no further point in studying an enemy that is greater and mightier than we are.

that I would be no exception. It is all right to know an overview of the enemy, but knowledge beyond that can quickly go wrong. I have a close friend who was a part of the military's Special Ops. He told me that they were always given just a short paragraph on the enemy's capabilities followed by extensive material on their own capabilities. They were supposed to especially focus on their own strengths. In our situation, when God is added to the picture, the discrepancy between the enemy's capabilities and our capabilities becomes even more pronounced. It really is true that *"if God be for us, who can be against us?"* (Romans 8:31 KJV).

The children of Israel were never told to ignore the "ites" of the Promised Land, but they were also never told to go study them. God had already told Moses that their enemies were greater and mightier than they—but only if He were out of the equation. Once the dynamic of God's presence is known, there is no further point in studying an enemy that is greater and mightier than we are. The point of discovering the strength of the enemy is to understand that our advance is going to have to be supernatural, with God as the presiding Game Changer.

When you know you require the supernatural dimension in order to step into what is yours, then you study the one Giant worth studying—the God of the universe. The level of your Caleb-vision is directly proportional to your God-view. I frequently quote A. W. Tozer, who said, "What you think about God is the most important thing about you." Giants aren't the problem. The inability to properly perceive God and/or His narrative is the problem. If we don't really believe that God has called us to be salt and light in every area of society (see Matthew 5:13–16), then we will never have Caleb-vision but will in fact be stuck with the same impaired vision that the ten spies had. Those ten spies so offended the heart of God by their lack of belief that they were stricken with a plague and died. (See Numbers 14:36–37.) Part of that consequence is the Old Testament paradigm of God, but He does want us to know that it is a serious affront to Him when we don't believe that He wants to give us special, promised land. You would think that seeing the deaths of the spies would have helped the Israelites to realize that the same God who struck down those seeing-impaired men could do the same thing to the giants, but they were a little slow on the uptake. How hard could the assignment actually be if you have an all-powerful God working on your behalf? Today, He will move heaven and earth on our behalf.

Treasure Hunting Versus Troubleshooting

The Bible says that *"the kingdom of heaven is like a treasure hidden in a field"* (Matthew 13:44). To me, this means the kingdom activity to be performed is to discover that treasure. It is not valuable to be able to discover the dirt of that field. The dirt is obvious and easy to find. The Hittites and the rest of their crowd were the obvious dirt of the Promised Land. Anyone would have seen that, but it required kingdom perspective, or Caleb-vision, to discover the treasure of the field. This is our prophetic call everywhere we go—to discover in everything and in everyone the gold or treasure that has been covered up by the dirt and to call out that promise into destiny.

Another truth the Holy Spirit has taught me is that if I want to stay encouraged and in Caleb-vision mode, I need to value treasure hunting more than I do troubleshooting. In treasure hunting, we live as Jesus did; He did only what He saw His Father doing. (See, for example, John 5:19.) Jesus did not go around merely reacting to Satan. That would have been acting according to a troubleshooting mind-set. In troubleshooting, we let the enemy set the agenda and create the battlefield, and then we show up. This locks us into counterattack mode, leaving us with no other agenda. With everything on the enemy's battleground of choice, it's hard to stay encouraged or to win.

Troubleshooting is valuable only at times when things are almost perfect and there is just a thing or two left to take care of. At some point in the future, that approach may be helpful for us. For the Israelites, there came a time years after they entered the Promised Land when God said to them, in effect, "Hey, you didn't finish the job yet. You still have some enemies in your territory." At that point, they were in some level of troubleshooting mode, but it was still connected to what was initiated by God.

However, when we first step foot into occupied territory, we need to be able to remain strong and courageous, just as Joshua was commanded to be. (See, for example, Joshua 1:7.) Upon entering enemy-infested territory, if all we can see is the enemy, then we will not stay encouraged for very long and will be tempted to use our expert troubleshooting gift to keep everyone, including ourselves, apprehensive and overwhelmed. This is something that is almost pandemic in the body of Christ today, and it simply must stop. The practical step toward ceasing this attitude is to commit yourself to being a treasure hunter and to report on the treasures you have discovered. Discovered treasure is the evidence that God is with us and that He is greater than every resistance, even that of giants. We stay valiant, encouraged, and joyful as we take note of the enormous grapes we are harvesting, right under the nose of the giants.

> *If you can learn to see potential fruit, you can learn to be a Seven Mountain champion.*

The greatest advancers of the knowledge of God and His glory will be those who can see it and value it even when it is in a limited state. The present Renaissance will be advanced by Papa's kids who have had their eyes fitted with Caleb-vision. Therefore, study the Father, the Son, and the Holy Spirit instead of the problems. God will give the strategy for overcoming the enemy. Become an expert at recognizing His voice, His narrative, His storyline, His possibilities. Then you will be like Caleb, who was as strong and courageous at the age of eighty-five as he was when he was a young man. If you can learn to see potential fruit, you can learn to be a Seven Mountain champion. But if you can see only the giants, you are doomed to be swallowed up by the very ground you are trying to take. In all your getting, get Caleb-vision. It is the spiritual art and discipline of learning to see.

Four

IT'S ABOUT INFLUENCE, NOT DOMINATION

In our excitement over this new Seven Mountain paradigm and assignment, we may sometimes get a little carried away in how we express it. I have noticed that Christians tend to like to use language such as "I'm going to 'take' the Mountain of _____." Likewise, I have heard of a lot of aggressive conversation about how we Christians are "taking over"—and we also seem to have a significant fascination with the word *dominion*. So, before we embark on bringing God's Renaissance into the mountains of society, we will really have to exercise wisdom as we describe our missional narrative. Society is listening in, and we need to be aware that the attention they pay to us will only increase as we move forward.

Now, humanity's dominion mandate from God is clear from the book of Genesis, but we must understand that none of the descriptions of dominion ever talk about it in regard to dominating our fellow human beings.

> *Then God said, "Let Us make man in Our image, according to Our likeness; let them have dominion over the fish of the sea, over the birds of the air, and over the cattle, over all the earth and over every creeping thing that creeps on the earth."….Then God blessed them, and God said to them, "Be fruitful and multiply; fill the earth and subdue it; have dominion over the fish of the sea, over the birds of the air, and over every living thing that moves on the earth."* (Genesis 1:26, 28)

Dominion is clearly laid out as a partnership between God and man over all other forms of life or existence, including the demonic realm. Therefore, whenever we use the language of dominion, if we don't immediately follow up with an explanation about what that means exactly, then we leave a huge open door for controversy, criticism, and a backlash of fear. "Having dominion" is not about Christians ruling over non-Christians, and we should always be aware of that fact. The dominion mandate was about the sons and daughters of God—all of humanity—having dominion over fish, cattle, birds, and all the earth, including every creeping thing and every living thing. Those last two categories would qualify as potential descriptions of demonic forces, and I think we all know that they should be the focus of the domination. Ephesians 6:12 tells us, "*We do not wrestle against flesh and blood* [people]*, but against principalities, against powers, against the rulers of the darkness of this age* [Satan and his demons]*….*" The purpose of "wrestling" is to gain domination over the demonic realm and the lies it promotes about God. The targets of our domination are Satan and demons, and we must make sure that we always understand that narrative and represent it correctly.

You see, based on the historical record, there really is a good reason for non-Christians to be scared to death of language that speaks of dominion unless we clarify the question, "Dominion over what?" The history of the world is rife with examples of attempted Christian domination over all other religions. About 300 years after Jesus, Emperor Constantine of Rome made Christianity the official religion of the people, and really since that day, it has been hard to keep religious domination out of the quotient. For many, many centuries, there was a pervasive atmosphere of religious imposition, and most of us would not have done well living in that reality. One needs only to read about the period of the Holy Inquisition to understand how a dominion mandate can get way out of hand. The true dominion mandate is stewardship over the planet, and it is to be seen as an extension of our carrying the image of the One who created us. It is a mandate to express His heart of love through every area of culture—and when that is done His way, the earth will rejoice!

The true dominion mandate is stewardship over the planet, and it is to be seen as an extension of our carrying the image of the One who created us.

Freedom of Religion Is a New Thing, and It's a God Thing

The idea of freedom of religion is a relatively novel concept. This fact can easily be forgotten, particularly in America in the twenty-first century. Religious freedom did not exist in Europe, or the Old World, before America was a nation. Church and state were essentially in bed together, and virtually all wars were over which religion was going to dominate the political landscape. Catholic Christianity dominated for over a thousand years. Then the Protestant Reformation came around AD 1500, and various nations experienced religious swings over the idea of which of those two forces would have preeminence. This situation led to cycles in which there were times of revenge, much like the situation in our day between the Sunnis and the Shiites, who take turns respectively in the seats of power in Muslim nations. Their cyclical fight for power looks very violent, extreme, and uncivilized to us today, but the history of Christian religiosity seems as violent and primitive as what we now see in those nations among those present-day religious sects.

We should know that the early settlers who came to America were not proponents of the idea of freedom of religion. In 1620, it was largely a group of religious separatists who arrived at Plymouth Rock on the Mayflower. This group did not advocate freedom of religion; in fact, it firmly believed that all non-Puritans were heretics that should be shut down if they did not conform. The early settlers, although often fleeing persecution or ostracism in Europe, failed to exhibit in their settlements the same freedom of religion to others that they themselves were so persistently seeking. Looking back at the Pilgrims, we would have to connect random bits of historical information if we wanted to piece together an idea that they somehow supported freedom of religion.

The Puritans were part of a Reformation-minded movement that came out of the Anglican Church of England in the sixteenth and seventeenth centuries (they started around 1560 during the reign of Queen Elizabeth I). They were a passionate group of people who were deeply distressed at the low level of spirituality that the Church and individual Christians exhibited. It had been a while since Martin Luther had led the Protestant revolt against the Catholic Church, and now there was a feeling among these purifying ones that the new church leadership was exhibiting as much debauchery and spiritual coldness as the church leadership they had left. The Puritan passion was not toward "presence Christianity" but toward "behaving Christianity." They were not trying to be better hosts of the presence of the Holy Spirit; rather, they were looking for universal conformity in behavior. Generally, to them, spirituality was about order.

As a group, the Puritans found themselves gravitating toward theologian John Calvin (1509–1564), with his very deliberate doctrines and clearly defined outcomes. Calvin himself became a prime example of the marriage of church and government, and for a season, Geneva, Switzerland, was his pride and joy—referred to as "a city of righteousness." Geneva was the original "city on a hill" example, which was spoken of fondly by many Christians of that day. The problem is that it is a horrible model for us today, as any of us would know if we researched and understood the prevailing atmosphere of the time. John Calvin believed that all dissent should be harshly and severely punished, and he followed through with this belief. He drew out of the Scriptures a phraseology he boldly announced and enforced—"He who resists the magistrate, resists God." With this as his inspiration and his permission to exercise his form of dominion, he proceeded to beat, imprison, and torture fellow believers and unbelievers alike.

Calvin was responsible for executing at least a hundred people who in our day would simply fall under the classification of being from a different Christian denomination.[1] Many Anabaptist ministers were drowned for their disruptions of Calvin's orderly society. The Anabaptists (re-baptizers) did not believe that infant baptism was enough; they claimed one needed a full immersion baptism for it to count. No "sinner's prayer" was used for salvation at that time; therefore, baptism was the route and the proof of one's Christianity. Baptism by immersion is basic baptismal orthodoxy for many people today, but it was a life-and-death issue back then. Calvin thought it

---

1. In the most famous case of the dissenting Servetus who was burned at the stake—a prison escapee when he arrived in Geneva whose personality happened to be just as unlikable as Calvin's—Calvin did write a defense of condemning heretics to death, but he also tried to switch Servetus' sentence to execution rather than burning at the stake. (For more information, visit http://www.thegospelcoalition.org/article/9-things-you-should-know-about-john-calvin or http://www.christianitytoday.com/ch/131christians/theologians/calvin.html?start=3.)

ironically appropriate to have the ministers who baptized by immersion be immersed until they drowned.

Now, to be more fair to Calvin, I should point out that his harsh and intolerant manner of dealing with those he disagreed with was largely in keeping with the religious culture of his day. He needn't be demonized beyond measure; we can assume that if he had lived in our day, he would have made some adjustments. However, it is relevant to critique his beliefs because although all honest studiers of Calvin would recognize that his ways of doing things would not work in any Christian setting of the twenty-first century, we have not equally recognized that his extreme behavior came from extreme doctrines, many of which are still with us today, that must be amended if they are to be of any value to us.

> *Don't forget that the kingdom of God is advanced by influence and not by imposition.*

The fact that the Puritans were drawn to Calvin tells you a little bit about their own religiously radical makeup. The Puritans eventually became so powerful in England that they took over the nation, beheading reigning King Charles I as part of that process. You think the radical Islamic beheadings of today are unparalleled in their extremeness? Well, our Puritan forefathers beheaded the actual king of England and took over the nation in the name of God.

I will continue this history lesson, as it is important—and will be even more so in the coming days when socially activated Christians become fully aware of what their power in some sort of concerted effort can accomplish. We don't want to repeat failed experiments, and we don't want to forget that the kingdom of God is advanced by influence and not by imposition. Therefore, dominion language has to be abstained from or properly allocated as dominion over anything other than people. Again, history is rife with examples of the damage brought about by dominion-minded Christians who imposed their beliefs on others. In contrast, if we exercise the kind of influence God created us to have, people and nations will love the solutions God provides for every problem that exists in all seven areas of culture!

From 1629 to 1642, more than 20,000 Puritans migrated to what would become the United States of America.[2] As they increased in number and in power, they began to manifest their severe brand of orderly Christianity. If I had lived in almost any part of New England during those days, I have no doubt that I would either have been imprisoned or executed, just for believing and speaking the things I do today. The atmosphere of the day was decidedly not one of religious freedom but one much more in keeping with Sharia law that might come from radical Islam. People were routinely imprisoned, beaten, and tortured for disagreeing with religious edicts that came down from the combination government/church beast that ruled in this land for the 150 years before we became a nation. Mary Dyer, a Quaker, was executed in Boston on June 1, 1660, by the ruling Puritans. Her offense? Refusing to cease preaching when she had been told to stop. In her preaching, she taught the common Quaker Christian values that women could speak and that all could hear the voice of God for themselves. In our very own nation, order-loving Christians decided that that was an executable offense. Famed Puritan Governor John Winthrop oversaw this process and sentence, as well as that of several other Quakers who were executed for similar religious reasons. This happened in America. These are some of the "Judeo-Christian roots" we speak of going back to.

The aforementioned Governor Winthrop is best remembered as the man who spoke of America as "a city on a hill"—a quote that President Ronald Reagan would famously use in speaking of America's destiny. Unfortunately, the governor was actually referring to Calvin's

---

2. Lynn Betlock, "New England's Great Migration," *Great Migration*, New England Historic Genealogical Society, https://www.greatmigration.org/new_englands_great_migration.html.

model versus the kingdom of God model of freedom of conscience. Winthrop also oversaw the trial of Anne Hutchinson, which was a horrific injustice to someone who seemed like a great woman of God of that day. Ultimately, she was excommunicated from Boston for not backing down from having Bible studies in her house. While establishing a new home in an area that is now the Bronx, she and fourteen of her children were killed by Indians. Among her descendants were two governors, President F. D. Roosevelt, President George H. W. Bush, and President George W. Bush, as well as presidential candidate Mitt Romney. She was a woman who, like Mary Dyer, believed that God could speak to anyone and that women could also hear from God. Back in those days—the days of our Judeo-Christian roots—that could get you killed.

Unbalanced dominionism is therefore in our roots, and we really need to see that it must not be brought back today or in the future. The apparent simplicity and orderliness of that time period appeals to us, yet it was not order from the inside out but from the outside in. The kingdom of God always advances with an inside-out dynamic. It is very important that we be sure of this truth as we move forward into unprecedented influence in society.

Again, many of our early American forefathers carried a very aggressive and impositional brand of Christianity. The theoretical motivation was the advancement of the kingdom of God, but, I repeat, this is not how the kingdom of God truly advances. In 1609, the London (Virginia) Company (an English joint stock company) authorized the kidnapping of Native American children so that they could be raised as Christians.[3] Early on in most colonies in America, church attendance was compulsory, and you could be publicly flogged, imprisoned, or both for not attending church. Is attending church basically good and advisable? Yes, it is, but if we were to resort to an incorrect version of dominion in this matter and force people to attend, it would cease to be a good thing.

---

3. *World Heritage Encyclopedia*, "London Company," World Public Library, http://netlibrary.net/articles/London_Company.

The infamous Salem Witch Trials of 1692 were overseen by this mix of Puritan clergy and government. It is quite clear that many, if not most, of those who were accused of being witches were not in fact witches. Any woman who claimed to have seen a vision or to have heard the voice of God was in danger of being executed, as such was the atmosphere of early American

> *God is still trying to get the Peters of our day to put down their swords.*

Christianity. Today, hopefully we all agree that even should a woman be an actual witch, she in no way deserves to be executed. God is still trying to get the Peters of our day to put down their swords. (See John 18:10–11.) Jesus sends us out as sheep among wolves, not as wolves among sheep. (See Matthew 10:16.) Sheep can only influence, not impose.

Then How Did We Get Freedom of Religion into Our Constitution?

Well, it certainly wasn't from the Puritans. We can thank a disgruntled former Puritan named Roger Williams who was a key proponent of freedom of religion. He is a greatly under-publicized American hero who initially came to America as a Puritan Separatist but then became convinced of the value of freedom of religion. He fell out of favor with the Puritans and was in essence forced to flee to what is now Rhode Island, which he turned into a haven for freedom of religion. Williams founded the city of Providence, stating that it was the providence of God for him. He gave many messages on the rightness of freedom of religion and appropriately proclaimed that "forced religion stinks in the nostrils of God!" He was largely the catalyst that led many people to embrace the value of practicing one's religion based on conscience rather than on governmental mandate.

Rhode Island became a place of refuge for non-Puritans; the Quakers, in particular, found safe harbor there. Roger Williams declared that his settlement was a haven for those "distressed of conscience," and his Rhode Island became the incubator that birthed the early concepts of freedom of religion. His was one of the initial strong voices rejecting the notion of a state church. Williams denounced any state's attempt to enforce any of the Ten Commandments that had solely to do with the relationship between God and man. He believed that the state had to limit itself to the commandments that dealt with relations between people, such as murder, theft, and lying.

As I wrote earlier, it is good for us to properly consider these things before making bold statements about "having dominion," "taking over," or even "taking our mountain for God." What level of domination would we exercise if we could do it by a sheer majority? We must think through those questions now, before our reformation train has too much speed and momentum to slow it down for proper restraint. A few decades ago, we had a "moral majority" movement that might have been headed for way too much forced dominion had it not been derailed. Any good thing to which we might add the destructive leaven of imposition would cease to be a good thing. Jesus said, *"Beware of the leaven of the Pharisees"* (Matthew 16:6). Such leaven entails hypocrisy and imposition.

Roger Williams and William Penn (a Quaker) were perhaps the key individuals whose thoughts and writings catalyzed our founding fathers to contend for religious freedom. The atmosphere was quite contentious during the days of the writing of the U.S. Constitution, but William Penn's Frame of Government of Pennsylvania (the constitution of that colony) was, in essence, the inspiration for our American Constitution. The Constitution embodied many of the Quaker values of freedom and championed the rights of the individual and of individual conscience. This was quite different from the Puritan atmosphere that had dominated America for 150 years.

It is also quite clear that the establishment clause of our Constitution was more concerned with keeping the church out of the state than the other way around, though both outcomes were clearly desired. Several years after the Constitution's ratification, in a letter to the Danbury Baptist Association, Thomas Jefferson penned that "religion is a matter which lies solely between Man & his God, that he owes account to none other for his faith or his worship." After quoting from the Bill of Rights that the United States Congress should "'make no law respecting an establishment of religion, or prohibiting the free exercise thereof,'" Jefferson added, "…thus building a wall of separation between Church & State."[4] He saw that wall as important to keep either church or state from intruding on the other. This was to guarantee both freedom *of* religion and freedom *from* religion, should that be an individual's choice. For the minority Quakers and others, this new law of the land allowed them the freedom to both believe and worship as they saw fit. For the ruling Puritans and offshoot denominations, this new law limited their ability to impose their religion. The same constitutional directive empowered the one and limited the other.

Influence Happens in an Atmosphere of Freedom

The great value of influence (versus imposition) is that it occurs under free will. In Luke 2:52, the Bible says this about Jesus: "*And Jesus increased in wisdom and stature, and in favor with God and men.*" Influence is the by-product of having favor. Favor is an irresistibility factor that often defies logic. True godly favor is that which comes by carrying a high measure of love. That high measure of love will manifest in actions that are attractive to people of goodwill and unattractive to people of devious intent. This must be our goal for how we desire

---

4. http://www.loc.gov/loc/lcib/9806/danpre.html.

> *There is a beauty of freedom that outweighs the beauty of order.*

to advance the kingdom of God: We must resist any and all impulses to impose upon the masses that which should be only a matter of conscience between man and God. May our writings and our spoken language begin to catch up with that important understanding. There is a beauty of freedom that outweighs the beauty of order. Again, the kingdom of God comes in freedom, and the order it brings is an inside-out order, not an outside-in order. We must watch how we use dominion terminology and make sure that we are at no time shifting toward order by means of imposition. God has always had the power to do in a mere instant what He needs to have accomplished. Yet He has chosen to endure the arduous process of winning over hearts and minds through love in order to accomplish His goals. As He is, so must we be in this world. (See 1 John 4:17.)

Five

RENAISSANCE ON THE MOUNTAIN OF RELIGION

The Mountain of the Religion is the sphere of society where there is a battle over whom one directly and intentionally worships as God. This is the mountain from which the church is based, and since it is the realm that will experience the most thorough overhaul of all the mountains, we will spend a little more time on it than the others. Over the next thirty-five years, a most intense reformation will take place both in the church and on this mountain overall. In this chapter, I want to address present and coming trends, as well as explore what Renaissance looks like on this mountain.

Current Statistics on World Religions

Though there is significant dispute over statistics about religion, and even some intention to deceive on the part of certain adherents through false reporting, I will share the numbers that seem most credible to me. These are from the Center for the Study of Global Christianity at Gordon Conwell Theological Seminary.[5]

+ There will be 2.6 billion Christians in the world by the year 2020. (I have read reports that we have already reached that 2.6 billion figure, as well as one that states that, as of 2014, we are at 2.4 billion. In any case, it is a rapidly growing figure that now approaches or exceeds one in every three people on the planet.)

+ Islam has between 1 and 1.2 billion adherents.

+ Hinduism and Buddhism both have adherents in the hundreds of millions.

These numbers mean that, mathematically, Christianity is taking over the world. It is at its highest percentage ever and is growing faster than the world's birthrate. Some projections have Christianity growing at more than 100 million a year over the next several years, and then only increasing after that.

The term *Christians* reflects all who claim to be followers of Jesus Christ. That includes Catholics who may or may not have had a clear conversion experience, as well as lukewarm or even hypocritical Christians. There are over 30,000 denominations in this category, and many within those groups don't believe that others fit their version of a "real" Christian. Clearly, there is a need to both acknowledge the mixed company that comes under the name *Christianity* and to state the need for allowing God to be the ultimate Judge on who is "in" and who is "out." My take is that it is my duty to accept whoever acknowledges that salvation is only through Jesus Christ and who believes that

---

5. Todd Johnson, et al., "Christianity 2015: Religious Diversity and Personal Contact," *International Bulletin of Missionary Research* 39 no. 1 (January 2015), http://www.gordonconwell.edu/resources/documents/1IBMR2015.pdf.

for himself or herself, as a brother or sister, and let God do the final judging.

The Geographical Trend: From Europe to Africa, Asia, and Latin America

Though Christianity has theoretically been popular for a long time, there is a real changing face to what modern-day Christianity looks like. Whereas before 1900, there were only a relative handful of Pentecostal/ charismatic Christians, there are now in the vicinity of 640 to 700 million followers of Jesus Christ who have doctrinal state-

Almost one tenth of the world is Holy Spirit-filled and empowered!

ments that prioritize the person, presence, and power of the Holy Spirit. This is, of course, a phenomenal trend, as it means that close to one in ten on the planet are such. Of this total, an estimated 120 to 160 million are Catholic charismatics,[6] and they are experiencing a tremendous growth spurt that will only accelerate as the influence of fellow charismatic Pope Francis expands. This, too, is a phenomenal trend. Wow, almost one tenth of the world is Holy Spirit-filled and empowered!

Another major trend is a moving away from European-based and European-style Christianity and a moving toward African, Asian, and Latin American styles of Christianity. In terms of Christianity, Europe was the center of the world for centuries. That situation has greatly shifted, to the extent that Europe is now largely seen as one of

6. Todd Johnson, et al., "Christianity 2015"; http://www.catholicnews.com/data/ stories/cns/1303443.htm; http://www.catholicworldreport.com/Item/2269/the_ charismatic_renewal_and_the_catholic_church.aspx.

the tougher mission fields. Both Europe and North America are declining in their percentage of Christians. Meanwhile, Africa has gone from nearly 115 million Christians in 1970 to about 540 million. Asia has grown from 91.5 million Christians in 1970 to about 376 million. Latin America has increased from about 263 million Christians in 1970 to more than 575 million.[7]

The Theological Trend: To the Person and Work of the Holy Spirit

What marks this shifting central face of Christianity to Africa, Asia, and Latin America is the new style of Christianity that is proliferating around the planet. For centuries, the Christianity that spread around the globe was a very heady, rules-oriented, Pharisee-like brand of Christianity that had no qualms about imposing itself on people, similar to the way ardent Islam does today. That particular brand of Christianity dominated much of the world with an expression that gave very little attention to the person of the Holy Spirit and His manifestations of power. In fact, the dominant brand of Christianity from 1500 to 1900 would heavily persecute those few believers who dared to believe that healing is still for today; that authority over demons is for today; that signs, wonders, and miracles are for today; that apostles and prophets are still for today; and so on. It's a good thing that brand of European-style Christianity is continuing to lose its traction and appeal. Across the globe, that form of Christianity is more likely to be the greatest enemy of the advancing church than the foundation for the new thing God is doing. It certainly doesn't have to be the enemy of the advancing church, but it is following the familiar pattern of an old, corrupted movement of God persecuting a new movement of God.

The new face of Christianity is much more passionate, emotional, and Holy Spirit-centric. It, too, has many excesses and needed upgrades,

---

7. Todd Johnson, et al., "Christianity 2015."

but it is a more preferable model of Christianity than the European-based model. It's less orderly and less predictable, but those two factors are the very thing that makes it more desirable. The new Christianity understands that it must advance through influence rather than force, and there is no greater influencer on the planet than the Holy Spirit. It's why the present growth and trend is unstoppable—because where the Holy Spirit has freedom to move, there is no slowing down.

The Two Competing Faces of Christianity: John Calvin and George Fox

Perhaps the shifting face of Christianity can best be seen as the final outcome of the fruit of two giants of the faith. These two are John Calvin, whom we talked about briefly in the previous chapter, and George Fox. If John Calvin is a snapshot of the fading face of Christianity, then George Fox embodies the emerging trend in Christianity. Let's look at the two of them and use this history lesson to assist us in knowing and agreeing with where the Holy Spirit is taking the church in this Era of Renaissance.

John Calvin (1509–1564)

John Calvin was a Frenchman who spent much of his pastoral career in Geneva, Switzerland. He was perhaps the most famous figure of the Protestant Reformation era other than Martin Luther. His lasting influence has been much greater than Luther's, mostly because of his extensive writings on Christian doctrine, the most well-known of which is his *Institutes of the Christian Religion*. Calvin was originally trained as a humanist lawyer, and that background surely influenced his approach to systematic doctrine and theology. He was greatly influenced by the writings and doctrine of Augustine, and it is from

Augustine that he derived his views on predestination and original sin.[8]

Through Calvin's presence and influence, Geneva became the epicenter of the Protestant Reformation movement. Calvin is widely seen as the intellectual father of all denominations that count predestination as a significant doctrine. Many people still think of him as a utopian leader, especially because of his ability to turn a city such as Geneva into the "Jerusalem" of that day, as it has been called. However, Calvin's overbearing tactics disqualify his methodology as having any value for us today. He had no qualms about implementing standards in the city that allowed him to imprison, beat, torture, and even execute those who bucked his orderly system of righteousness. As I stated previously, he personally oversaw the execution by drowning of Anabaptists ministers, as well as the execution of scores of other believers who disagreed with his views. Though he was a brilliant thinker with redemptive ideas—mixed in with views that weren't redemptive—he is still a clear picture of what we are moving away from.

George Fox (1624–1690)

Englishman George Fox was not born until sixty years after the death of Calvin, but he came from a strongly Puritan village of firm Calvinists. George Fox was the founder of the Quakers, who exist to this day but with only traces of the truth and grace that Fox carried. He was a very influential leader in England and also in America, which he visited in 1672, only sixteen years after the first Quakers arrived there. In both England and America, Fox's Quakers were greatly persecuted by Calvin's Puritans, yet the Quakers carried so much of the Holy Spirit that, during Fox's lifetime and for a season after his death, it

---

8. The doctrine of predestination asserts that God has freely and unchangeably ordained whatever comes to pass. This includes every evil thing that occurs. God also has predetermined who will be saved and who will not. Thus, the decision about your eternal destination has already been made for you. The doctrine of original sin maintains that the whole human race sinned in Adam when Adam sinned. Therefore, all people are born guilty before they make one decision. Even newborn babies are under the wrath and curse of God, already guilty and condemned.

seemed that they would become the dominant brand of Christianity in both of those nations. When William Penn founded Pennsylvania in 1682, it became a Quaker stronghold, as did much of New Jersey and North Carolina. By the early 1700s, the Quakers were a prominent political, social, and economic group in the colonies. They were the largest religious society in Rhode Island, and for many consecutive terms won all of the governorships there.[9]

Throughout the colonies, the reputation of the Quakers was that they were hardworking, trustworthy, industrious, prosperous, socially respected, and very spiritual. As the eighteenth century settled in, they seemed to

Virtually every societal reformation advance was spearheaded by a Quaker, and almost every societal reformation attempt was fought against by a Puritan or by the denominational descendants of Puritans.

be poised as *the* defining Christian religion of America. All of that changed as they drifted from Fox's primary, defining tenets of spirituality, which combined "inwardly to God, and outwardly to man."[10] Their moving away from the "outwardly to man" principle caused them to later lose their preeminent place in American influence. And yet, for the next 200 years, it would be Quakers who would lead most of the initiatives for societal reform.

---

9. "Quaker History," Downington Friends Meeting, http://downingtownfriendsmeeting.org/quakerhistory.htm.
10. George Fox, *George Fox's Journal* (London: Isbister and Company Limited, 1903), 2, http://www.markfoster.net/rn/George_Fox_s_Journal.pdf.

John Woolman, a Quaker, became the apostle of the abolitionist movement; he should probably be the most honored spiritual leader in American history. Through his writings, Woolman influenced abolitionist William Wilberforce in England. He also influenced the Quaker denomination, which, for decades, stood alone in opposing slavery, supporting just treatment of the Indians, and validating women and their rights, both inside and outside of church.

The following are other Quakers who led societal reform in America and England. Levi Coffin, called the "President of the Underground Railroad," was responsible for rescuing and taking care of thousands of slaves. Lucretia Mott and Susan B. Anthony were the principal figures in bringing women's rights to the forefront as they fought not only for a woman's right to vote but also a woman's right to earn wages, to keep her wages, to own property, to have rights to her children should she be divorced, and other similar justice realities of today. Joseph John Gurney and Elizabeth Fry were the initial campaigners for prison reform, and because of their efforts, many prisons were upgraded in every way, starting with the treatment of women in prisons. All in all, virtually every societal reformation advance was spearheaded by a Quaker, and almost every societal reformation attempt was fought against by a Puritan or by the denominational descendants of Puritans. Therefore, I say that George Fox represents the better picture of the new face of Christianity.

Competing Doctrines of Calvin and Fox

I want to list several competing doctrines between Calvin and Fox that I believe exemplify why we are headed away from Calvinism and into that which more closely resembles Fox's doctrinal approach.

1. Original Sin Versus Inner Light

The central idea behind the doctrine of original sin, represented by Calvin, is that man is a wretched sinner worthy of hell, but if a person will recognize this reality and how distasteful he is to God, then God will forgive him and Jesus will come into his heart, thereby enabling the person to be acceptable to God and to have eternal life. (Consider Jonathan Edwards' sermon "Sinners in the Hands of an Angry God.") On the other hand, the central idea behind Inner Light, represented by Fox, is that man's origin is from God, the Father of Lights, and therefore all people have an inner light available to be addressed and spoken to.

Although the doctrine of original sin does reflect biblical truth about fallen human nature (see Romans 5:12–19), the problem is that it causes people to focus on their sins and failures, thus forming a wrong foundation for their identity as human beings. In contrast, the doctrine of Inner Light shifts the focus from humanity's sin to humanity being made in God's image; thus, the missional task, rather than making people feel condemned, is to get people to agree with that understanding and to, in essence, return to God as their Source. In this view, the only path to a restored relationship with God is still the blood of Jesus, which atones for our sin; although Fox didn't explicitly talk about the blood of Jesus as necessary for salvation, it is clear from his writings that that is where he stood.

The Inner Light focus is illustrated for us in the parable of the prodigal son. (See Luke 15:11–32.) This parable demonstrates that all people originally come from the Father, and that the real rejoicing in the Father's house occurs when a son comes to realize who his Father truly is and thus desires to return to Him. In my view, this emphasis is far more effective for winning to Christ those who don't yet know they are indeed sons of God. Rather than imagine that our Father can't stand them until they come to Jesus (the idea promoted by the original sin doctrine), they can know that He is waiting with open arms every day for them to recognize that they belong in His house and that, through Jesus, they can have access to return home. I believe this approach to be the evangelistic trend of the future. Again, it is not that God hates us apart from Jesus; rather, we came from God, He has always loved us, and He ever waits for us to come back to Him. God doesn't embrace us only after we come to Him though Jesus. It is in fact because of His profound love for us that He sent Jesus to die for us *"while we were yet sinners"* (Romans 5:8).

2. Predestination Versus "There Is That of God in Everyone"

As mentioned earlier, the Calvinist doctrine of predestation is that God has, in essence, already planned everything out, and we are just fulfilling the role He has assigned us. God has already determined who gets saved and who doesn't. He made that decision before the foundation of the earth, and there is nothing we can do to change His mind. This doctrine seems to be one of the most illogical and damning doctrines on the planet because, in effect, it makes God the author of every evil that occurs on earth. Though I believe the weight of Scripture to be entirely in the free will camp, it is still possible to isolate certain passages in the Bible to seemingly validate this horrendous doctrine of predestination, which turns God into a megalomaniacal monster. When a theology of God is invented that makes Him into One who does not hear the cry of the oppressed, who is not just and fair, who gives no second chances, who cannot be entreated, who can ignore His very image in those whom He has created—then, to me, it qualifies as a horrendous doctrine. This doctrine twists the true character of God.

> *There is a very logical reason why the Puritans and subsequent denominations were the spiritual defenders of racism and sexism, while the Quakers were the resisters of racism and sexism.*

If, in trying to prove God's sovereignty, you have to preclude His very character, then you are doing Him an astronomical disservice. Furthermore, there is a cultural consequence or societal ramification of this way of thinking—it creates a seedbed for racism and sexism. When you believe that God has already decided people's lot in life, whether for good or for bad, then it makes it convenient to believe, for example—by extension of logic—that slaves were made to be slaves and thus should not buck what has been predestined by God. It makes it easy to believe that women were called to be subservient to men and therefore should just accept their predestined role. There is a very logical reason why the Puritans and subsequent denominations were the spiritual defenders of racism and sexism, while the Quakers were the resisters of racism and sexism. I submit that Calvinism laid the foundation, through the doctrine of predestination, for blacks, Indians, and women to essentially be considered disposable. Again, predestination lays a seedbed for racism and sexism, as well as every other kind of discrimination. This does not mean that every Calvinist automatically embraced discriminatory beliefs, but the doctrinal foundation for them was certainly put in place. Original core Calvinism was fraught with doctrinal error that carried great negative societal implications. In my opinion, the doctrine of predestination leads its adherents to ask, subconsciously if not consciously, "If God does not equally love human beings of all genders, races, and nationalities, then why should we love them equally?" That is why I say this doctrine distorts God's image by disregarding or misunderstanding our Father's universal love for all people.

George Fox, on the other hand, taught and believed that there is "that of God in everyone who Christ Himself seeks to speak to." He believed the mission was to search out this God in everyone and to seek to get the individual to agree to live in accord with who God made them to be. As you see, this is closely related to the first doctrinal comparison we made in which Fox recognized an Inner Light in all. Though we might call this a difference of doctrine from predestination, it is actually stronger than that. It is a difference of God-view. Remember that A. W. Tozer said, "What you think about God is the most important thing about *you*." Nowhere is this truer than with this matter. Fox's teaching that there is "that of God in everyone" was not only a theoretical belief, but it also carried societal ramifications. Fox applied it first in church meetings, where he believed it was possible for anyone to be moved on by the Spirit and to share something that would benefit all. Therefore, in his meetings, women were free to speak, as were even children. He believed the biblical insight that *"there is neither Jew nor Greek, there is neither bond nor free, there is neither male nor female; for you are all one in Christ Jesus"* (Galatians 3:28).

The cultural consequences of this style of meeting were profound. The Quaker God-view, established by Fox, made it explicitly clear that all people carry intrinsic value because of the Light that is in them and that this inherent value extended to women, blacks, Indians, slaves, children, and anyone else. In the centuries after Fox, it would be his followers, with this doctrinal underpinning, who would contend for the abolition of slavery, for fair treatment of the Indians, for women's rights, for prisoners' rights, and more.

Many subsequent denominations were not at the forefront of the abolitionist movement and other social movements until very late in the game. By and large, these groups were the resisters of such change. For example, there was no denomination other than the Quakers contending for eliminating slavery during the Great Awakening (1730s–1740s). Individual pastors and other leaders joined in abolition efforts, but not whole denominations. So again, this was not just a doctrinal debate—it was a significant difference in God-view that had profound societal ramifications. Let us look at one case in point.

George Whitfield is one of the foremost revivalists in British and American history. Many wonderful things could be said about him, and, in fact, have been said about him over the years. However, here I wish only to point out a societal ramification of the Calvinism that he believed.

In 1735, over 125 years before the Civil War, the American colony of Georgia outlawed slavery, under the leadership and inspiration of James Oglethorpe. Stop and think about that a moment. A full 125 years before America went to war over slavery, there was enough awareness of the wrongfulness of slavery for a whole colony to outlaw it.[11] So when and why did Georgia revert to allowing slavery? The answer to the "when" is 1751; on January 1, the ban on slavery was rescinded, making it legal again to own slaves.[12] The answer to the "why" is George Whitfield.

British George Whitfield and American Jonathan Edwards were the two great religious figures of the Great Awakening. During that time, Whitfield made a couple of tours through the colonies. It must be understood that Whitfield stands out as perhaps the most famous preacher in England and America in the eighteenth century. In 1749, Whitfield came into Georgia on one of his revival tours, but besides doing that, he also intensely campaigned for the ban on slavery to be overturned. He expounded in detail how the colony would never be prosperous without the work of slaves. He came back to Georgia in 1751 and again campaigned heavily for the legalization of slavery. He wrote passionate pleas to the Georgia Trustees advocating slavery, so that even his own plantation in Georgia could be profitable. Largely through his significant influence, the ban on slavery was removed sixteen years after it had been instituted.[13]

It is truly appalling to realize that at about the same time that a Fox disciple named John Woolman was touring the colonies pleading with people to end the abominable slave trade, a Calvin disciple named George Whitfield, who was perhaps the key figure in having slavery reinstituted into a colony, was arguing the opposite. How different our entire nation's history might have been had Georgia been permitted to lead the way in showing economic prosperity apart from slavery. Perhaps more appalling is that today, throughout evangelicalism, it is

11. Some economic reasons contributed to the decision as well. See Betty Wood, "Slavery in Colonial Georgia," *New Georgia Encyclopedia*, http://www.georgiaencyclopedia.org/articles/history-archaeology/slavery-colonial-georgia.
12. Ibid.
13. Kyle Painter, *Constructing the Past*: Vol. 2: 1, Article 5 (2001), 32–36, http://digitalcommons.iwu.edu/constructing/vol2/iss1/5; Thomas Walker, "George Whitefield," Our Campaigns, http://www.ourcampaigns.com/CandidateDetail.html?CandidateID=230048.

often the name of Whitfield that is championed as ministers call for another revival, while the name of the heroic reformer John Woolman is hardly known. The following is George Whitfield's penned defense of slavery, in a letter to a friend:

> As for the lawfulness of keeping slaves, I have no doubt, since I hear of some that were bought with Abraham's money, and some were born in his house. And I can't help thinking, that some of those servants mentioned by the Apostles in their epistles, were or had been slaves. It is plain...though liberty is a sweet thing to such as are born free, yet to those who never knew the sweets of it, slavery perhaps may not be so irksome. However this be, it is plain to a demonstration, that hot countries cannot be cultivated without negroes. What a flourishing country might Georgia have been, had the use of them been permitted years ago? How many white people have been destroyed for want of them...I should think myself highly favoured if I could purchase a good number of them, in order to make their lives comfortable, and lay a foundation for breeding up their posterity in the nurture and admonition of the Lord. You know, dear Sir, that I had no hand in bringing them into Georgia; though my judgment was for it, and so much money was yearly spent to no purpose, and I was strongly importuned thereto, yet I would not have a negro on my plantation, till the use of them was publicly allowed in the colony. Now this is done, dear sir, let us reason no more about it, but diligently improve the present opportunity for their instruction.[14]

When, through his influence, slavery was reinstated in Georgia, Whitfield purchased slaves to work at his Bethesda Orphanage and to run his Bethesda Plantation. Is this all supposed to be overlooked as unimportant history because Whitfield was a fiery revivalist? I think not. Whitfield's segregated way of thinking of Negroes versus white

---

14. George Whitefield, *The Works of the Reverend George Whitefield, M.A., Vol. II.* (London: Edward and Charles Dilly, 1771, digitized by New York Public Library), 404–405, https://archive.org/details/worksreverendge04whitgoog.

men is a natural outcome of predestination and elect thinking. If, in his mind, God had no qualms about predetermining that blacks were meant to be slaves, then why would Whitfield have a conscience about it? The societal ramifications of predestination expose it as the horrendous doctrine that it is.

I would like to not be so harsh on Whitfield and say that he just didn't know better due to the times in which he lived. Keep in mind, however, that in this same period, there was an entire Christian denomination, the Quakers, that was increasingly raising the consciousness of the nation as to the evils of slavery. James Oglethorpe himself was an Anglican man of privilege, and he was already known as an avowed abolitionist.[15] How was it possible for a man of God to not know that God would value the lives of those known as Negroes? The answer is that to embrace full Calvinism is to embrace the ramifications of its doctrines—believing in a God who is not merciful, or just, or humane but who rather cold-heartedly sticks to an arbitrary plan, assigning lives of comfort to some and horrible existences to others. I don't know if I have the right to do this, but on behalf of George Whitfield, who is surely now aware of his great errors, I ask

> *God must be bowed down to, but not because He is the neighborhood bully and we have to play by His rules, but rather because He is the epitome of kindness, justice, and love.*

---

15. Edwin L. Jackson, "James Oglethorpe 1696–1785," *New Georgia Encyclopedia,* http://www.georgiaencyclopedia.org/articles/history-archaeology/james-oglethorpe-1696–1785.

all blacks for forgiveness for the profound ignorance and darkness of heart revealed through his words.

I should also point out that Jonathan Edwards himself had no qualms about slavery, and history records that in 1747, even after leading two rounds of the Great Awakening revival, he purchased a slave named Venus for 80 pounds. It seems clear that one of God's desired outcomes for the Great Awakening was to awaken the American consciousness to the evils of slavery. Though that seemed to happen with others, it was not the case with the two great revivalists themselves. A purpose of revival is always to address matters that need reforming.

Because of all of the above, I believe the moving forward trend of Christianity must take us away from the possibility of proclaiming a God who would choose a destiny of pain and misery for certain unfortunate people (as in predestination). Ultimately, God must be bowed down to, but not because He is the neighborhood bully and we have to play by His rules (as predestination and the accompanying elect doctrines imply), but rather because He is the epitome of kindness, justice, and love—and His very image in us yields to that representation of goodness.

3. Word Priority Versus Spirit Priority

George Fox got himself in a lot of trouble with Calvin's followers for proclaiming that the Spirit was superior to the written Word, or the Bible. Actually, Fox loved the Scriptures, but he summed up his thoughts in this way:

> I was to direct people to the Spirit that gave forth the Scriptures, by which they might be led into all truth, and up to Christ and God, as those had been who gave them forth."[16]

---

16. George Fox, *Journal of George Fox*, Street Corner Society, http://www.strecorsoc.org/gfox/ch02.html, chapter II.

He understood his assignment to be this: to connect the people not to the Bible but to the Holy Spirit who was the One who would teach His people through the writings He inspired. Fox contended for the reality that the Source of the Scriptures had to be greater than the Scriptures themselves. Though this seems obviously true, many people have a great doctrinal fear of acknowledging the Holy Spirit to be greater than the Scriptures He inspired.

The Calvinistic position on the supremacy of the written Bible is easy to understand. It is based on the idea that if people have the freedom to stray from precisely what is written in the Sacred Constitution, then there is no mechanism for doctrinal control. Anyone can claim to have been inspired by the Holy Spirit and seek to advance an idea or doctrine based on that inspiration alone. There is no doubt that those who cherish the Scriptures because of this concern have a valid caution. Fox himself had to rein in some of his disciples who did not understand the delicate balance of priorities. Fox understood that balance:

> Yet I had no slight esteem of the Holy Scriptures. They were very precious to me, for I was in that Spirit by which they were given forth; and what the Lord opened in me [revealed to me] I found afterwards was agreeable to them.[17]

Fox saw and declared that, though the Spirit was greater than the Scriptures, what the Spirit spoke would always be in agreement with the Scriptures. That is the fine balance.

Of course, there is significant fallacy to the belief that, by solely sourcing the written Scriptures for our doctrines, we can avoid error or promote some higher level of unity. There are over 30,000 denominations that have each chosen to separate from other Christians over a matter of interpretation of the supposedly clear instructions of the Bible. Obviously, the fear-based reasoning for disallowing extra-biblical revelation has not held up. Additionally, it is quite amazing how the most fervent defenders of the priority of the Holy Bible

---

17. Ibid.

are the very ones who "dispensationalize" out of the Word all truth that doesn't rationally appeal to them.[18] Miracles, signs and wonders, apostles and prophets, speaking in tongues and prophesying—all are repeatedly validated, endorsed, and modeled by Scripture itself, yet somehow dispensationalist John Nelson Darby and others have pulled off an amazing feat of scriptural elasticity, allowing those things to be tossed out of the very Book they idolized.

What is so disturbing about the dispensational grid is that you can apparently use it to evict from the Bible any truth you are not comfortable with. This is further proof that the Spirit is greater than the Word, as the Spirit reins us in from foolishly throwing out the parts of the Word that we don't have the faith to live out experientially. The biggest difference between charismatics and evangelicals is not that the former strays from the Scriptures and the latter stays grounded on them. The biggest difference is that charismatics value much more of the Scriptures, while evangelicals tend to have a dispensationally reduced Bible. It is the Bible itself that repeatedly prioritizes the Holy Spirit and all of His signs and manifestations. The point of the Manual (the Bible) is to engage with the Author of the Manual (the Holy Spirit) without fear, hesitation, or apathy.

> *Minus the Holy Spirit, the Scriptures can be an instrument of death, as proven time and again in history.*

Again, the clear trend moving forward for Christianity is the recognition that the Spirit is greater than the Word because it is the Holy Spirit who makes sure we properly assimilate the treasures contained in the Bible. As George Fox contended, if the Scriptures were equal to

18. "Dispensationalism" includes the belief that signs, wonders, and miracles are not for today but were only for a certain dispensation, or time period.

the Spirit, then you should be able to have a relationship with God simply by purchasing a Bible. This we know is impossible. Furthermore, 2 Corinthians 3:6 says, *"For the letter kills but the Spirit gives life."* Even the devil, when tempting Jesus in the wilderness (see, for example, Matthew 4:1–11), resorted to quoting Scripture. The Scriptures can be twisted and used to authorize some horrendous things. Minus the Holy Spirit, they can be an instrument of death, as proven time and again in history. The Inquisition, the murderous Crusades, Calvin's executions of other pastors, the Puritans' executions of Quakers—all were done surrounded by quite a bit of biblical quoting. Only the Holy Spirit can put the brakes on the deadly foolishness people commit with the supposed validation of the Bible.

George Fox, based on his Spirit-priority perspective, went around healing the sick, casting out demons, and prophetically "reading people's mail" (receiving discernment or a word of knowledge from the Lord about them). The members of the group he founded were known as the "Quakers" because when they would wait on the Holy Spirit, He would show up, and individuals and sometimes even whole buildings would quake with the impact. A Spirit-led life does not afford you all the guaranteed but limited outcomes of living only by biblical principles. A biblical principle should always lead to the essence of the Word—the Holy Spirit. If you give preeminence to the Holy Spirit, He just might mess up your orderly plan, but He will also supernaturally infuse you or the place where you are with an answer from heaven. When He shows up in power, His visitation is rarely the epitome of order. (See, for example, Acts 2.) Religion often brings order, but it's usually stifled order. The Holy Spirit brings life. John Calvin was into order. George Fox was into life. The advancing church will always prioritize life over order.

4. Anti-Semitism Versus Honoring the Jews

Perhaps no aspect of the old face of European Christianity is more disturbing and regrettable than its anti-Semitism—its prejudice or hostility against the Jews. It is the ultimate indicator of the weakness of the brand of Christianity that has principally been exhibited throughout the history of Christianity from right after the apostles' days up until the last few decades. It is not coincidental that, to the same degree that the person and work of the Holy Spirit has been high-lighted and valued in recent years, anti-Semitism among Christians has been rejected.

I have done as much research as possible on George Fox and his views on the Jews. I must point out the obvious—we can't refer to his views on Israel as a nation because such a thing did not exist in his day, nor did it seem possible. Yet, to the best of my ability in deciphering his thoughts, words, and actions, he seems to have been a man who felt passionately toward Jews and earnestly desired to reach them. From his theological premise that there is "that of God in everyone," we know that he was constrained from believing the lie that God had predestined the Israelites to fall away and become reprobate. It is quite remarkable that Fox could resist the tide of Christian anti-Semitism of his day, as it was so pervasive. It seems clear that if he were not a man of the Spirit, he also would have been deceived, misunderstanding the Scriptures and joining in the anti-Semitism accepted by much of what was called the church in that day.

Fox did write several treatises that attempted to convince the Jews that Christ was their Messiah. He and his wife, Margaret Fell Fox, had their messages translated into Hebrew, showing their passion to reach the Jews. He clearly considered it a valuable use of his time and saw it as something of importance to the Holy Spirit, whom he priori-tized at all times. We must understand that Fox was not looking for conversions in the sense we think of today, because they thought about it in a different way; he did not ask people to repeat a "sinner's prayer" that would once and for all seal them for eternity. So, when Fox and his wife were reaching out to Jews, it was not in order to get them to pray the sinner's prayer but that they might know that Jesus was their Messiah.

John Calvin, on the other hand, was decidedly anti-Semitic, as were virtually all of the fathers of the Protestant Reformation and the leaders of the Catholic Church. It was not that Calvin started anti-Semitism, but he did yield to the prevailing Christian thought of his day and was also strongly influenced by the centuries-old belief that the Jews were a damned race because of their role in the crucifixion of Jesus. There is a good reason why Jews today are slow to trust Christians; if they know their history, they can easily shake their heads over why many Christians suddenly respect, love, and honor their race when for centuries Christians dismissed them. However, we are finally beginning to model a Christianity that is less offensive to the God we serve because the Holy Spirit is making us into a people who understand His heart.

Part of the frustration toward Jews that John Calvin carried was their lack of response to the Christianity of the day—a Christianity that I, too, would not have responded well to. The Jews of that time had almost no interest in the brand of Christianity being bandied about by the reformers. Calvin's views on God having elect ones did extend to the Jews; he knew by the Scriptures that at least a remnant of Jews must come to recognize Jesus as Messiah. The problem was that none of the Jews were buying what the Protestants were selling from a theological perspective, which was really irritating to both him and Luther, who was an even more severe anti-Semite. Calvin said of the Jews,

> Their rotten and unbending stiffneckedness deserves that they be oppressed unendingly without measure or end and that they die in their misery without the pity of anyone.[19]

When you believe it is proper for anyone to "die in their misery without the pity of anyone," it can be revealing that this is your perspective of who God is and what He is capable of. That Calvin would address the entire race of Jews in such a hopeless manner is disturbing. He also wrote of the Jews,

---

19. John Calvin as quoted in Gerhard Falk, *The Jew in Christian Theology* (Jefferson, NC: McFarland and Company, 1931).

> I have had much conversation with many Jews: I have never seen either a drop of piety or a grain of truth or ingenuousness—nay, I have never found common sense in any Jew.[20]

This statement reveals a general anti-Semitic character to his thoughts about the Jews, and it really is important to identify this as a significant matter. Honestly, the negative role of Protestant Christianity in promoting anti-Semitism must be underscored. Martin Luther wrote some of the most vitriolic things about Jews that have ever been written anywhere, and there is strong connective evidence that Hitler and the Nazis felt validated by Luther and his writings.[21] It is not just a coincidence that the nation that produced Luther is the same nation that produced Hitler. It seems almost obvious that the anti-Semitic seeds that Luther planted in Germany were harvested in Hitler's life. It is well-established that Hitler's soldiers would go from their day at the extermination camps to taking their families to their Lutheran churches. Yes, some of the Lutherans were misled by Hitler, but honestly, most of them had already inherited this anti-Semitism. It was already in their religious DNA.

The Jews are supposed to reject all inferior brands of Christianity, and they will ultimately accept only that which is birthed and bathed in the Father's love.

---

20. John Calvin, "Daniel 2:44–45," *Calvin's Commentary on Daniel*, Christian Classics Ethereal Library, http://www.ccel.org/ccel/calvin/comment3/comm_vol24/htm/viii.xxviii.htm.

21. See, for example, Robert Michael, *Holy Hatred: Christianity, Antisemitism, and the Holocaust* (New York: Palgrave Macmillan, 2006), 119.

Therefore, when we look ahead to the Christian trends away from the old face of Christianity toward the new, we must recognize the supremely important shift taking place to honor Israel and the Jews. The Jews are the original root that we are grafted into through faith in Jesus Christ (see Romans 11:17–24), through which we have access to the original covenant that God made with Abraham. Abraham is the common bond, but it is through our faith in God (by Jesus Christ) that we connect to the same promises Abraham attained through his faith in God. It is not our primary assignment to attempt to transactionally convert Jews; rather it is our privilege to love and honor them for belonging to the original root that brought forth our Lord and Savior. Our biblical commission is to provoke them to jealousy with the level of God-likeness we display. (See Romans 11:11–12.) A significant sign that we are finally carrying the correct brand of Christianity is that it will be attractive to the Jews, not so much in an intellectual capacity but on a heart level. Their internal "knower" will go off, convincing them that they are hearing truth. If we do our part, we can trust the Holy Spirit to do His part. The Jews are supposed to reject all inferior brands of Christianity, and they will ultimately accept only that which is birthed and bathed in the Father's love. They will one day look at Him whom they rejected and mourn for Him, but we are to be the vehicle of the grace that God will pour out on them.

> *And I will pour on the house of David and on the inhabitants of Jerusalem the Spirit of grace and supplication: then they will look at Me whom they have pierced. Yes they will mourn for Him as one mourns for his only son, and grieve for Him as one grieves for a firstborn.* (Zechariah 12:10)

Final Thoughts on the Comparison Between Calvin and Fox

My purpose in reviewing the contrasting beliefs of Calvin and Fox is to give us a practical picture of the changing face of Christianity today. Again, John Calvin is representative of where we have been, and George Fox is representative of where we are going. I cannot ultimately vouch for every theological statement or doctrine of Fox, but suffice it to say that as far ahead of the pack as he was almost 400 years ago, I am certain that if he had lived into the twenty-first century, he would have been the lead domino for the church today.

In fact, in 2012, I had a special encounter with the presence of the Lord one night in which He told me that I was a carrier of George Fox's torch. It wasn't that I was the only one carrying his torch, but that I was one of those who came in the same spirit as Fox. This led me to a time of deep research into Fox's writings and into who he was. During this process, I had the privilege of visiting his gravesite in London, England. I believe that as the church and as a nation, we owe a great debt of gratitude to this man of God. He truly was a forerunner in many things that are only now becoming characteristic of the church as a whole.

Fox didn't have a clearly developed theology on many things, because he went totally outside the box and tried to live by simply being responsive to the Holy Spirit. Women thrived under his ministry because he was a very early voice validating the abilities of women to carry leadership and the anointing of God. He was imprisoned many times for his views, once specifically for declaring that women were also made in God's image. If you think our brand of Christianity is weak today, just know that it has been enormously upgraded from what it was. The Protestant Reformation reformed almost nothing compared to what is left to be reformed. Luther gained for us the truth that salvation was by faith in Jesus Christ alone, which is huge. But he did not advance in much else of significant value. It took great courage for him to do even that, and thus we applaud him, but there is still an immense amount of forward progress in reformation to be made. In the next section of this chapter on the Mountain of Religion, I want to specifically address coming areas of Renaissance that will be taking place through the year 2050.

The Church Renaissance: 2015–2050

I should point out that in my last prophetic book on the Seven Mountains, entitled *The Seven Mountain Mantle*, I covered basically what I could see up until 2015. I really could not see much further than that; I perhaps even felt that things were progressing at a quicker pace than they really are. Though things are advancing at an unprecedented pace, there is the reality check that the things that need to be accomplished before Jesus comes will take decades or centuries to complete; they won't be completed in just a handful of years.

Generally, as leaders in the church and other believers age, it is customary for them to begin to believe that their own approaching end of days means the wrapping up of things for everyone. My own very godly father thought he would be here when Jesus returned, and yet he died over nine years ago. I grew up in a movement that believed that the end of days, in one way or another, would be upon us shortly. I remember being concerned as a teenager that I would never really get to experience life, because I was taught that all signs were pointing to an imminent end. Yet decades have gone by, and those supposedly clear signs of the end have had to be reconsidered. I have also studied enough of church history to be aware that an end-times mentality has affected every single generation since the apostle Paul encouraged the unmarried to remain so because Jesus' return was imminent. (See 1 Corinthians 7.) Paul, too, thought Jesus would come back to earth in his lifetime. This means you can be very spiritually mature and even have many revelations and visions but still be wrong about how soon Jesus is returning or how soon your end-time scenario is going to play out. At least consider what I am saying.

Why a 100-Year Plan Is Wise

Before I begin to explain various aspects of the church in Renaissance, I want to share why I think it wise to make long-term plans. Short-term thinking has been extremely bad for Christianity, and it has many negative repercussions. First of all, we find ourselves with very few enduring institutions because of our shortsighted expectations. For example, we complain about the extreme humanism and similar ideas in our colleges and universities, yet we haven't really prioritized the founding of new institutions of higher education. Certainly, one part of reformation is to change the old, but the other part is to create the new. When we live by a narrative that says, "It's all going to be over in a few years," then we don't find value in building enduring institutions. As a result, we have many shooting-star institutions that rise up quickly and collapse just as quickly. It's as if we can't envision anything beyond five years, and so everything we are contending for must happen in that time frame. We operate with a microwaveable Christianity that rarely leaves anything of substance for the next generation. That is now going to change.

Even as I have carried and advanced the Seven Mountain message, many have asked me, "Where have we seen that this actually works? Tell me of a nation that has been transformed." I respond that, first of all, this message has only had any real traction for about five years, and it is highly unlikely we are going to correct centuries of neglect and societal absenteeism within that short time frame. Second, I am still able to give remarkable testimonies and examples of great advancements in nations (even if we are not yet able to point to such and such a nation as an example of complete transformation). It is all a work in progress, and we need to temper our eschatologically induced impatience, which is not helpful for advancing things to the next generations and positioning them for greater advances.

Consequently, as you age, you have some very clear choices before you. Ask yourself, "Do I continue to invest time and resources in advancing myself, or do I look to advance my children...or grandchildren?" I believe the Holy Spirit guides us in wisdom for how to do both, because both are needed, but surely there is an urgency to begin to prioritize the next generation.

What would happen if we built churches not thinking about only the next five to ten years? What would happen if we set up learning institutions thinking beyond that, to the next 30, 50, or 100 years? What would it look like if we established Harvards rather than simply schools of ministry—or rather in addition to our schools of ministry? Why aren't we presently very influential in Hollywood, or in government, or in education, or in media, and so forth? I believe it's generally because we don't go after positions and options that might require some real time and effort. I previously mentioned eschatologically induced impatience. Well, that mind-set also breeds eschatologically induced laziness. When we believe that either Jesus or the Antichrist is coming right around the corner, we develop shortsighted plans and have shortsighted dreams. I know these things because I realized that, until fairly recently, that is how I myself operated.

> *When we believe that either Jesus or the Antichrist is coming right around the corner, we develop shortsighted plans and have shortsighted dreams.*

I have finally become convinced that we are not as close to the end-of-days scenarios as most of us think. It was initially a little depressing for me to accept the idea that I will get old and apparently die one day without seeing the fullness of this Renaissance manifested, but once I got over that hurdle, it has been very healthy for me and has allowed me to begin to care and plan for my children and their generation.

Moving Past the "Sinking Ship" Mentality

A mind-set of making long-term plans has other implications. For example, we as Christians have been perhaps the most negligent group at caring for our planet. This, too, is eschatologically induced, resulting in poor stewardship of the world God has given us. We have held the idea that, since Jesus is about to return, there is no real point in taking care of our rivers, lakes, oceans, varieties of species, air quality, and so forth. Famed Bible teacher J. Vernon McGee (1904–1988), whom I listened to as a kid, was a typical voice devaluing any attempt to fix things on this planet. One of his key phrases was, "There is no sense polishing brass on a sinking ship." He viewed the world as a lost cause; hence, there was no reason to improve anything. As I have been pointing out throughout this book, many of our doctrines do not stay confined within the walls of our churches. Rather, what we believe has a huge effect on how we respond to our day-to-day society. When one of our doctrines is faulty, it can release considerable damage in the world. We simply must begin to think long-term, while all along acknowledging that we are in the general scope of the last days. Again, the apostle Paul called his days the last days, and yes, we are closer to the end than ever before; but we are still probably a few generations away. Believe it, and it will help you to be more effective in the world.

Renaissance Trends

As we look at the forthcoming church trends, please note that they are all part of an ever-increasing knowledge of God. This Renaissance period is when His better ways of doing everything will be made evident. As a result, God will increase in fame throughout the earth. The church in Renaissance will be about each church finding more ways to reveal who and how God is. We will learn and manifest in more nuanced ways all the various ways that He loves. His sacrifice on the cross embodied how much He loves us, but He also has many more ways that He desires to show His love for us. Our goal will be to discover His many manifestations of love and to display them in every area of society. Though there will always be enemies and some level of peril, now is the time to increase in wisdom and in favor with God and man. I believe that over the next two generations, the kingdom of God will so advance that it will become a popular thing to be a Christian. Darkness is going to begin to be pushed back to the outer fringes of society in many to most nations. This really is going to happen. Believe it, and you will become one of God's transformative hope ambassadors on the planet.

Trend #1: Transitioning from Revival-mindedness to Reformation-mindedness

There is nothing wrong with wanting revival. We want many new people to come to a living relationship with Jesus Christ, and we also want the church to be and to feel revived. Whatever revival means to you, it is in fact a good thing. However, now it is time to make the switch into prioritizing reformation-mindedness. Whereas revival is about souls (and perhaps also a passionate and fully alive church), reformation is about the structures of society itself being addressed by the presence and the solutions of the kingdom of God. Reformation-mindedness thinks in multigenerational terms, while revival thinking is usually connected to the unhelpful end-times thinking that currently grips many people—the idea that we have to get everybody saved because Jesus is coming any day now.

In Matthew 5:14, in Jesus' first recorded address as the Son of God, He said, *"You are the light of the world"* and then described the light as being on a lampstand that will light up a whole city or nation. (See verse 15.) This connects well to the Seven Mountain mandate that I've spoken of in my earlier books. (I do recommend you read those books because they further lay out the fact that our assignment extends beyond just making converts to Christianity.) Jesus preceded that statement about being light with this one: *"You are the salt of the earth"* (Matthew 5:13). He continued by saying that if you don't show up with your proper saltiness, you are good for nothing but to be trampled upon. This mandate also makes it clear that we have a responsibility beyond revival and that we must be reformers or transformers of society. In those days, salt was used to preserve meat because people had no means of refrigeration. Jesus was saying, in effect, "You are the preservers of your society. Whatever part of society you do not preserve will come back to trample you." He could have added, "And don't think I will return just because you are being trampled. It just means you stayed in your revival salt shaker and refused to step out into reformation." Reformational/transformational thinking takes us back to Jesus' original message and His original mandate. We have somehow limited being salt and light to giving our testimony of salvation and contending for others to also get saved. Clearly, we have not fully understood the assignment, and that's why much of society has the smell of rot in it, despite the large presence of Christians. This, too, will begin to greatly change over the next few decades. Believe it, and you begin the process of being salt and light. Proper behavior and action follow true believing.

> *Proper behavior and action follow true believing.*

As important as it is to want people to one day live in heaven, it is equally important to be aware that Jesus' very first message was more about trying to get heaven on earth than about trying to get people into heaven. In that same message, He said, *"In this manner, therefore, pray: …Your kingdom come. Your will be done **on earth as it is in heaven**"* (Matthew 6:9–10). Somehow, we have become stuck with a narrative that prioritizes getting people prepared for heaven, yet Jesus came proclaiming a different priority—a priority of heaven coming down to earth. He didn't present the sinner's prayer in His first message but rather, in essence, pleaded for partners in reforming society. Obviously, He also cared for people's eternal state, but the scope of the kingdom of God—His better way of doing everything—is broader than that.

It is the famous Lord's Prayer that informs us of heaven's priority of reformation over revival (focusing only on the saving of souls). Let us look at Jesus' words again:

Our Father in heaven, hallowed be Your name. Your kingdom come. Your will be done on earth as it is in heaven.
(Matthew 6:9–10)

The typical revivalistic, getting-saved thinking is about prioritizing the hereafter. Kingdom-come thinking is about how heaven can show up on earth today. When it says, *"Your kingdom come...as it is in heaven,"* it's not talking about the transaction of getting saved, because that doesn't happen in heaven. God doesn't have periodic meetings in paradise where He asks for every head to be bowed and invites whoever wishes to raise their hand and pray the sinner's prayer. So the kingdom coming to earth is not about salvations; it's about functionality and the institutions of heaven. The kingdom is the rule and reign of heaven, and so the mission is to manifest the rule and reign of heaven on earth. It is to showcase heaven's better institutions.

Heaven is not just a place filled with happy people but a place filled with happy institutions. The Seven Mountains on earth also exist in heaven. As a reminder, the Seven Mountains are religion, education, family, government, economy/business, media, and celebration/arts. These are the seven primary spheres or structures of society in every nation. Jesus' prayer was that heaven's model of these structures would come manifest *"on earth as it is in heaven."* This is absolutely going to happen, because Jesus' prayer cannot go unanswered. Let's briefly take a look at each of these areas:

1. Religion/Worship

Religion, properly understood, exists in heaven. Our religion is our choice of who we intentionally worship. The Mountain of Religion can also be called the Mountain of Worship. In heaven, our Father is honored as God, and everyone is fully aware of that reality. All around the throne, worship of Him and to Him is constantly breaking out. This is also what's happening throughout heaven. It is not by compulsion that He is the ongoing object of worship and honor. Literally no one can hold back from worshipping and honoring Him because the sevenfold beauty of who He is compels all to do so. It starts with the overwhelming awareness that we do not deserve to be in this place called heaven, and that God so loved everyone that He did everything possible to allow humans the privilege of living in His ecosystem, where every structure shouts with His goodness. As we learn what truly causes people to be unable to resist worshipping and honoring Him in heaven, that will greatly serve us on earth in defeating the counterfeit competition for worship and honor. So, Jesus was essentially saying, "Papa, let true religion show up on earth as it is in heaven." In reality, the only true religion that exists is the worship and adoration of the Father, Son, and Holy Spirit. All other so-called religion is just a counterfeit designed to steal that which belongs to Him.

2. Education

There is continuing education in heaven. When we go to heaven, we will fully know as we are known (see 1 Corinthians 13:12), but we will not fully know all things. There will be ongoing learning and instruction throughout eternity. Mystery after mystery will be revealed throughout the ages. Even as here on earth, whoever is hungry to learn will have endless opportunities. There is in fact a glory to education because, ultimately, true education expands our hearts and minds into the greatness and majesty of God. The more we are educated about Him and His ways, the more we will live in awe.

I believe that the twenty-four elders in heaven spoken of in Revelation 4 and 5 are constantly casting their crowns at His feet and saying *"Holy, holy, holy"* because they have just been shown something they hadn't previously seen. They do not cast down their crowns and emote because some megalomaniacal dictator has ordered them to. They simply can't help doing so as they learn more about God's ways. This is another means by which the Father shows His love to us—by satisfying our love of learning and exploring; by rewarding our curiosity with insights that instill satisfaction and joy. Our assignment on earth is to ponder and learn through the Holy Spirit how the glory of instruction and education advances in heaven and then to manifest it on earth. The standard for education is in heaven, so we must learn from there, for here. This we can do through the instruction of the One who is the Spirit of Truth. Again, He was saying, "Papa, the way education functions in heaven, let it function here on earth." This is what reformers from this mountain long to step into—praying, doing, and seeing heaven on earth.

3. Family

Not only is there family in heaven, but we are all one big family in Him. We all came from Him, and all who are in heaven are those who recognized that He is indeed our Father and that He provided access to His family via what His Son Jesus did on the cross. Ephesians 3:14–15 speaks of our Father's whole family in heaven and on earth. Our God in heaven is also our Papa. It is yet another strand of His love that He shows us from the seven primary ways He reveals His love to us. Think of the seven colors of the rainbow as each color representing another nuance of His love. God as our Papa in heaven provides an atmosphere of absolute belonging and absolute nurture. In the Lord's Prayer, Jesus was saying, "Papa, the way family functions in heaven, let it function here on earth." As we learn by the Holy Spirit how that works, we become empowered to manifest that rule and reign of heaven on earth. We are made in His image and are designed to reveal His image. There are seven *"Spirits of God"* (Revelation 1:4; 3:1; 4:5; 5:6), and we are to see and reflect each of

> *Our God in heaven is also our Papa.*

those on earth just as they are in heaven. The further studying of Him, and the subsequent revealing of Him in this expanded perspective, is what the Era of Renaissance is all about.

4. Government

There is government in heaven. This may be a surprise to many who despise government here on earth, but heaven is not anarchy. Father God is fully in charge, and things run totally by His rules. However, everyone loves His rules and there is no rebellion. There is a glory to a properly run government, and it is one of the ways in which our Father shows His love to us. Everyone feels safe, and everyone knows that only just decisions are being made. When Jesus says, *"On earth as it is in heaven,"* one of the things He is saying is, "Papa, let the way government functions in heaven come function here on earth." As we look to how heaven runs government, we the sons and daughters of the kingdom can demonstrate on earth what we are shown by the Holy Spirit about how heaven's government runs. The principles of that government may be found throughout the Scriptures, ready and waiting to be mined by us.

5. Economy/Business

Yes, there is business in heaven. Heaven will not be about sitting around; rather, we will all be gainfully employed in what we were originally wired to do. Business in heaven is not about what makes you money, since there's no need for money there. It's about connecting your uniquely wired skill set with what needs to be done. This is how we are supposed to function on earth, as well.

Father is the great Provider who covers all our needs as we fulfill our calling. This is yet another way He showcases His love in heaven. He gives us the opportunity to do and to be what we were originally wired for, and He's the One who takes care of economizing everything. He doesn't just have billion-year-old structures and resources in heaven, but He continues daily to be Jehovah-Jireh, the Lord our Provision.

He is continually and constantly renewing heaven. We really do have mansions, and they are being built with His ongoing resourcefulness as we gain eternal rewards on earth. In the same way that He resources heaven, He is prepared to do on earth. Jesus was in essence praying, "Father, the way you run the economy of heaven, let that system and reality come to earth." As we learn His heavenly system and download it here on earth, we further advance the on-earth aspects of our reformation assignment.

6. Media/Communications

This may also be a surprise to some, but there is media in heaven. In heaven, communication is not only important but is an essential part of who God is. John 1:1 says that *"in the beginning was the Word, and the Word was with God, and the Word was God."* If we know about the power of the media here on earth, then we can imagine just how knowledgeable our Father is about that which is His essence. Everything in heaven runs on good news. Think about it: The inhabitants of heaven know better than we do what is going wrong on earth. They know exactly how many people went to hell in the last twenty-four hours, yet that is not repeated on the evening news in heaven. The news in heaven is always good and always looks for the silver lining behind everything. God cares deeply about all the tragic things that happen here on earth, but He doesn't consider the reviewing of those tragedies as helpful. He will tell only of the heroism within the tragedies, and this keeps everyone encouraged, hopeful, and expectant.

Our Father is a brilliant Communicator, and His way of communicating is another facet of His love. Our earthly assignment is to discover the wisdom and glory of God's communication system and to implement those principles here on earth. Referring to how we defeat Satan, Revelation 12:11 says, *"And they overcame him by the blood of the Lamb and by the word of their testimony."* The word *"testimony"* means evidence given, a record, report, or witness. Satan is overcome not just by what Jesus did on the cross but also by our repeating the correct "eyewitness news." As we learn this standard of heaven, we can implement on earth the rule and reign of heaven that coincides with this structure of society. We agree with Jesus when we pray, "Papa, the way media and communications work in heaven, let them work on earth." Reformers will look into this and cause a Renaissance in our media reporting.

7. Celebration/Arts & Entertainment

Celebrating through creativity is huge in heaven. In Psalm 16:11, it says, "*In Your presence is fullness of joy; at Your right hand are pleasures forevermore.*" When God's throne room is described in Revelation 4 and 5, it becomes clear that it is a place of supreme creativity, with amazing creatures, sounds, colors, smells, and angels all in some kind of elaborate creative flow or orchestration. Our Father is introduced to us in Genesis 1:1 as Creator, and this is clearly a prime way He shows His love to us. In the Lord's Prayer, Jesus was therefore also declaring, "Papa,

> *A major aspect of our assignment on earth is to have the world in awe of God's creativity.*

let the way creativity is celebrated in heaven become a reality here on earth, as well." A Renaissance in arts and entertainment will take place as we better understand the model in heaven and learn to reflect it here on earth. Presently, Christians are not particularly known for their creativity or innovation. That will be greatly changing in this Era of Renaissance. We will fully recognize that a major aspect of our assignment on earth is to have the world in awe of God's creativity, just as the elders and angels of heaven themselves are in awe of His majestic creativity. Our God loves to celebrate with that which is new, and it will be a great joy for the coming generations to carry that aspect of who He is to the masses. It is a primary way that He loves.

So this is a taste of how we go from revival thinking to reformation thinking. It starts with knowing how much more there is to God, His kingdom, and His narrative, and then contending for it. The irony, of course, is that once we finally get on with the reformation mandate, revival and souls will come in like a deluge. When Jesus is lifted up, He draws all to Himself. (See John 12:32.) We have primarily been counting on people's fear of hell as their motivation to get saved, but there is a better way. Up to now, a sense of eternal insecurity has brought in much of the harvest, but in the coming days, the beauty and glory of God will win the hearts of the masses, and that harvest will be immense.

Trend #2: Transitioning from Church-mindedness to Kingdom-mindedness

After reading "Trend #1: Transitioning from Revival-mindedness to Reformation-mindedness," this next trend could be seen as fairly obvious, but each trend progresses toward the next. One aspect of revival thinking is all about the church. When you expand the purpose of revival into reformation, then you also expand into a kingdom-first focus. Jesus said, *"But seek first the kingdom of God and His righteousness…"* (Matthew 6:33). Again, the kingdom of God is about a way of doing things and not just about conversion transactions.

The reason that a church focus presently dominates and permeates the Mountain of Religion is that churches are, by and large, led by pastors. When pastors lead, they think of their mission in terms of "my church." A true pastor is wired with many great qualities, but it is totally unnatural and therefore rare for him to think at a macro city-church level. This is why the biblical model for church leadership is first apostles and prophets: *"Having been built on the foundation of the apostles and prophets, Jesus Christ Himself being the chief corner stone"* (Ephesians 2:20).

Both true apostles and true prophets are gifted with macro vision and see all they do in the context of society, culture, city, nation, and God's master narrative. The word *apostle* in the original Greek was not religious terminology. It was a military word used for the military leader that was in charge of bringing the culture of Rome to the most recently defeated nations and tribes. Rome had discovered that defeated nations and tribes would rebel and seek to revert back to their old identities unless Roman culture was intentionally transfused into the region. Therefore an "apostle" was sent to make sure that not only did a people militarily submit, but that they also would begin to culturally reflect Rome by speaking the same language, using the same money, adopting the same holidays, and so forth.

That God would transform and commission His twelve disciples into twelve apostles tells us that He not only wanted conversions, but He also wanted heaven's ways of doing things to begin to be implemented. He wanted heaven's culture on earth. A local pastor in the truest sense has a basic inability to think that broadly, which is precisely what makes him so good at loving the local sheep. We definitely want true pastors, and we definitely don't want to resent or negate them—it's just that they are mismatched for the role they are generally expected to play. Militarily, it's sort of like the MASH unit doctor trying to fulfill the role of a general.

If a church is going to be kingdom-minded and raise kingdom-focused people, then it must be led by the primary voice of an apostle. Presently, many who carry the title of apostle are just insecure pastors with baggage and extra pride. However, that will change. There are still real apostles, and they will continue to increase and populate the church until we are more in line with the biblical mandate of apostles first, with the other gifts following. (See 1 Corinthians 12:28.)

Once a church, a movement, or a denomination is led by an apostle who sees from a macro perspective, we will begin to experience a much greater advance of the kingdom of God at large; the size of the apostle's personal ministry will be a secondary matter. Many of the largest churches in the world have almost no apostolic influence on the culture, and it's because they are led by either a very charismatic pastor or someone who knew how to leverage marketing in order to grow. The masses are often drawn into adulation of gifted people, but if the gifted one does not also equip them for real life and for influencing the culture, then it's a tragically wasted opportunity. These leaders may have effectively accomplished the first step of attracting a potential army, but they have failed to train, equip, and deploy them. A true apostle will always care more about training, equipping, and deploying than about the size of the crowd that follows him. Large congregations are notorious for being spectators rather than participants, and sadly that's often because it satisfies the demands of the charismatic leader's ego. Having a large congregation makes you famous on earth, but a crowd of nodding heads does nothing for a community or city. When you are a leader involved in training, equipping, and deploying, it makes you known in heaven. Soon there will be great churches that excel at both. Those leaders who truly seek first the kingdom of God will be satisfied with nothing less than reformation-minded congregants.

Kingdom-mindedness is about getting the salt of influence into society. Church-mindedness is about salt being in the shaker and every grain of salt (the congregants) being accounted for and fought over with the other salt shakers (churches). Kingdom thinking has you occupied with getting light into the city, as Jesus instructed. Church thinking has you trying to extend only your own church's fame. Kingdom thinking is more concerned about the nine-to-five, Monday-through-Friday window, whereas church thinking just wants to have a successful Sunday meeting (and, of course, a great offering). Renaissance will come to the church as kingdom thinking grows, creating a trend for the next several decades.

Trend #3: Transitioning from Kingdom-mindedness to Church-mindedness

Yes, you read it correctly. This may sound confusing and even contradictory, in light of the previous trend of going from church-mindedness to kingdom-mindedness. Here is the explanation—it's all about proper placement and proper priority. In the same way that we would not build a foundation on top of a first floor, we cannot put first what needs to come second. But once the foundation is laid, the building now becomes the priority. The church is immensely valuable, but it must be built upon a kingdom grid. Once we make the transition from being overly focused on church to being focused on the kingdom first, we can then transition to building *the* church.

Many people have mistakenly assumed that *the* church and the local church are really not important, but nothing could be further from the truth. Once we understand that the foundation is the kingdom, then it is in fact the church that is the most important part of the kingdom. This is going to become increasingly important for us to be aware of as we advance. The church has lost much of its luster because of its improper placement and leadership. But have no doubt about it—the church will be a glorious thing in the coming days. Jesus said, *"I will build my church; and the gates of hell shall not prevail against it"* (Matthew 16:18 kjv). He didn't say that the kingdom would stem the gates of hell but that the church would. In Ephesians, when instructing husbands on how to love their wives, Paul said, *"Husbands, love your wives, just as Christ also loved the church and gave Himself for her"* (Ephesians 5:25). We must remember that the church is still the bride of Christ, for whom He gave His life, *"that He might present her to Himself a glorious church, not having spot or wrinkle or any such thing"* (verse 27). To further establish the church's coming value, let's read Ephesians 3:10:

> To the intent that now the manifold wisdom of God might be made known **by the church** to the principalities and powers in the heavenly places.

There is something that God is going to showcase even to principalities and powers and it will be by the church!

And another portion of Ephesians:

And [God] *put all things under* [Jesus'] *feet, and gave Him to be the head over all things* **to the church, which is His body,** *the fullness of Him who fills all in all."*   (Ephesians 1:22–23)

Ultimately, nothing will ever be more important than being Christ's body—and ultimately, all opposition will be put under the feet of the church, with Christ being the head. Therefore, I repeat, once we lay the foundation of the kingdom, there is nothing more important than the church. The kingdom is the divine mission, but the church is the divine romance, and together they give us the divine narrative. God is not just trying to get something done; He is producing and directing the greatest story ever told. So let's become those who seek first the kingdom of God while not losing sight of the great value of His bride, the church.

Trend #4: The Explosion of New Church Wineskins

I believe that we will soon experience such a great harvest of souls that the existing church wineskins won't do well at holding what comes in. (See, for example, Matthew 9:17.) When I talk about "wineskins," I'm speaking of church structures. The coming harvest will bring in so many broken and fractured people that the existing churches will struggle with how to

> *Much of the church is presently a bit schizophrenic, not knowing if it is more important to be the standard of righteousness or the example of unconditional love.*

properly assimilate them. Much of the church is presently a bit schizophrenic, not knowing if it is more important to be the standard of righteousness or the example of unconditional love. This is something we will begin to resolve and address better and better as we advance in this Era of Renaissance. The answer to that dilemma is in the most common verse of the Bible:

> *For God so loved the world that He gave His only Son, that whoever believes in Him should not perish but have everlasting life.*
> (John 3:16)

Note that this verse doesn't start with, "For God so *needed* the world to *know the rules* that He gave His only Son…." God didn't allow His Son to be crucified just to rehash the Ten Commandments. He needed the world to know that He was about relationship, not about rules. Furthermore, Jesus Himself told His disciples that when He would send them the Holy Spirit, it would be the Holy Spirit who would convict the world of their sins. (See John 16:8.) Things quickly turn into a mess when we try to do the Holy Spirit's work for Him. To connect this point with a previous one, Calvin-based thinking declares, "We have to get the world to behave." Fox-based thinking, on the other hand, emphasizes, "We must make room for the Holy Spirit, because He is the One who convicts of sin."

A very great harvest is coming, made up of homosexuals, transvestites, druggies, the abused, the displaced, and the rejected, as well as the "up and outers" of society. Up and outers are those with social and economic privilege who are yet very broken. This harvest is going to require a lot of patience and love, and many church structures and denominations (old wineskins) will not be ready for the task. The tendency of churches will be to worry about their holiness reputation; as a result, they won't want to dirty their hands cleaning the new fish (baby Christians). This will initiate the dynamic that accompanies most revival seasons, such as the Azusa revival in the early 1900s and the Jesus Movement of the 1960s, when multiple denominations were formed to hold the harvest of individuals who didn't easily fit into the already established churches. Once again, people will be having such intense and personal experiences with the Holy Spirit that most churches will not feel comfortable with them. Churches will once again theoretically want the Holy Spirit to show up, as long as He doesn't *really* show up. Churches will once again accept the God who brings a tear to the eye, but not One who shakes the whole body. Once again, the "fish" will be so messy and stinky that churches will be torn between protecting what they already have and making room for the new. In this vacuum, many new churches will arise, along with many new ways of "doing church." This will be a key component to the coming extreme make-over of that organization that calls itself the church.

Seven Mountain Micro-churches, Daily Churches, 24/7 Churches, Home Churches, and Stadium Churches

Let's go through a quick rundown of some other things that will be coming into view. These are meant to be understood more as examples than an exhaustive list. There will be Seven Mountain micro- or mini-churches that will meet around their mountain assignments. These will be those that are so reformation-minded and kingdom-minded that they will seek the vehicle of advancement with the least distraction from their core assignment. It would be my recommendation that there be at least two mountains per micro-church, as it creates greater perspective. Certain mountains best facilitate certain other mountains. For example, the Mountain of Economy/Business and the Mountain of Celebration/Arts would go well together. The Mountain of Education and the Mountain of Family would also jointly function well. The Mountain of Media and the Mountain of Government would similarly team up well. Other combinations could also work. Obviously, the Mountain of Economy/Business would be a good match with any one of the other mountains, because all advances require funding. Official or unofficial micro-churches have the opportunity to be for the kingdom what Special Forces are to military advances.

I believe we will have so many new people coming in needing or wanting to encounter God every day that there will be churches that open their doors nightly for meetings. I also see 24/7 churches being raised up for the same reason, churches that will stay open and have services all day. People will be hungry and needy for encounters with God, His presence, His principles, and His people. A soon-coming revival will be the impetus for many 24/7 churches exploding onto the scene of Christianity.

Home churches are already exploding all over, and I expect that trend to increase indefinitely, as well. There will be some networks of these home churches that will have developed a healthy model for experiencing true relational Christianity. The present home church phenomenon is primarily about people seeking true connectivity and relationship. In the coming models, genuine reformation-mindedness will also be part of the DNA of many of these home church streams. Presently, many of these streams carry an end-of-days narrative as part of their identity, but this, too, will begin to change in a positive direction. True apostolic oversight and vision-casting will be key to this taking place. Some of it is already happening, but it will greatly increase as a home church dynamic in this Era of Renaissance.

Ultimately, there will be every kind of church expression and every size of church, including stadium churches, because of the immense size of the harvest. There really is no biblical ideal as to where the church should meet. The early church met in homes, not because it was ideal but because it was the only place they could meet. Jesus clearly attempted to speak anywhere a crowd would come. He went to the temple and to synagogues, and He also went to individual homes. He spoke in open fields and mountain settings—anywhere two or more would gather in His name.

There is nothing wrong with multiple styles and models, and I think we are finally going to get comfortable with that reality. God made no two people on the planet the same. He is the Author of many looks and many styles, and He is okay with that as it relates to church models, too. This will allow for every person with every type of personality or background at any particular season of their life to be able to find some place to call home. Many will move around to other churches after they have grown as much as they can where they were attending. When you think according to a kingdom grid, it's no longer tragic for someone to leave a church and go to another. Yes, there is a danger in becoming a spiritual vagabond, but excessive loyalty to one place can also lead to spiritual stagnation. The key in all of the above is obedience to the Holy Spirit. Whatever He is orchestrating will be good, and He must be the object of our focus and attention.

A Special Note on Apostolic and Prophetic Churches

This is a unique niche of churches that is presently exploding all over the globe. These churches attempt to intentionally fulfill the biblical paradigm of apostle and prophet leadership. That is a very bold endeavor, and this group of churches will be a most important one to observe. They will make some of the greatest blunders with their new models, but out of this stream will ultimately come the greatest foundations for the advancing church. Out of this classification of churches will come the models that show the greatest ability to advance the kingdom of God in a sustainable way and properly champion the reformation of society. Many of the early mistakes among churches in this niche have had to do with overemphasizing titles over function and with authoritarianism. As the years pass, there will be ongoing upgrades in this reformation-minded group, and by 2030, we will have New Testament-caliber apostles and prophets leading some of these networks.

Trend #5: Unprecedented Unity

I believe that one of the most significant trends we will see in Christianity between the years of 2015–2050 will be in the area of unity. Presently, one of the most damaging mentalities that exists among Christians is the one that fears false unities and one-world churches. There is more fear over ecumenism than over disunity. Many believers carry such paranoia and expectation of end-time disaster and chaos that they find the dark lining in every silver cloud. For example, Pope Francis is a genuine Christian with a true heart for love, respect, and unity in the body of Christ. He has reached out across the Christian aisle to leaders of various movements and denominations, speaking on Jesus' heart for unity as expressed in John 17. However, many Christians are releasing warnings of how the pope's efforts at unity portend the end of days because it is a false unity between a harlot church and the real church. There are several problems with this perspective. First, we must cease calling the Catholic Church the "harlot church," since we, too, have played the harlot all over our own religious spectrum of Protestantism. Second, this belief falls way below the standard of endeavoring to keep the unity of the faith. Might Pope Francis have some imperfect doctrines? I am sure that is true. Might I have some imperfect doctrines? I am sure that is true, as well. However, we both agree that salvation comes only through the blood of Jesus Christ, and we both love and cherish the Holy Spirit and His work on earth. That is a basis for a significant amount of unity.

> *It is a Pharisee spirit that separates over relatively trivial matters.*

Catholics have over a billion adherents around the world, and in that group are many, many true believers who love God and are filled with the Holy Spirit (120–160 million). If there is unacceptable idolatry and too much veneration for Mary in the institution, nowhere in the Bible does it give permission to reject as brothers and sisters those who overly respect Mary—particularly so if these are ones who clearly have a living relationship with Jesus Christ, whom they see as their Redeemer. The Scriptures tell us that whosoever calls upon the name of the Lord will be saved (see, for example, Romans 10:13); it doesn't say that whosoever has perfect theology will be saved. Once we have the central theology correct—that salvation is through Jesus Christ—then much of the rest of it has to be left to the judgment of God. It is a Pharisee spirit that separates over relatively trivial matters.

To generalize, some say that the Catholics have their doctrinal door too wide open, allowing too many extraneous beliefs. However, to generalize again, I say that most evangelicals have their doctrinal door too restricted by not even allowing the Holy Spirit Himself to show up. If I had to choose which is the worse offense, I believe it would be the latter. I think that it is perhaps better to have excessive veneration for Mary and the saints and yet be very open to the Holy Spirit and His presence, His power, His gifts, His healing, and His authority over demons and so forth, than to have the correct view on the matter of Mary and the saints and yet be closed to the work of the Holy Spirit and all its fullness.

Ultimately, I can think of almost no doctrine that is worse than one that squelches the Holy Spirit, because He is the Promise sent by the Father to assist us in bringing heaven to earth. Without Him, we are just warring with concepts and ideas. It's the Holy Spirit who makes the difference because of His presence and power. Also, unless we embrace the Holy Spirit, the desired unity will not be forthcoming. He is the Helper for all things, and not least of what He helps with is unity. So, despite the naysayers—who will always be among us—a progressively increasing element of the church will desire unity. A reformation-minded church will always have a greater heart for unity than will a revival-minded church. Reformers realize the need to join forces with other reformers.

A Final Note on the Mountain of Religion 2015–2050

I have spoken very little about the other religions on this mountain. Islam has over one billion adherents, and Buddhists and Hindus number in the hundreds of millions each. There are also lesser religions, such as the Jews, who alone number approximately 14 million worldwide. The kingdom of God will continue to press into these religious strongholds, and over the next thirty-five years, there will be multiple millions from each of these major groups who will be attracted to the love of Christ flowing out from those who know Him as Lord and Savior.

Christianity will be progressively more attractive in the coming years. There is presently a war over the identity of Christianity, but the forces of love will continue to strengthen, and the forces of dead religion will continue to weaken. Those who carry a hope-filled narrative will continue to lead and thrive, and those who carry the religious wet blanket of doom and judgment will increasingly lose their audience (though they will always retain some audience because misery does, after all, love company).

The battlefield within the church is over the true nature of God. By 2020, there will be greater and greater agreement about who He really is. There will always be distorters of His image on this Mountain of Religion and even in the church, but our children's generation will be much more comfortable with the idea of a God who is good, loving, relational, and merciful—as opposed to a God who is stern, obsessed with behavior, and prone to explosions of vengeful judgment. Yes, as stated earlier,

> *An on-fire, loving church that has a hopeful perspective on life will be globally advancing by 2050.*

God is concerned about sin, but only because He loves us. His hatred of sin is based on the fact that it separates His children from Him; it's not based on some ethereal hatred for unrighteousness. Our God is utterly relational, and this characteristic far supersedes any other aspect of Him we might want to highlight. When your identity is one of love, as His is, you have identified yourself as relational at a core level.

By 2020, the advancing church will be known for her hope. By 2030, the advancing church will be known for her faith. By 2040, she will be begin to be known, as never before, by her love. An on-fire, loving church that has a hopeful perspective on life will be globally advancing by 2050, walking in unprecedented signs, wonders, and supernatural manifestations of power. There will be resistance, and there will be war, but this "age of the restoration of all things" will be in full bloom at that time. There will be at least fifty nations that will be walking in a high level of national transformation. In these fifty-plus nations, evil will be in full flight mode, and it will actually be popular to be a Christian. This is going to happen. Believe it, and help it to become your nation's reality.

Six

RENAISSANCE ON THE MOUNTAIN OF EDUCATION

Nowhere will the coming Renaissance be more powerfully felt than on the Mountain of Education. Since Renaissance is all about a rebirth in learning and paradigms, we can expect this mountain to greatly lead the way. Because the church of Jesus Christ structurally sets up shop on the Mountain of Religion, that mountain will always be the most important, but the Mountain of Education certainly could be next. The church is meant to function as the central volcano of God's love that then shoots out its members as living lava stones to all of the rest of society. We are to be His *"living stones"* (1 Peter 2:5). The Mountain of Education is to be filled and ignited with the wisdom and solutions that will overflow from those who gather as the church of Jesus Christ.

Education Is Religion Taken to a Deeper Level

In my last book, *Rainbow God: The Seven Colors of Love* (coauthored by my wife, Elizabeth Enlow), we identified a color coordination between each hue of the rainbow and a corresponding sector of society. Religion was represented by the color blue, and Education by the even deeper blue color of indigo. As this progression may lead you to understand, I believe that education is really just religion taken to a deeper level.

Religion is often that which you pick up on your weekends or special weekday services. Education is that which you are taught for at least twelve years of all-day instruction. We could say that religion is the inspiration, while education is the discipleship. In America, education was initially designed to indoctrinate the next generation into the Puritans' version of Christianity. Reading, writing, and arithmetic were added to that religious training, and the subjects have progressed in various ways since then.

Problems in Today's Educational System

Currently, the educational system in America is viewed by many as being in crisis, with systemic failures on multiple levels. A high student-teacher ratio, inadequate discipline, sub-standard teachers, non-pertinent curriculum, violence, drugs, and high dropout rates are among the areas most frequently mentioned as contributing to the crisis. However, I believe that there are two greater reasons for the general weakness of our educational system. One is the predominance of left-brain curriculum and teaching style. The other is the fact that education, as I stated above, is actually religion taken to a deeper level—we could call it "Religion 2.0." Because there is this close connection between religion and education, the government is intruding beyond the wall of separation that was designed to exist between church and state. Let me expound on both of these ideas.

The Problem of Left-Brain Education

We have two processors in our brain, connected by a mass of nerve fibers that allow for messages to be sent between them. Our left-brain processor is verbal, and it processes information analytically and sequentially—in a step-by-step, linear manner. Words are the primary means it uses to remember information. This side of the brain is logical, rational, and objective; it is good at organizing, planning, rule-keeping, time-keeping, and producing desired intentional outcomes. This side always looks for the *what* of things.

In contrast, the right brain is visual and processes information intuitively and simultaneously. It looks at the whole picture before examining the details. This right brain is a creative processor, as opposed to the left brain's robotic capacity to regurgitate what it has been fed. Unlike the methodical approach of the left brain, the right brain processes information concurrently and immediately, producing what we might call discernment or a gut feeling. Pictures (in the mind) are its key memories. The right processor is not highly organized, but is organic and responds in an as-needed fashion. This side is always after the *why* of things and is not sensitive to the issue of time. While the left brain is more the spectator, the right brain is a player and enjoys participating by touching and feeling. It loves patterns, metaphors, analogies, and visuals, and it can be subjective and random, particularly when judged by the left brain. The left brain doesn't really understand the right brain and develops an intelligence-assessment test that primarily values the left brain's operations.

As I stated, a central weakness of our educational system is that it is mainly education for the left brain. When entering school, most children are predominantly right-brain processors and thinkers. However, after just a couple of years of formal education, more than 90 percent of these children have shifted to left-brain dominance. The further they go

A central weakness of our educational system is that it is mainly education for the left brain.

in higher education, the more left-brain dominant they become. Both sides of the brain have a voice, but it is as if they arm-wrestle for dominance; and the one that is rewarded and certified by the values promoted by the student's daily schooling becomes stronger and stronger and routinely wins. Once a student steps into the level of a master's or doctoral program of study, they are almost hopelessly locked into left-brain processing.

Most IQ and scholastic aptitude tests measure left-brain skills. Verbal skills, abstract thinking, most mathematics, and inferential logic are all left-brain operations. Our educational system determines students' intelligence almost entirely based on the proficiency of their left brain. This can be very toxic to the right-brain processor who has to switch from their natural right-brain thinking to left-brain thinking.

We obviously need both of our processors functioning and doing their distinct jobs. However, we were designed by birth and wiring to be right-brain dominant. The left brain was designed to be complementary and to assist the right brain. It is helpful to have a "reminder processor" that can tell us what time it is and the general parameters of the assignment at hand. It is like the value of having a picture frame that harmonizes with a picture—the frame itself is not the thing of beauty, but it frames that beauty, causing it to stand out the way it should. Our education system seems to reward the "frames" and those who can make them more than it does the "pictures" and those who create them. As you can imagine, a world that is all about frames is infinitely more boring and tedious than a world that is all about art. This is a major reason why many kids hate school and why they are increasingly dropping out from the rigors and dryness of the school system.

Many organizations are now making adjustments in their IQ testing because the weakness of a straight left-brain IQ score has been evidenced. Sports teams and businesses have now developed alternative testing that seeks to discover emotional intelligence (EI, or EQ) and social intelligence (SI, or SQ). Both of these come out of significant participation from the right brain, and the results of such testing allow a boss to identify the leadership abilities of thinking on one's feet and adjusting to unplanned circumstances and dynamics. These tests endeavor to identify a type of genius that our educational system would consider significant only if the person also had a superior capacity to remember. Remembering what one has been instructed is of good value, but the ability to think outside the box and successfully innovate is of greater value. For example, if you are a quarterback, and your offensive tackle missed the block he was supposed to make, thinking outside the box could save your face from getting smashed into the ground.

The Problem of Education as Religion 2.0

As I mentioned earlier, the second great weakness in our educational system is related to the fact that education is, in effect, Religion 2.0, but it doesn't follow the rules of separation of church and state. Again, the history of education in America will bear out to be a Puritan endeavor to codify learning á la John Calvin, thus promoting and producing conformity. The goal was not to awaken the genius within each child but rather to ensure adherence to the doctrine of the land. The original educational model was designed to squelch any outside-the-box, hard-to-manage curiosity that might arise in a right-brain dominant individual.

Given this reality, it should be no surprise that the city (Boston) and region (New England) that was the bastion of forced Puritan education has today become the nest and hotbed of American humanism and nonreligious thought. Boston was the center of American Puritanism, where all nonconformists were severely and efficiently brought into compliance in their thinking. I once wondered how a university like Harvard, founded on Christian principles, could turn into the center of humanistic thinking. It appeared to have been hijacked from its original intent. Yet with a better understanding of the realities of that historical era and Harvard's role at that time, it all makes more sense. Harvard, as it turns out, was specifically founded to stifle the advances of the right-brain thinkers of Christianity of that day, such as Anne Hutchison.

Harvard was actually formed in 1636, during the trial of Anne Hutchinson, which was the dominant story in Boston and New England at the time. She was a right-brain-thinking Christian who believed that God's revelation was not limited to the Bible and that He, being the Word, was still speaking. She also believed that women could hear from God and speak for God. Anne was a champion of making room for the Spirit of God and not just the Word of God. Obviously, we could easily make the valid point that left-brain Christianity will value the written Word of the Bible, with its less fluid and random possibilities, as opposed to right-brain Christianity, which believes in access to the Holy Spirit, His presence, and His power—along with all of the outside-the-box possibilities that stem from that grid. Anne Hutchinson became the most influential person in Boston through all her right-brain spiritual gifts (such as healing, prophesying, and knowing how to host God's presence). This did not sit well with the establishment Puritans who executed the most unjust trial imaginable against her, ultimately managing to have her excommunicated from the church and thrown out of Boston. Today, she is appropriately honored as a heroine in Boston. Back then was a different story. Because of her tremendous following, Harvard was quickly formed as a needed thought-police to rein in dangerous doctrines such as those advanced by the right-brain,

Spirit-led Quakers. This all enabled me to understand that it was a natural progression for Puritanism to become the seedbed for humanistic thought through its cause-and-effect dynamic. Wherever a forced feeding of religion takes place, the eventual fruit will be a backlash of humanism that even denies the God that its founders in theory championed. The prioritizing of left-brain thinking is the seedbed for humanism. Left-brain Christianity will ultimately attack itself, eliminating the movement of God that is alive and real for today, while championing the memory of the God of 2000 years ago.

> *The prioritizing of left-brain thinking is the seedbed for humanism.*

As we are seeing, education and religion are completely intertwined. Schooling, in essence, disciples us in how to respond to the real world. This is in effect the secondary role of religion. Religion (or spirituality) is first designed to connect you with your God, but its second mission is to give instruction on how to morally and practically respond to the issues of life. The Puritans knew that education was supposed to instill religious thought and paradigms, which is why Harvard, the elite center of education, was formed in order to stem undesired and uncontrollable religion.

Thomas Jefferson's proposed wall of separation between church and state has simply not been properly extrapolated. Government truly is not meant to be the instructor of religious matters and matters of conscience between man and God. For example, when a government begins to legislate which curriculum it approves based on whether it agrees with its morality on human sexuality, then, in effect, government is intruding past the wall of separation and dictating into matters of conscience between God and man. Today, by being the instructor of public conscience matters, government has overreached into religious implementation, thereby violating the establishment clause. In the next section, I have some solutions to present on this matter.

Seven Mountains Curriculum as Solution to the Present Curriculum Deficiency in Public Schools

I have already established the fact that left-brain based curriculum carries intrinsic deficiencies. By not connecting and relating to the whole person, but only to the intellect, it does not properly prepare a person for life. The present purpose of education must be to prepare a person to interact with and successfully respond to real life. In other words, any and all schooling should in some way prepare a student for something they most likely will face. They should be getting tools for coping and thriving in life. Though this seems simple and logical, it's amazing how the reality is the opposite.

For example, I personally have yet to use algebra or trigonometry in real life, despite being over fifty years old, having owned a business for many years, and having pastored a church. More than 95 percent of the people I know and have asked have never used it, either. Yet it's obligatory for all students, and it truly saps the joy of learning for many who would otherwise be excited to advance in knowledge. It is illogical to force 100 percent of the population to take advanced mathematics when less than 5 percent will use it in any even incidental way. To me, doing this is, at some level, insane! Of course, we need some people to have the option of advancing with higher math so they can go on to create the things that require those skills, but the fact that only a tiny percentage will actually do something with it doesn't justify putting everyone else through the mental torture. It makes no more sense than forcing all kids to study about raising pigs, because 5 percent of them will be farmers one day.

Isn't it obvious that every subject should address a present or future reality in life that at least more than 90 percent will actually face? If it is not in that above-90-percent category, it just shouldn't be standard curriculum. For example, in school, I had to attend an art class that forced me to practice drawing, cutting things out, gluing, and so forth, even once it was discovered that art was not going to be my thing. I could go on and on about many things I was force-fed at school that have added no real benefit to my life. It's as if I was taught to scratch an itch that I never had. Meanwhile, I was given no instruction on matters that could have really benefited me in life. I was never taught social skills, never taught real communication skills, never extensively taught about other religions (even though over 90 percent of the world is religious), never taught alternative historical perspectives, never instructed on how to start a business, and so on. I do realize that, depending on where and when one went to school, the realities may have been different—but this is my straightforward and honest evaluation of my personal schooling and its benefit to my life. I would love to hear how it compares with your own (theoretically, of course).

I do love that I was taught to read, which afforded me immense benefits. I love that I was taught to handwrite—less important today with our new technologies, but still important. I even enjoyed all the basic math I was taught; I'm so thankful that I can add, subtract, multiply, and divide, even though I acknowledge that such knowledge is less valuable now with so many devices available to do calculations for us. I love that I was taught history, particularly American history (although I do wish I had been given multiple perspectives on historical events). Regarding science, I guess I'm still trying to figure out how much less of a person I'd be if I hadn't learned about *meiosis* and *mitosis*, although I can still see the value of basic science being taught. Spelling was very important, but even if that isn't someone's strength, they can always use spellcheck. Health and nutrition was somewhat of a weird situation because almost nothing I was taught still stands as accepted fact. Physical education was always my favorite class because I was finally out of my left brain and could actually enjoy something that still qualified as education. Geography and social studies were helpful, especially considering the globalism of modern society—to not know about the rest of the world is to be truly ignorant; it will handicap you in interfacing with other nations and cultures. My main point is that if learning doesn't have a future application or benefit, then it very possibly should be weeded out and replaced by something more important and relevant to real life.

Our educational problems demand solutions, which leads me to present the Seven Mountain curriculum for public schools. Each one of the Seven Mountains is a primary sphere of society. As we have noted, the seven general areas are government, arts and entertainment, religion/spirituality/worship, media/communications, economy/business, family, and education. Each one of these is an area of society every person in every nation interacts with. Therefore, if a curriculum were to be designed around the goal of teaching individuals how to successfully interface with each of these mountains of society, then we would have developed a direct benefit link between what is studied and what is applicable to life. I will lay out my Education Reform Proposal, believing that many people will agree with at least the essence of what I present here.

State Education Reform Proposal— Seven Mountain Curriculum

The Subject of Government

Though not necessarily needed before fourth grade, government is a vital subject that should be taught over the course of multiple years. The goal behind this subject would be to develop an informed and productive citizen. In fact, the subject could be called "citizenship" or "civic responsibility." The most indispensable part of the subject of government is its instruction in understanding and participating in our present government. Government needs to be taught much more in depth than it has been, particularly its historical aspect; history is ultimately the greatest teacher for almost all of the other subjects. Every citizen should be very familiar with our Constitution's history and, even more specifically, the reasoning behind the various articles and amendments. Studying the Bill of Rights should be of highest priority; we should strongly consider requiring students to memorize it. America has modeled the greatest freedom in the history of governments, and it's important that all present and future citizens understand the origins of that freedom. Our system of checks and balances between the executive, legislative, and judicial branches of government should be expounded upon long enough that students will not merely be able to pass a test on it but will have a working knowledge of it. All aspects of our political parties and electoral processes should be thoroughly covered, as well as the freedoms and limitations of lobbyists. Certainly, this should be a subject that is taught with increasing complexity from at least fourth grade through twelfth grade. Significant, ongoing review of this material is also called for so that it will remain working knowledge for us throughout our adulthood.

> *America has modeled the greatest freedom in the history of governments, and it's important that all present and future citizens understand the origins of that freedom.*

Many current, hot-spot issues, such as immigration, could be better examined if students were given a strong historical grid and were fully saturated in understanding the foundations of our nation and our law. The tax code, the Internal Revenue Service (IRS), and the history and purpose of the Federal Reserve should also be key elements of instruction. Studies continue to show that we are largely illiterate about both our government's history and its present-day operation. If we want to provide a scratch for an itch that will eventually come, then we should fully instruct students in governmental structures and their function. Such a foundation will enable them to become informed and productive citizens. Some level of civic involvement, such as writing letters to Congress, should be incorporated into the learning process, since the practical use of knowledge must always be a goal. And, where curriculum can be created to appeal to the right brain, it will have a better chance of being enjoyed and therefore absorbed. Remember, anything that comes in story form or is interactive appeals more to the right side of the brain.

The Subject of Sports, Arts, and Entertainment

Though I complained earlier about having to take art class while I was growing up, it's not because I don't think art instruction belongs in school. The point is, rather than subjects being one-size-fits-all, there must be strategic, forward thinking behind them.

In curriculum associated with sports and arts, the goal would be to expose a student to enough different forms of sports, arts, and music that their core creative bent would be discovered and then developed. The instruction really should be about finding a student's inner passion and joy, rather than about forcing all students to have some base level of artistic capability that they may not even have an interest in. Obviously, we all need to learn the basics of staying physically fit, and we all need to be introduced to the general art forms that exist; but fairly soon in the educational process, we must help the student to connect to their particular area of passion and gifting.

Again, this requires a different thinking grid where the educational system exists to serve the student, rather than the student existing to serve the system. In the model I am proposing, students would spend the first three grades being exposed to various forms of art, sports, and music with the intention that by grade four, a student (with their parents' full involvement and participation, of course) would then choose a primary track or, if desired, still continue to explore multiple tracks. As you can see, the recurring concept here is to make education that which prepares a student for success in life. The goal would not be just to entertain the student but rather to properly balance enjoyable study with hard work and preparation. As all professional athletes or artists know, hard work inevitably accompanies success. But by nature of it being a participatory subject, it already makes it something more enjoyable and rewarding.

The Subject of Religion or Spirituality

Religion is a subject that has to be addressed, but as I have already stated, we also must get the government out of the business of approving or disapproving people's personal choice of religion. This subject therefore requires thoughtful navigation. The goals of this area of study, as an obligatory school subject, must be to encourage freedom of religion, as well as understanding and respect in relation to religious beliefs that are different from one's own. Since 90 percent of the people in the world consider themselves to be religious in some capacity or another, and since the majority of the wars in the world are fought over this matter, it leaves no small incentive to prepare students for entering this kind of world.

First of all, I don't believe that this subject should be compulsory until the sixth grade. This allows time for parents to lay whatever foundation they wish before a student ever has instructive exposure to alternative beliefs. (I believe that the government should be supportive of such a policy in relation to public school education.) The practice of reading, which students will have been taught to enjoy in earlier grades, will be an excellent preparation for the study of religion.

The Question of Church and State

Now we must navigate through the thorny relationship between church and state. Please hang with me through this, even if you find yourself disagreeing. The worst that can happen is that we will think outside the box together! Though the state (public schools) cannot be involved in the indoctrination of religious or antireligious thought, it can play a vital role by providing a level playing field for exposing students to religion and guiding them in discussions about it. A state-paid religion teacher or professor must know that their goal is not indoctrination of any sort. Rather, their role would be to teach the history of the major religions—Christianity, Islam, Buddhism, Hinduism, and Judaism—and any other religious perspective represented by the students in the classroom. The goal would be to build understanding toward other perspectives, thus eliminating the barrier of ignorance.

> *The goal would be to build understanding toward other perspectives, thus eliminating the barrier of ignorance.*

Now, in providing that level playing field, the state would equally allow a minister/priest/religious leader of any of the primary religions, plus any other religions represented in the classroom, to come into class to explain the foundations of their worldview and God-view. By simple majority, the parents of the students in each classroom would be given the opportunity to choose which particular religious leaders would come to speak. The state's position would be that it is not in the business of promoting or rejecting any religious beliefs but is serving only as a facilitator of the freedom of religion and of the knowledge of religion. If atheists or agnostics were represented in the classroom, they too would be allowed to present their case. (Generally, parents who were not comfortable with their children being exposed to other religions would have the option of sending their children to a private school or of homeschooling. But remember, this instruction would not be given in the public schools until sixth grade.)

Additionally, the religion teacher would teach various perspectives on the origin of the earth, including Darwinism, creationism, and whatever other theories exist among the main religions. The teacher would abstain from disclosing their personal religion since they would be representing the state. The teacher's primary role would be to keep the presentation fair. After the initial instruction on each of the major religions of the world, the teacher would facilitate the visiting representatives of the religions or beliefs reflected in the student body of that classroom. The students would already have benefitted from gaining an overall awareness of the major religions, and it would no longer be necessary to give time to views that no one in the classroom held. This would create fluid options, depending on the number of religious views represented in the classroom, in terms of how many times a representative of a religion might come in and speak. The representative could not force any student to pray, nor could they officially proselytize, but they themselves would be free to pray in front of the students.

As you can see, this format would give parents a substantial voice in their children's religious formation, which would surely be considered in accord with a constitutionally neutral stance on religion. The state would be well within its rights to consider it valuable that students be taught to appreciate the freedom of religion and to respect those who have religious beliefs that are different from theirs. From a governmental standpoint, it should be considered essential for all citizens to value and experience the freedom of religion. This type of educational format would ensure that government is neither involved in the promulgation of religion nor interfering in the free exercise thereof. Under the present format, government seems to be perpetually doing one or the other. As a parent, if you have been given the opportunity to be the sole spiritual mentor of your child through the fifth grade, then you should not feel alarmed at their subsequent exposure to other religious beliefs, particularly when their own is also continually validated at home.

The Question of Prayer in the Public Schools

Next, let's discuss the issue of prayer in the public schools. Since this is such a hot topic, I must address it, even though it has indirectly been covered by what I have already written. Obviously, government has no right to speak to the theme of prayer in school beyond the realm of the public schools. Only when the schooling is recognized as having governmental oversight does the prayer in school debate become relevant.

Though many Christians are very unhappy that prayers can no longer be made over the P.A. system of a school, it really does have to be acknowledged that, in a melting pot environment, this is the only constitutional way to proceed. It is also the only fair way of operating. Built into the separation of church and state is the understanding that the majority cannot impose on the minority, but that religion must be allowed to be a matter of freely chosen conscience. If the majority religion in America was Islam and not Christianity, Christians would not wish to be forced to be under prayers made to Allah in a public school setting. It would also be wrong to say, "Ah, but we are the majority; therefore, it is okay to impose *our* prayer." First of all, it violates our constitutional value of freedom of religion (which I believe to be godly); second, even among Christians, there are significant divisions over particular beliefs and emphases, so of the 30,000-plus denominations, who should get to decide exactly what kind of Christian prayers are said? The only sensible way of advancing is to reflect the way God Himself treats us—He provides us with the freedom of choice and time to discover for ourselves who and what we will believe in and follow. The way this manifests in the classroom is to help students learn to properly respect the various differences of religion and conscience held by people today.

Many Christians have wrongly prophesied America's demise because of the removal of prayer from the public schools. (We should keep in mind that, as long as kids are required to take tests, some level of prayer in school will exist!) Government has not forbidden praying in school; it has forbidden only the school/state-sponsored platform for religious prayers. This is the right decision for the melting pot reality that we have in this beautifully diverse nation. However, I believe that government could do a better job of providing a non-hostile perspective toward religion if it allowed a two- to five-minute time slot during the school day for students to pray or spiritually connect with the god of their choice. As Christians, if we really have the truth, then all we should care about is maintaining a level playing field where all religious ideas get an equal chance to compete. Genuine, New Testament-style Christianity is obviously the only religious option that is self-validating by means of the very presence of the living God that it carries. I believe we often fear the level playing field because, for many, Christianity is just an argument and not faith that experientially carries the presence of the Holy Spirit. When it's all said and done, the religion that carries the presence of peace and the power of love is the one that will prevail. We need to be okay with the challenges that arise from the counterfeit religions, especially when it's all within the context of being informational.

The Subject of Media and Communications

As common sense will quickly tell us, in the twenty-first century, media and communications are absolutely essential for societal integration and advancement. This is a significant enough subject that it's clearly worthy of being part of the compulsory schooling in a state-sponsored education system. I will begin with the goal for this curriculum: preparing students to be socially and technologically skilled in order to meaningfully engage in and with society.

In the early grades, in relation to being socially prepared with communication skills, instruction in things like proper manners, social ethics, and protocol should be a very high priority, accompanying the foundations of the normal subject of language arts. Due to

America's historical background of rebellion against Britain, I think many Americans have perhaps never had the proper foundation of politeness and etiquette that should be a mark of an advanced civilization. First Corinthians 13 lays down many guidelines for operating decently among people. Verses 4 and 5 reveal the foundation for manners and ethics in communication: *"Love is patient, love is kind. It does not envy, it does not boast, it is not proud. It is not rude, it is not self-seeking, it is not easily angered…"* (NIV). In this passage is also the foundation for forgiveness: "[Love] *keeps no record of wrongs"* (verse 5 NIV). This cannot be viewed as mere religious instruction, because the government has already spoken up about matters such as hate speech and bullying, which are clearly covered here. If the state can charge someone with speech crimes, then it must first, out of necessity, give instruction in what an ethical foundation of tolerant speech is. We must recognize that the very idea of tolerant speech is biblically based, although the state has clearly overreached by warring against even matters of conscience. As I said earlier, by being involved in education already, the government is in fact involved in Religion 2.0. Therefore, we must wisely navigate through this reality in the coming years. As it stands now, government is in effect a religious instructor (versus a neutral informer) of our children, and that must change.

How foolish is it that we are still teaching students how to properly address and format a letter while giving no attention to how they're actually communicating?

A secondary stage of media and communications preparation for students must obviously be the area of the latest electronic technologies. In today's world, if you don't know how to navigate and protect yourself on the many social media platforms, then you are truly communications-impaired. Because social networks are in a constant state of flux, this educational approach must be continually evolving. How foolish is it that we are still teaching students how to properly address and format a letter while giving no attention to how they're actually communicating? Additionally, students would benefit from receiving instruction on Facebook etiquette or how to respect others on Instagram. We have a reality that kids are, by and large, teaching themselves life outside of the classroom, while the school systems are giving them curriculum that was relevant a hundred-plus years ago. This is changing slowly, but it must and will change in a more meaningful way.

The Subject of Economy or Business

This subject can be highly effective as an endgame for the study of mathematics. I believe studying mathematics is a hard sell to students when the perceived goal is the satisfaction of being smart or just passing a class. Nothing should be learned merely so that one can be looked at as intelligent; instead, there should be long-term purpose behind learning. As I said before, students should be learning a scratch to which there will be a forthcoming itch. Math should be taught in the context of helping students understand economic realities and how to operate in the business world. This attaches a storyline to the number crunching that makes it meaningful and, furthermore, right-brained. If we keep in mind that the goal of education is preparation for real life, then it becomes increasingly apparent what issues should be covered in the classroom. Somehow, most of our kids seem to be finishing school without a basic knowledge of or skill in budgeting, after having had ridiculously advanced and obscure concepts forced down their throats. Wouldn't it be beneficial if kids finished school having an understanding of mortgages, leases, taxes, the stock market, how to take out a business loan, and so on? As the Era of Renaissance comes into this Mountain of Education, we will begin to make these wise and reasonable adjustments.

The Subject of Family and Human Relations

This is a subject that carries huge ramifications. It's an area that students absolutely must be given instruction in, but that instruction must not intrude into matters of conscience or religion. Knowing how to do that nearly requires the wisdom of Solomon. We are possibly the most fractured society in memory, and it's producing dire consequences in our nation. The state, in its attempt at political correctness, finds itself in a major catch-22. They know family is the most important institution, yet they wish to validate all expressions of human sexuality, and they find themselves conflicted on how to validate both. To overemphasize one is to inflict some degree of damage on the other.

So, how do we navigate this minefield in the classroom, since navigate we must? First of all, the state must realize its responsibility to abstain from interference in matters of conscience while protecting issues of human rights. How would that look, as it relates to the gay discussion? The state does not have the luxury of having an opinion on whether or not a certain religion can consider homosexuality a sin—that is a matter of conscience and religious dogma. For the state to rule on that matter is to cross the boundary of the separation of church and state and to engage in legislating its own religious persuasion. However, the state can instruct that no discrimination against homosexuals may exist and that homosexuals must be given the same practical and legal treatment that heterosexuals receive. The state must also refuse to overreach into religious institutions and dictate to them their hiring practices because, if they do, they will have again breached the intended wall of separation that our forefathers rightly established. The state may protect human rights in every sphere outside of the religious spheres, but by constitutional law, the state must refrain from intruding into matters of religion. This is foundational.

School curriculum on the subject of family and human relations should explain this tension in depth so that it is clear for students moving forward how it all works. The centrality of family in an enduring society must be made clear. The connection between mental health and one's family situation must also be made evident. A recent CNN article (July 10, 2014) stated that over 27 million Americans take over-the-counter drugs for mental health. Additionally, over 90,000 emergency room visits were made last year in the United States by these individuals related to something going wrong with their drug medications. There is also interpretation of research that suggests that more than 90 percent of all illnesses come from psychosomatic causes connected to unhappy family dynamics. We can bury our heads in the sand and pretend that family is only nominally important, but the statistics will bear out that an unhappy family life often leads to loss of mental health, physical health, and/or spiritual health; it can even incite someone to criminal activity.

That's why schools must teach students about all aspects of human relationships, beginning with the dynamics of a family. Obviously, family starts with a couple, and so instruction must start from that point of reference. The state should have no qualms about affirming that the majority of all families are a husband/wife or male/female nuclear household and then providing instruction that assists this group. It would be fine to throw in the fact that different states recognize same-sex marriages and that in those states these couples can apply the relational instruction that applies to the other families. Once same-sex couples are validated by a state, being backed by state law, that is reason enough for schools in that state to instruct students about same-sex marriage. Anything more than that crosses the line between church and state.

Teachers of this subject need to be experienced in counseling and in all aspects of human relationships. We really must start using education as the time when we equip our kids with what they will need to be effective in life. Consider that most challenging or disruptive elements in our schools are directly tied to relational dysfunction. Bullying is a result of a broken ethos for human relating, as is school violence. The problem of a lack of discipline cannot be separated from this issue, either. Kids don't need just to be told to behave; they must be walked through areas of pain that they carry that are related to difficult family dynamics. They must be taught how to forgive, how to draw boundaries, how to confront, and so forth. This is exceedingly more important than learning trigonometry!

I understand if the idea of the state teaching about human relationships seems a bit frightening. However, consider two points: first, it is already teaching about them, and it needs new parameters for doing so; second, the current system will be in full-scale implosion apart from significant reform. Keep in mind that there is always the option of private schooling for those who want to more closely manage this area of instruction in their kids' lives.

The Subject of Education Through the Lens of History

When viewed as the seventh strand of curriculum, the Mountain of Education should be introduced through the subject of history, for history is the ultimate educator. Edmund Burke said, "Those who don't know history are doomed to repeat it." In other words, if you don't allow history to educate you, you will remain ignorant. Winston Churchill said, "The farther backward you can look, the farther forward you are likely to see." Nathaniel Hawthorne said, "The past lies upon the present like a giant's dead body." These quotable quotes establish the huge instructional potential of an objectively related history.

> *Whoever is allowed to tell our history has the power to shape future generations.*

This, of course, is a very significant matter. It can be said that whoever is allowed to tell our history has the power to shape future generations. If a distorted history is being bandied about as truth, then we lose the fundamental value of history as an instructor. Many people see new versions of history as being revisionist texts, but it is of the highest importance that what is taught in schools be as objective as possible. Because of that fact, I believe it vital to always give at least two historical perspectives on the same important information. Jesus Himself provided four versions of what He did on earth, expressed through the four gospels of Matthew, Mark, Luke, and John. There is great overlap in these records of what Jesus did, but each writer also presented his account with a distinct flavor, using slightly varying details, which together help to provide a more complete picture of what occurred.

Therefore, it would be instructive to consider American history through the eyes of a Native American, a white European settler, and the British government. Maybe we Americans had a little more rebellion in us than we would like to admit, and maybe that still affects us negatively. Not to properly learn the lessons that history affords us is a great travesty of life. Hindsight does offer something close to 20/20 vision, and we should not waste the profitability of that perspective. The idea of education and the proper examination of history absolutely go hand in hand. We can miss out on the greatest instructor by not being willing to recognize a past historical reality. The worst thing imaginable is an educational organization or association with a preexisting agenda that has the authority to officially sanction curriculum. History is to be desired for the truth-telling that is available in its rediscovery and remembrance, not as a means to force an agenda on others.

Though I have taken some time to discuss future public school reforms, it is truly through the private schools that the front edge of educational renaissance can quickly come into play. The great value of private schooling is that you do not have to operate within all the boundaries of the separation of church and state, and that really does allow education to become what it was originally meant to be—instruction in God's ways. The Bible says that the earth will be filled with the knowledge of God as the waters cover the sea. (See Habakkuk 2:14.) As I stated before, there is currently significant knowledge about the fact that God saves, but very little knowledge about anything else that He does or knows. This situation will begin to change institutionally as the new Renaissance schools come into alignment with their original assignments and advance the nuanced knowledge of God, starting with the Seven Mountains of society.

Seven Mountains Curriculum in Private Schools Will Teach a Nuanced Knowledge of God

Each one of the Seven Mountains is meant to reflect a specific aspect of how God is available for us today—in the real world, in real life. Here are some examples of what will be taught in the Seven Mountains curriculum of private schools:

Government

Proper education about government begins with instruction on how all governmental authority and mandates come from God. Heaven is not anarchy; rather, it is a manifestation of the glory of a properly exercised government. When citizens feel safe, cared for, and rightly judged, there is a beauty of life that they can enter into. Jesus taught us to pray, *"On earth as it is in heaven"* (Matthew 6:10); we must see this as connected to the manifestation of *heaven's* Seven Mountains on earth. We are to seek to learn as much as possible about God's structural ways in heaven and then, as His children, re-image Him and His ways on earth.

Government is ultimately one of seven primary manifestations of who God is. He is King, Lord, President, Prime Minister, Governor, and so on, and government is one real-life means through which He shows us His love. If private education can explore in-depth and then validate this reality (because it covers all the other basics of government), then we will have, in fact, done a great service to our children. Somebody will develop curriculum from this perspective, and it will set so many things in order—including awakening in our children a desire to properly represent God and His values in government. We need to raise up generations who are passionate for bringing God's better way of doing things into government. This should start during our kids' initial education experience.

Celebration of Arts/Entertainment/Sports

A proper curriculum in this area would have, as its starting place, the reality that God is a God of creativity and celebration. This act is initially established by His introduction to us in Genesis 1:1, which says, *"In the beginning God created...."* It's further established by Scriptures such as *"In Your presence is fullness of joy; at Your right hand are pleasures evermore"* (Psalm 16:11). Once we understand that He is a creative and celebratory God, we can embrace as instructional all the various outlets through which He expresses these qualities and how they connect to specific ways we were wired by Him. Again, the great advantage of having non-state-sponsored education is that it can start with the premise of expanding our knowledge of the God who designed our very existence. Because He wired us with creative passions, it is of utmost value to discover them, develop them, and activate them.

Religion, Spirituality, and Worship

Obviously, this subject gains the greatest freedom for instruction when removed from the public school setting. God can now be intentionally spoken of and advocated; and, in a private Christian school, salvation through Jesus Christ and life in the Holy Spirit can be openly taught. Unlike in some former educational settings, such instruction does not need to take a fear-based, indoctrination approach. Truth will be self-validating by the internal resonance of the Holy Spirit in an individual. When we believe we must indoctrinate (i.e., brainwash) in order for the truth to stick with our children, it reveals our own lack of proper relationship with God. Moreover, to the degree that a private Christian school can be fair to other religions, people from other religions will desire to send their children to be taught there.

True Christianity is not just the right religion—it is the *only* religion—the only spiritual pathway—that will be internally confirmed because we are made in God's image, not in the image of any other god in the world. The Holy Spirit is the convincer of truth, and He must be trusted to fulfill that role. And since the Holy Spirit is the definitive Helper for all matters having to do with life, to the degree that a school assists a student in connecting to the Holy Spirit, it has prepared them for life. Beyond this primary goal, there are, of course, many other valuable God-perspectives to be learned, starting with the fact that God is the Creator of the universe.

Media and Communications

In private education, not only can all the usual knowledge about media be expounded upon, but there is also the opportunity to expand a student's knowledge of God. The following truths must come out in the Renaissance curriculum: God is the Governing One, He is the Celebrating One, He is the Redeeming One, and He is the Communicating One. He loves communication and has wired us for communication, as well. John 1:1 says, *"In the beginning was the Word, and the Word was with God, and the Word was God."* This verse makes it abundantly clear that communication is intrinsic to God's very essence. If our curriculum narrative can have, as a starting point, the fact that God is at the center, then everything else will make sense. This is not to say we shouldn't teach the practical aspects of media and communications but rather to show how all advances in media and communications are extensions of who God is. This curriculum will be effective when it can substantiate that reality and move forward from it. Thought must be given as to how God runs communications in heaven and how to apply that on earth. More instruction on that matter will be forthcoming in the chapter on the Mountain of Media.

Economy or Business

I already pointed out how math should be very intentionally connected to business, and that idea still applies in a private school setting. Additionally, another facet of God's character can be revealed through this subject—His role as Provider. One of His names in Scripture is *Jehovah-Jireh*, which means "The Lord My Provider" or "God Is Provision." The fact that Provider is one of His names means that it is a core element of who He is and what He does. If this narrative doesn't get woven into instruction on economics and business, then truly we have raised our kids to think through an orphan mind-set. But we are not alone on this earth; God didn't leave us here by ourselves, expecting us to figure out how to live solely by our own efforts. That approach may seem like good capitalism, but it denies the One who is as *the* Source of all. The fact that He is our Provider isn't just a religious concept. The reality of how His principles and His guidance are incorporated into daily life must be shown and established. There will be a Renaissance curriculum that will cover all the basics of economics while expanding a student's faith and belief in a God of the marketplace who still provides on earth as He does in heaven.

Family

In the context of a private school, family is an incredibly broad and important subject to be explored, free from the constraints of the separation of church and state. The Renaissance curriculum can come out fully valuing God's moral standards. From these standards, we learn that God is not merely trying to determine who's a good rules-keeper; He has actually given us standards that reveal how life works. He is Papa of us all, and His standards show us the best way in which a family can function. They provide a path to the most satisfaction, joy, and safety for us.

But even beyond that value, a new curriculum will be written that, in essence, does the job of counseling and helping students to receive inner healing from past wounds. This shouldn't be considered a matter for just church or special counseling. Many of us as adults have taken classes to assist us in being healed from childhood pain. Spiritual and emotional healing programs are available, such as Sozo, Life Skills, Elijah House, and Theophostics, all of which are designed to help us break free into true adult living. But why should we wait until we are thirty, forty, or fifty before getting whole? This should be established as a curriculum that allows children to go ahead and deal with pain they would normally stuff away for years or decades. Of course, this all has to be handled delicately and with wisdom, but I tell you that I see a future school that will have such a great track record with the mental state of the students who attend that parents of even non-Christian homes will want their kids to be taught there. I promise you, kids need this instruction much more than they do calculus. Again, schooling should prioritize instruction on everyday life matters.

Education Through the Lens of History

All that I said earlier about the study of education in relation to a public school setting applies here, as well. However, once more, we now insert the intentional God-component that can be offered in private Christian schools. Wisdom and understanding is valued time and again in the Scriptures as primary facets of who God is. The very fact that we are curious and love learning new things establishes that we are wired in His image. Education itself must be seen as God's central purpose for each and every one of us. If the endgame is the whole earth being filled with the knowledge of who He really is, then we must understand and teach our children that this is the goal of life—to grow in the nuanced knowledge of who God is. Within the nuances of *who* He is, it must also be revealed *how* He is. That is where the greater ignorance presently exists. Almost everyone seems to know that Jesus saves, but almost no one seems to know that He also governs, creates, communicates, provides, and much more.

Proverbs 9:10 says, *"The fear of the LORD is the beginning of wisdom, and the knowledge of the Holy One is understanding."* In this verse, we get the foundational value of education: To be in awe of the Lord is the beginning of wisdom, and to learn all about His many facets is understanding. All instruction should have as its goal to somehow lead to a further understanding of who and how God is.

> *Though the history of man is valuable, it is the history of God at work with man that is even more valuable.*

A future Renaissance curriculum will understand these dynamics and will also understand that the best rendition of history will always be the discovery of what God has been doing. Though I have spoken of presenting an objective history that comes from several vantage points, this type of history will always pale in comparison to a view of history that discovers how God has been involved in nations and societies down through the ages. It will require a uniquely gifted person or persons to be able to look through the annals of history and find the evidence of God at work. Though the history of man is valuable, it is the history of God at work with man that is even more valuable. This is what gives students a worldview and a God-view that can sustain them throughout life. One of the reasons it is often so hard to find God in the midst of everyday life is that our twelve-plus years of education have weeded Him out of the picture, and we have great difficulty overcoming that distorted discipling. We have grown up in our education having God as an absentee Father. However, if a child can go through a system of schooling that emphasizes God's very present Fatherhood in all aspects of life, then that child will grow up with an ability to see God in all of life.

Again, I am not talking about overdoing the religious rhetoric, but I am speaking of making known a very real, practical, and present God of all life. Currently, I don't know of any school that is doing this, but such schools will come forward and become game changers on the Mountain of Education because people will notice that the kids from this instructional base outperform others. We don't need more "religiosity" in our schools. We need more reality, and God is the most real Being on the planet. Furthermore, He's the Person who's the most interested in desired outcomes. In the Bible, He told Israel about His rules of life and then virtually said, "If you will keep them, this is what will give you your desired outcomes. You will live in abundance, your children will be blessed, you will be protected, you will be the head and not the tail," and so forth. (See Deuteronomy 28.) God is the most practical Person on the planet, and when we reduce Him to ethereal-ness or to having relevance only in the future, we have ignorantly mini-mized Him out of any real life value. The coming Renaissance curricu-lum will be based on the fact that it has a foundational assignment to find, reveal, and give instruction about a near and present God who has always been there for us. Sometimes, it will take an anointed historian to find evidence of Him as the treasure hidden in a field, but we will see that He has always been at work in the midst of every day of our past.

Final Thoughts on the Coming Renaissance in Education

Obviously, there are many more challenges on the Mountain of Education than the ones I have addressed. There is a great problem of indiscipline, overcrowded classes, under-qualified teachers, violence, and other things. However, I truly believe that those are secondary matters compared to what I have presented and that there will also be forthcoming solutions for all of these issues. I believe many of these sec-ondary matters will begin to dissipate when highly relevant curriculum comes into the picture. There will, of course, always be other challenges, but they can be significantly abated as classrooms become what they were intended to be. I believe that by 2020, there will be some bright, shining examples of these new Renaissance schools that will begin to pioneer with such excellent results that mass duplication will follow. By

> *By 2050, upgrades will have been made on the initial breakthrough Renaissance curriculum that will cover age two through higher education.*

2030, I believe we'll have the same breakthrough at the higher institution level; and by 2040, people will be having conversations about the methods of education we used in 2015 in which they will say, "Can you believe that we used to...?" By 2050, upgrades will have been made on the initial breakthrough Renaissance curriculum that will cover age two through higher education.

While many people are waiting for Superman to come and rescue education, it's the arising sons and daughters of God who will jointly be the "super kids" who bring real solutions to the educational system. Education is the practical discipling of the next generation, and it is of the highest priority imaginable for God's kingdom kids to rise and shine on this mountain with God's better ways of doing everything. Believe this is possible, and become part of the solution.

Seven

RENAISSANCE ON THE MOUNTAIN OF FAMILY

There seems to be no sphere of life that requires more attention than the Mountain of Family. In fact, I've spoken to many people who feel that this is the most important of all the other mountains because everything and everyone flows out of family. If we can get families to be healthy and all right, they claim, then society will also come into line. Although this claim holds some merit, the reality is that a healthy family cannot be produced unless some of the other areas of society are healed, as well, because all the mountains are interconnected. Family is not an isolated area of life that can be easily pursued independently of the overall Seven Mountain mandate of bringing solutions to all the mountains. Let me briefly explain the overlapping family-affecting dynamics from the other six mountains of society.

+ *Religion/Worship:* Healthy churches are one of the most important aspects of bringing stability and ministry to hurting families. Even if you were to adopt a family-first approach to life, it's virtually impossible to sustain healthy family dynamics apart from some spiritual family connection. Religion definitely affects the Mountain of Family.

+ *Education:* The ability to find or to afford a good school is also a major ingredient in a healthy family. If a family's economic situation doesn't allow them to find a reasonable place for their children to attend school, they can be forced to place their children at risk by the limited schooling options available to them. Furthermore, the current humanistic and otherwise morally damaging curriculum that exists in our public education system adds another risk factor. Education clearly impacts the Mountain of Family.

+ *Media:* The incessant regurgitation of bad news through most communication outlets greatly affects everybody's morale. Add to that the often negative, yet intangible, impact of social media and you have an area of society that has invaded your private household dynamic. Media certainly has an effect on the Mountain of Family.

+ *Economy:* We've just discussed how economic need can limit a family's options for the education of their children, but it can also limit many other options, such as being able to live in a part of town that's safe. In addition, it takes resources to provide for children's extracurricular activities, like music, sports, and the arts. A lack of resources is a primary stressor for families and a leading cause of divorce, with its devastating repercussions on families. Economy greatly shapes the Mountain of Family.

+ *Celebration/Arts/Entertainment:* The truth is, from about the age of ten, most of our kids are being ideologically discipled by Hollywood and the rest of the pop culture. Yes, we do need to work on protecting our families from the inside out, but if we can't shift the entertainment culture out of the gutter and into a positive influence, then our task is very, very tough. Sex outside of marriage and perversion, which are both highly promoted through this area of culture, are leading causes of family fractures. When arts and entertainment aren't produced according to God's better way, they seriously erode the Mountain of Family.

+ *Government:* In the last several decades, many governmental laws have ended up being enormously destructive to the well-being of the family. For example, although the original idea of welfare was to assist the needy, the incompetent way it was set up ended up rewarding many people who shouldn't have been given the aid, while giving little incentive for people to improve their lives. Moving to another issue, government potentially has the oversight and ability to greatly restrict the flow of pornography to children, but it lacks the resolve to instill the protective measures it must. A failure to protect children from pornography brings some level of destruction to most families. Government assuredly touches the Mountain of Family.

The point here is to show that no mountain of society exists in a vacuum, especially in the case of the Mountain of Family. I theoretically agree that if families could be made healthy, then it would impact all the other mountains—but truly it requires change in the other mountains in order for the Mountain of Family to thrive the way it was meant to.

If you are one who's called to bring solutions to the family, this is a most honorable calling. It's important for you to know that we are only at the beginning stages of the Era of Renaissance for families and that the best solutions for the Mountain of Family will come from those who most understand what our Papa God is like in His relational

> *The best solutions for the Mountain of Family will come from those who most understand what our Papa God is like in His relational dealings with us.*

dealings with us. Those who see Him as the great Adopter and Accepter of us all will be successful in their advances in this area. Many people come to the Mountain of Family to defend the institution of marriage and for similar reasons, but priority must be given to heal the rejection that people feel in their hearts; we must show them the acceptance that comes with God's unconditional love. We have to learn how to demonstrate His Fatherhood in the world. He is Father to us—above every other title we may give Him. Those who truly know Him as Father will develop the best solutions for this significant need in society.

Five Essentials for a Healthy Family

There are a myriad of books and resources already being used to assist families, as well as great ministries advancing with solutions and resources for healing and stabilizing families. These resources will continue to improve and abound with new insights and solutions as God's sons and daughters show up on this mountain full of hope and resolve in the face of real challenges. God is greater than the challenges, and if you feel called to the Mountain of Family, this must be your posture. You can never embrace hopelessness for any segment of society while remaining an advancer of Father's heart. I want to share five essentials that every family must incorporate into its DNA in order to become or remain healthy:

1. How to discipline

2. How to forgive and receive forgiveness

3. How to resolve conflict

4. How to have fun

5. How to make and respect relational boundaries

Whoever can help instruct families in these specific areas—whether through books, seminars, personal counseling, or any other avenue—is, in a very practical way, giving families invaluable tools that can enable them to be the safe and dynamic place they are called to be. Families nowadays need more than just church picnics to foster healthy dynamics. There's a need for real, practical help in knowing even the basics of how to structure a family and how to operate as a family. Each one of the five essentials I have listed above are worthy of at least a full chapter. Because I wouldn't be able to do them justice in this book, I'll simply add that I believe greater and greater wisdom on these essentials will be available in the coming days as our own Father's love is more extensively revealed to us. All solutions for families come out of knowing Him better. When you know Him well, you know Him as a Father who provides discipline that isn't abusive, who is quick to forgive, who wisely provides a foundation for resolving relational conflict, who is fun Himself, and who has designed relational structures to work best with good boundaries. Understanding how to advance these five essentials is key to bringing wholeness into family life. All five essentials lead to increased feelings of acceptance and honor among the members of a household.

Health and Medicine Are on the Mountain of Family

One of the questions I am frequently asked is, "What mountain is the medical profession on?" As I have already stated, all matters having to do with health are aspects of the Mountain of Family. Some believe that up to 90 percent of all illnesses can be attributed to broken family relationships. This is not all that hard to understand, as we know that family members generally have the ability to cause us the greatest emotional joy or the greatest emotional pain. Most disease is psychosomatically advanced or hindered as the body's immune system is degraded by stress and strengthened by the joy of good relationships. Therefore, issues related to health and the practice of medicine cannot be separated from a family's overall mental health.

Speaking of mental health, research from the Web site of the Department of Health and Human services revealed the following:

- Nearly 44 million U.S. adults had a mental health issue in the last year (18.6 percent of the total).
- Nearly 10 million were diagnosed with serious mental illness.
- Nearly 9 million had serious suicidal thoughts.
- 1.3 million attempted suicide.
- 25 million Americans over age 12 needed treatment for drug use.

> *Many families don't know how to run their homes, and they are sicker because of it.*

These disturbing numbers are all outcomes of acutely broken and fragile family structures. Eighty-one percent of youths between the age of twelve and seventeen who received mental health attention indicated they were feeling depressed and having problems at home. Many families don't know how to run their homes, and they are sicker because of it. This will begin to radically change in the coming years as advanced wisdom on the five essentials for healthy families are incorporated into this mountain.

In another example, obesity is possibly the greatest health hazard in the world right now, the incidence of obesity having doubled since 1980. The World Health Organization (WHO) has stated that for the first time ever, more people are dying as a result of obesity than from hunger. Obesity has a direct link to heart disease, type 2 diabetes, and stroke—among many other illnesses. Thirty-five percent of all Americans are significantly overweight.[22] Millions die every year from the effects of some level of obesity. Not all obesity is directly related to overindulging per se. More and more evidence points to people developing systemic malnutrition by poor eating habits—by consuming "dead" food (containing little or no nutritious elements) or toxic food; then, as a result of being malnourished, they tend to overeat as their body pleads for nourishment. So, more than one root issue can lead to obesity.

Even when obesity seems to be tied to gluttony or overeating, the underlying cause is often unhealthy family habits. American families—and many families in other nations around the world—rarely sit around the table for a home-cooked meal anymore, receiving the benefit not only of nutrition but also of companionship and a sense of emotional security. As a result of this broken family dynamic, people are getting fatter and fatter. It's not due merely to a lack of willpower. They are eating for comfort, as well. They are substituting family relationships for a relationship with excess sugar, carbs, and so forth, because eating foods with these ingredients can make us feel soothed and consoled—temporarily.

For example, if we've had a bad day and have just blown up at our sister, brother, mom, or dad, we head to Starbucks and console ourselves with a Java Chip Frappuccino. I'm not knocking an occasional treat, but this dynamic of consuming food to cover up relational pain occurs all around us and can have devastating effects. Health and family are totally connected—if you improve someone's health, you will help their family life, and if you help someone's

---

22. See "Overweight and Obesity Statistics," National Institute of Diabetic and Digestive and Kidney Diseases, http://www.niddk.nih.gov/health-information/health-statistics/Pages/overweight-obesity-statistics.aspx.

family life, you will improve their health. The Renaissance solutions that will be available for the Mountain of Family will come from those who completely understand this connection. They will begin providing holistic solutions for restoring the image of God in families.

All this to say, if you are in the medical profession, your assignment is actually on the Mountain of Family. As you become more aware of that connection, you'll be positioned to have an even greater impact. If your giftedness involves bringing health to individuals in any manner, then you should know that you are, in essence, a minister on this mountain. If you are an observant doctor, you understand that disease causes stress, and stress causes disease. Healing and family go together.

The arising sons and daughters of the King will soon begin putting together so many pieces of the puzzle having to do with family and health that we will see a tremendous renewal of family life. Don't be distracted by wrong narratives and by wrong battlefronts. Though many are saying that the family is under assault by the "gay agenda", including the legalization of gay marriage, the truth is that even if all gays voluntarily moved away to their own island (which I am not suggesting), the family's core issues and challenges would remain. Most of the significant challenges for families have almost nothing to do with the battlefronts we expend so much time and money on. Often, it is easier to scapegoat our own issues onto someone else's sin in society,

> *Most of the significant challenges for families have almost nothing to do with the battlefronts we expend so much time and money on.*

rather than to acknowledge and deal with those issues. I have had to counsel many couples over relational matters, and not once has anyone ever said, "I'm having this problem because gay marriage was legalized." Couples are generally struggling with issues related to communication, money, boundaries, pornography, or forgiveness. They need direct practical help for these challenges—and we will begin to do a better job addressing them.

Premarital Counseling

At its micro level, a family is comprised of a husband and wife. And a husband and wife begin as an engaged man and woman. Therefore, significant Renaissance solutions are going to be forthcoming in the area of premarital counseling. Today, premarital counseling is generally weak and ineffective at properly preparing couples to be the all-important foundation of a healthy family. There are many reasons for this, but the good news is that there are going to be premarital programs that are so remarkable in their outcomes that they'll go viral. Prophetically, I see one in particular that becomes, as it were, a silver bullet that is embraced everywhere. It will go after generational curses, arrested development issues, unforgiveness, and childhood wounding, as well as train in household structuring. I am seeing a program that will walk with a couple for five years—or even a lifetime—assisting them in the various transitions of marriage. This will be done so well that certain states will even pay for these family services and will financially incentivize prospective couples who participate, realizing that it will ultimately save the state money. This will be a very important development between the years 2015 and 2025.

The Manufacturer's Guidelines for Sex

Perhaps nothing is as destructive to family strength, life, and health as illicit sexual behavior. By illicit sex, I mean that which takes place outside the parameters laid out by the One who originally created sex. It is interesting that in virtually every area of life, it is understood that rights or privileges must take place within the context of rules. Yet we seem to prefer sex without any rules.

If you have a job, it comes with very specific guidelines. You show up at a certain time and work at a certain work station and under specific oversight and established conditions. If you violate the conditions, you could lose your job. Similarly, if you take advantage of the freedom or right to drive a car, it comes with a myriad of restrictions, too. You can't go faster than the posted speed limit, you can't cross lanes without signaling, you can't drive against traffic, you can't drive a vehicle that hasn't been governmentally approved, you can't drive a vehicle that hasn't had its emissions checked, and so on. You're free to drive a car, but you must follow the operating rules so that your freedom doesn't endanger yourself or others. I may be overstating the point, but we really must see that sex was invented by God, and it is meant to work by His rules of operation. Life itself works well only when we live it according to the Manufacturer's guidelines.

God is the Manufacturer, and He is the One who designed this extreme human pleasure called sex. He has amazingly simple guidelines for sexual activity and how it works best, and yet it seems as if almost no one wants to play by the Manufacturer's rules. God says that in order for sex to be what it's supposed to be—a blessing and not a harm—it must occur only within the boundaries of marriage. Furthermore, God says that marriage is to be between a man and a woman. He made the anatomically connecting counterparts obvious so that there would be no question. Sex must be between a man and a woman *after* they have pronounced lifetime vows to each other. These are His only clear rules. Wow, what simple rules, and yet how intensely we wriggle to try to shake free of them. Sex works counterproductively unless it is engaged in as the Manufacturer designed it. In this context, I'm not even entering into the *legal* debate over gay union or marriage. Beyond the legal arguments, the simple reality is that sexual activity will backfire and do harm to any and all who ignore the Manufacturer's guidelines. The gift of sex will bring you pain, disease, and heartache if you fail to follow the instructions for use that the Manufacturer, or Designer, spelled out.

God doesn't tell us what sin is merely so that we would know if we were breaking the rules of the game or not. He isn't a Pharisee who likes rules just for the sake of rules. All of His rules have a divine wisdom behind them and are for our good. It's wisdom about how love is best protected and enhanced, and such love simply cannot be given and received correctly without His guidelines. God's boundaries provide the dynamic that allows sex to be as awesome as it was designed to be. Again, beyond moralizing and beyond the legal arguments, sexual activity just won't work outside the boundaries of marriage. Outside of that boundary, it becomes, in some way, an assassin of true love. All sexual activity outside that of a husband and wife will always cause serious erosion to the family unit. If you are called to serve the Mountain of Family, you really must see and embrace this fact or you won't be able to be an effective ambassador of God our Father, who is the One who designed the family unit.

> *All sexual activity outside that of a husband and wife will always cause serious erosion to the family unit.*

The Collateral Damage of Illicit Sex

There seems to be no real way to properly quantify the emotional health toll that illicit sexual behavior has taken on individuals and society. Studies can't make the connection directly enough, but there is no doubt that many of the mental health issues mentioned earlier are highly connected to illicit sex. As we know, sexual behavior and emotional behavior are strongly related. However, beyond even the mental health toll, there is a more concrete physical health toll due to sexually transmitted diseases (STDs). The Center for Disease Control and

Prevention (CDC) numbers for 2013 show that 1,401,906 Americans contracted chlamydia; 333,004 were treated for gonorrhea, and millions more for other STDs, such as syphilis, genital warts, AIDS, herpes, and so on.[23] Each year, there are 12 million people who contract a sexually transmitted disease, and that includes 3 million teenagers. The cost of all these diseases is a whopping 16 billion dollars. The price we pay for not accepting God's guidelines is emotional, physical, spiritual, and financial.

Though not all STDs are contracted outside of marital sex, most are. In fact, the only way a sexually transmitted disease makes it into a marriage is if someone along the way has been engaging in sex outside of God's rules. Obviously, there are exceptions, such as in cases of rape or incest; but in general, if you follow God's guidelines for the family, you'll be protected from these costly and harmful diseases. Once again, this proves the connection between family and health. Family done God's way will strengthen and protect you in all kinds of ways; in contrast, to not follow His better way is to open yourself up to disease, demons, heartbreak, divorce, depression, and all kinds of other maladies of body and emotion. His guidelines are truly given to us because He loves us so much. He doesn't tell us it's easy to follow His guidelines on sex, but He knows that if we learn to value family and relationships, we'll do whatever it takes to follow His better way of doing relationships. The pleasure of sex is a minimal taste on earth of pleasures that will be available in heaven; hence the restrictions surrounding it. What we can be trusted with in eternity is partially being determined by how we follow God's earthly guidelines. Sex is always to be entered into in the context of fostering a marriage relationship that's based on a lifelong covenant.

Even Hollywood cannot find a more emotionally riveting narrative than a love story ending in a marriage where the couple look at each other and promise to be faithful forever. Every time they stray from that narrative into a more modern twist of just living together, it loses emotional steam and appeal. Sex done God's way creates much better

---

23. See "Reported STD's in the United States: CDC Fact Sheet," Center for Disease Control and Prevention (December 2014), http://www.cdc.gov/nchhstp/newsroom/docs/std-trends-508.pdf.

storylines. If Hollywood were to add an ending where the lovebirds promised to prioritize each other over their other sexual partners, it would totally fail at inspiring an audience. It's the promise of exclusivity of love and sex that makes the love story appealing.

Hollywood also knows that perhaps the greatest emotional pain you can depict on the big screen is the painful rejection someone feels when they have been cheated on. The entertainment industry bucks the restrictions of the Manufacturer's guidelines for sex, yet when searching for an emotional connection with an audience, it instinctively knows that the effect of sexual infidelity is a great source of passion and emotion. We are wired by our Designer and Manufacturer to know that sexual faithfulness is the only way a love relationship will work. It's still a lot of work even when we're faithful, but without that faithfulness, the relationship has very little hope of surviving or avoiding a major relational earthquake.

The Coming Medical Breakthroughs

In the previous chapter on the Mountain of Education, I mentioned the wholesale need to upgrade even the science of education in our school curriculum. Curriculum that was more relevant 100 or 150 years ago is still being produced, ignoring the new priorities in life. The health industry is in an even greater crisis, with extremely conflicting, fluctuating, and supposedly scientific information being advocated. Public fear, confusion, and frustration is rampant and has led to millions leaving conventional medicine for alternative medicine.

The mainstream medical profession has clearly been corrupted by the billions of dollars brought into play by the pharmaceutical industry. It has become particularly easy money to collect millions and millions of dollars through blood pressure and cholesterol medications. I will single out these two, although they are just cases in point. I was actually shown in a vision a massive demon of fear assigned to everything having to do with blood pressure. Ninety-seven percent of all blood pressure medicines have serious side effects, and yet fear and medical pressure cause

The mainstream medical profession has clearly been corrupted by the billions of dollars brought into play by the pharmaceutical industry.

tens of millions of Americans to faithfully take these "medicines." I put the word *medicines* in quotation marks because I've read many studies, and they show that no lives have actually been saved by blood pressure medicine, nor can it be proven that such medicine has stopped even one stroke! This is truly astounding. I invite you to Google this topic and see for yourself.

The medical wisdom from a few decades ago was that healthy blood pressure (the top numerical figure) was 100 plus your age, because, as you age, your blood pressure increases. This would mean that if you are fifty years old, an upper number of 150 would be within the normal range. In more recent times, when the pharmaceutical industry realized how much money it could make just by lowering the standard, suddenly 140 was the highest permissible number considered to be safe blood pressure. Wow, that was easy money. With no statistical proof to validate the new recommendation, this new low became standardized. As you know, at a traditional doctor's office, the first thing medical personnel check is your blood pressure; and between the new standards and the nervousness many people feel about being at the doctor's office, you find that your blood pressure numbers are less than ideal. Your doctor will come in and say, "You know that blood pressure is the silent killer. Even if you have no symptoms, this could be killing you. The medical industry standards say you have high blood pressure and need medicine, so I'm going to prescribe medicine for you." I've had multiple nurses acknowledge to me that not only is this scenario accurate, but they have had to convince their own spouses after a doctor's visit that they don't need to use the blood pressure medication the doctor prescribed.

You may be eighty years old, but you'll still be evaluated by the same lowered standard as patients who are younger than you are. Apparently, whether you are eighteen or eighty, whether you weigh 120 pounds or 350 pounds, whether you're five feet tall or seven feet tall, your heart is ideally supposed to pump blood at the same level of pressure. Doesn't common sense itself tell us that this is illogical? Of course, millions and millions of dollars are in the balance with this standard and approach, so the disservice to the world continues. Just a few years ago, somebody apparently looking after the pharmaceutical industry's bottom line had a brilliant suggestion: "What if we lower the recommended standard to 120?" With a new wave of fear of hypertension, taking that simple step would make them multiple millions more. Of course, this was supposedly new science—and it's worked like a charm for them. Again, I've researched and failed to find *any* proof that blood pressure medicine is saving even one life, but it sure is filling the pharmaceutical coffers!

This same faulty, money-motivated science has been applied to cholesterol levels, and we again have millions of people unnecessarily taking a medicine that not only is costly but is also removing the very protection our blood vessels require. Yes, it's possible to have blood pressure levels that are too high; and yes, it's possible to have undesirable cholesterol levels—but the science for addressing such levels has been corrupted and contaminated by the pharmaceuticals mafia. I'm calling it a mafia because that's how it functions, which is no real surprise. The Era of Renaissance is going to bust up this mafia, as fearless sons and daughters of the King in the medical industry no longer bow before mammon but instead risk it all by telling the truth. Know that if you were to break up the pharmaceuticals mafia, which extends far beyond these two health matters—you would actually be doing a commendable work on the Mountain of Family. I've already been shown by the Lord in another vision that His bulldozer was about to come in and virtually level the existing medical playing field because it's so systemically corrupted by greed. Of course, there are some awesome doctors and nurses in the healthcare industry, but the mainstream system has become totally compromised by what is going to be uprooted from

An aspect of the Renaissance on the Mountain of Family will be an overhaul of the health industry.

this part of the Mountain of Family. The new knowledge of God and His ways is coming into medicine, and it's going to change everything.

By and large, the mainstream medical profession won't even recognize a disease or illness unless there's a drug that can be offered to treat it. Go to a traditional doctor with an adrenal problem, and you'll discover that most of them don't recognize something like adrenal fatigue as being a legitimate health concern because the pharmaceutical industry doesn't have any drugs to sell us to treat it. I could go on and on, but obviously there are already many articles and books that are now informing us about these corruptions, as well as many doctors and nurses who are boldly ratting out their industry.[24] I will state it again—an aspect of the Renaissance on the Mountain of Family will be an overhaul of the health industry and what's considered health science. It's amazing that there is still a substantial percentage of doctors who treat symptoms apart from recognizing a mental health quotient. That almost defies logic.

Great change is coming to all that comprises the health industry on the Mountain of Family. This will come in great leaps and bounds, especially between 2015 and 2025. By 2025, much of what

---

24. See, for example, Marcia Angell, M.D., "The Truth About the Drug Companies," Want to Know, http://www.wanttoknow.info/truthaboutdrugcompanies; "Health News Stories," Want to Know, http://www.wanttoknow.info/healthnewsstories-131-20; "Pharmaceutical Corruption News Articles," Want to Know, http://www.wanttoknow.info/pharmaceuticalcorruptionnewsarticles; Sherry Rogers, *The High Blood Pressure Hoax* (Solvay, NY: Prestige, 2008); Joseph Mercola, M.D., *Dark Deception* (Nashville: Thomas Nelson, 2008); Joseph Mercola, M.D., *Sweet Deception* (Nashville: Thomas Nelson, 2006).

is presently considered to be mainstream medical practice will have been bulldozed and replaced by better wisdom on health. Multiple medical breakthroughs will be attached to this Renaissance explosion, and many health sciences of today will be disproven in such a public and convincing way that we will look back to today and think of it in some ways as the medical dark ages. Medical science will move away from treating symptoms and toward treating the actual causes of illness. Even medical schools and training will be overhauled so the focus can be on the real cures. There are countless wonderful doctors and nurses in the health industry today, and in the coming days, they will be called upon to team together and make a stand against the systemic corruption in the medical industry. They may face losing their licenses, resources, and credibility, but if they will stand up for what they know is right, they'll be covered and properly recompensed by God. His care is substantially better and more dependable than national healthcare plans. (Obviously, there are areas of medicine such as the treatment of fractures and various surgeries that function very well today. I don't intend to demean all of the health industry by this broad brush with which I'm painting.)

I believe that by 2020, a massive breakthrough in reversing the immune deficiency of AIDS will have taken place; and by 2025, both cancer and AIDS will essentially have cures. AIDS and cancer will both eventually, completely, bow before the light of God through His Renaissance sons and daughters. There will always be illnesses brought on by sinful behavior, but in God's kindness, He will continue to allow us to find cures for the most horrible diseases. Every single dastardly virus that ever shows up will have an answer for it out of the wisdom that God will provide for those who look to Him. Never doubt that He desires to give us the cures for even those things that are the result of our own sin. Satan comes to steal, kill, and destroy. Our Papa comes to heal, restore, and give life. (See John 10:10.)

Unraveling the Homosexual Dilemma

Because this is such an explosive issue, and because this entire book could be marked by my following comments and observations, I must first go on the record saying a few things regarding homosexuals. All homosexuals are entitled to equal rights and protection under the laws of the land, as any other citizen is. They should not be bullied, badgered, insulted, belittled, shamed, picked on, or in any other way persecuted. It is almost unpardonable that any group or individual calling itself "Christian" would march with posters implying God's hatred for homosexuals or emphasizing eternal damnation. Whoever does that is more likely to face a severe judgment than the very ones they are judging. God deeply loves every single homosexual, and anyone calling himself or herself a Christian must likewise represent Him.

Can a Homosexual Make It to Heaven?

"Can my gay Christian relative make it into heaven?" This is a question that haunts parents and other family members of homosexuals. I will quickly go on the record and then explain. I believe the answer is yes, that someone can be homosexual and still make it into heaven. The famous verse John 3:16 says, "**Whoever** believes in him shall not perish" (NIV); it does not make exceptions for any particular classification of sinner. Mark 16:16 says that he who believes in Jesus will be saved, and whoever does not believe will not be saved. Romans 5:9–10 makes it clear that we are justified by believing in the reconciling work Jesus completed through His blood when He died on the cross, and not by any of our own righteousness. Many other Scriptures make that clear, as well. If a homosexual knows Jesus Christ as their Lord and Savior, and they are trusting His blood that was shed as the source of their salvation, I believe that makes them heaven-bound. For parents concerned or heartbroken because their son or daughter announced himself or herself as gay, just know that this doesn't equal their going to hell. Of course, the devil would love for that to be their end, but our God's mercy clauses always prevail over His judgment clauses. His justice always looks for mercy, as He is perfect in His emotions. He is desirous that none should experience hell; no matter how tormented a soul may be under any burden of sin, should that person somehow manage to find Jesus in the midst of that torment and believe in Him as their Savior, I believe even that tormented sinner can make it into heaven. If you read the Bible, you would conclude that those who will not forgive could be in danger of missing heaven, and unforgiveness would seem to be by far the worst of all sins. It's the one sin where you yourself chose to sit in the judgment seat of God—and the exclusion from mercy comes to those who do so.

God's mercy clauses always prevail over His judgment clauses.

I believe that it is possible to be a homosexual who loves God, who knows and believes in Jesus, and yet who doesn't believe that it's possible to be free from a homosexual drive and has thus embraced it as a viable alternative. I'm not saying it is a viable alternative, but that it's possible for a homosexual to believe it to be so. I make this claim because many of us believe similarly about our own pet sins and might be hoping for the same grace. Maybe we are 100 pounds overweight, and we know the Bible condemns gluttony, but we haven't been able to find a way through our weight problem, so we have lost any hope of correcting the weight and have concluded that being obese is a viable option. Maybe we have frequent explosions of anger, which is condemned by the Bible, and yet we cannot free ourselves from them, so we count on the grace of God to be our righteousness. Maybe we repeatedly fall back into any number of sins, but yet we know that we love Jesus and that we're born again. If you can imagine the presence of some sin in your life and yet still believe in a grace greater than your sin, then just apply that same reasoning to homosexuals.

The Scripture says that, ultimately, we become judged by the same measure with which we judge. I don't want sin to be justified, but I do want grace measured back to me for my niche of sin, even if it's not on the abomination list. Our heart's desire must be to see all those lost in any kind of sin be in relationship with Jesus and filled with the Holy Spirit. When Jesus comes in, He makes room for the Holy Spirit, who is the One who convinces each of us of right and wrong. The same Holy Spirit who works on us in our areas of weakness can be trusted to do His job in others, whether they're homosexual or not. I like it better when the Holy Spirit convicts than when people point fingers—don't you?

Are Homosexuals Born Homosexual?

This question, too, is a hot topic of debate. Many people feel that the answer would provide definitive proof of the rightness or wrongness of homosexuality. I believe that it ultimately doesn't matter what you may or may not have been born with. Homosexuality is not validated or invalidated by who we are at birth. To those who say God would not allow a person to be born homosexual, does He not permit children to be born with transgender realities, two heads, missing eyes, missing limbs, and so forth—all of which occur? We live in a fallen world that carries, incorporated into it, generational sin that can manifest in any number of ways. Not everything born is born perfect. It doesn't matter how we are born; the vital issue is to seek to come into alignment with God's best for us. God's best will always come about as we embrace what He clearly lays out as truth, either from a scriptural standpoint or from a self-evident standpoint. A child born without a leg will function best in life if he can be fitted with an artificial leg. A blind person is best served by measures implemented to assist him in dealing with that particular disability. We can sometimes enable a legless person to walk, but so far we can't make a blind person see. A person born with both male and female parts creates a huge ethical dilemma, and we as Christians are best served by not being overly black-and-white in areas where there is more gray than we care to admit. Remember, our assignments on the Mountain of Family are designed to showcase the adopting and accepting Father rather than heap coals of shame or guilt on someone born with one or two strikes already against them.

The "what we were born with" debate rings hollow on several fronts. Nobody is born as a conscientious, law-abiding citizen who is automatically faithful to his or her mate, and yet that is the expectation for a Christian adult. I have been married for twenty-six years to a beautiful wife whom I've been faithful to, after having been a virgin up to age twenty-nine when I married her. However, I was not born faithful and monogamous, and it has taken me going *against* what I was "born with" in order to maintain what I have maintained. I was not born wired for monogamy. I have had to walk contrary to what feels natural or instinctual.

In fact, as a pastor, I have counseled many men, and I have yet to find a single one who feels like he was wired at birth for monogamy. Yet monogamy is the standard from our Manufacturer and Designer as to how life will best work. For much of society, it's considered too harsh or unreasonable to ask someone who feels they were wired to be a homosexual not to give in to those feelings. It's even considered cruel. But if another person said they felt compelled to have sex with children, their desire would not be societally validated just by the feeling alone, and a moral standard would need to be introduced into the picture. Society suddenly

Society hates the idea of a sexual standard from God.

wouldn't care about how unreasonable or not it might be for someone to have to suppress sexual urges when the safety of a child is at stake.

Now, I'm not equating homosexuality with child abuse; I'm simply invalidating the argument that emotions or feelings, however ingrained, provide an authorization for action. Our society's hypocrisy is revealed in situations like this. Society might send you to jail for the rest of your life simply for acting on what your sexual wiring tells you, if it's telling you to be a pedophile. Such laws are supported by the culture. Yet conversely, you can get in a lot of trouble with society if you suggest that a man shouldn't have sex with another man or a woman with another woman. Society hates the idea of a sexual standard from God, but when people overly commit to standards based on individual sexual preference, they quickly realize the holes in their argument. My point is that innate sexual preference is not an authority on rightness. Your feelings of sexual desire are not validated just because you feel they are your core drive. There is right and there is wrong, no matter what drives you—and, by and large, all of our consciences recognize that fact, if we are completely honest with ourselves.

All Excessive Appetites Must Be Suppressed, No Matter What You Were Born With

There, I said it. This is the central tenet to be embraced. We are such a feelings-driven society that at times we believe we are self-validated by those feelings, while responding hypocritically toward others and *their* innate feelings. Above and beyond our fickle feelings, however, there's an absolute right and wrong. God's way is always the right way, and it will *always* entail suppressing or curtailing our natural (fallen) bent.

Too much of just about anything good, is bad. Every appetite for pleasure that God has given us is meant to operate within limitations. For instance, He gives us all kinds of amazing foods and food options, but if we don't learn to say no in our consumption, if we don't suppress the excesses of what seems to be our natural appetite, we can become ill and may even shorten our lives. The older I get, the more I have to say "No" in relation to my eating. Obviously, if I had embraced more

"No's" earlier on, then it would be easier now. For health reasons, I recently had to cut out caffeine, gluten, and most white sugar. These are all my favorite foods, going back as far as I can remember, and it sure did feel like I was wired to eat them. I'm certain I was born for Boston Cream donuts and Starbucks coffee, yet now I'm having to say no to them. How painful! It can't be right that I should have to deny my appetite! Yet somehow I'm feeling better than ever, and I've managed to easily drop the twenty pounds I had been asking God to supernaturally help me lose. I have also learned to enjoy other foods that weren't previously in my repertoire. The end result is that coffee and donuts are definitely out, but I still enjoy eating—and I'm healthier.

Sex Is an Appetite

Everyone is wired for sex. It's truly the rarest of rarities for someone to claim never to have had any sex drive. We are sexual beings, and sex is the closest thing on earth to a taste of heavenly pleasure. That's part of its design—to convey to us that a God who can provide that kind of euphoric pleasure for brief moments here can also have a future home for us where that level of pleasure will be the normal environment.

Sex is an opportunity for us to be pre-stewards of heaven. Chew on that for a while. Once you do, though, the implications are significant. If you abuse or misuse this gift of God while here on earth, then you could actually be setting limits on what He can trust you with in eternity. It is one thing to scrape by into heaven as a citizen, and it's another thing to make it into heaven as a spirit being who can be entrusted with significant responsibilities. Our heavenly roles and assignments will be directly tied to our stewardship of the life He gave us on earth. Everything here is the testing ground for greater authority, privilege, and influence. Even here on earth, most of our promotions from God will come after we have had to say a tough no to something.

The ability or opportunity to have or experience a sexual pleasure is such a great test of hearts—especially for men, but in some measure for all. Will we stay within the guidelines He clearly laid out, or will we ignore the Manufacturer's guidelines? There's the issue of morality, the issue of what's best for you, and then the issue of eternal consequences. The church has generally stuck with presenting sex as a moral issue—emphasizing that it's all about sin and guilt. Beyond that, I've been pointing out that suppressing our appetites isn't just about keeping the rules; it is actually about what's best *for us*.

The eternal consequences matter is likewise huge. Salvation is the free gift that comes solely through trusting in what Jesus did on the cross. Heavenly rewards are connected to how we respond to and obey God's instructions for life. You see, Lucifer failed the test of handling pleasure, even though he was already in heaven in a place where no sin existed. He was given a supremely pleasurable position in heaven and in God's heart, but he wanted more. (See, for example, Isaiah 14:12–15.) He made a decision not to keep the Manufacturer's guidelines and coveted even more power and pleasure for himself. In essence, it was similar to the idea of our going after illicit sex. It is why that's still his most effective weapon for tripping humans up. He decided he would make up his own guidelines based on what he felt like doing. That, of course, is core satanism. "Do as thou wilt" is the operating principle of the satanic bible.

God's Two Clear Rules on Sex

I state that these are clear rules because there are some matters that are not clear. Where the Bible is either silent, vague, or unclear—I will remain so, as well. But there are two clear rules on sex that are from the Ten Commandments:

1. Don't commit adultery. Adultery is consensual sex between two adults when at least one of them is married to someone else. (Any nonconsensual sex is rape.)

2. Don't commit fornication. Fornication is consensual sex between unmarried individuals. This second rule is really just meant to undergird the first one.

Both of these rules can be reduced to the one idea that God is looking at. In essence, the great gift of sex was meant to be the reward and the glue for choosing to embrace the bold, courageous endeavor of creating and raising a family. God released a drop of heaven into the Mountain of Family to be this great motivator and incentive. Sex was made for family. All of us are sexual beings because we all come from families and were essentially made for the further reproduction of families. If you aren't in the business of family, whether you can have children or not, sexual intercourse with another human being wasn't something created for you. Sex is for securing and enhancing the marital relationship and/or for producing family. All sexual activity outside of marriage will reap something negative. It may be a toll on our emotions, our health, our spirit, or even on our eternal destination—but there will be a toll. Of course, through repentance and forgiveness, one can always come back into right standing with God in this area. But *all* premarital sexual intercourse between humans is against God's will, is harmful for the humans who engage in it, and carries with it potential eternal ramifications.

> *The great gift of sex was meant to be the reward and the glue for choosing to embrace the bold, courageous endeavor of creating and raising a family.*

Adultery and Fornication Are Equal to Homosexual Acts

Many believers want to add an "abomination factor" to homosexual acts, but although these acts go against nature and against the proliferation of family, they cannot be considered a greater sin than adultery or fornication. In fact, I will contend that adultery and fornication are worse. "How?" you may ask. Well, significant research (though most researchers are very unwilling to go on the record because of the potential backlash) seems to show that most homosexuals were victims of some kind of abuse at a very young age. Many homosexuals have reported that they experienced a sexual sin perpetrated against them as a child,[25] and it's become a factor in their present sexual identity. It's extremely difficult to recover from sexual abuse as a child, whether one now sees oneself as homosexual or not. Many simply opt for a route of sexual promiscuity with people of the same sex, or some other sexual deviancy. For these, even while they are choosing sex outside of His guidelines, God has great compassion and understanding. However, although He does not endorse their present route of sexuality, He understands the sins against them that placed them in this sexually precarious place. He will do everything in His power to give them a chance for healing and restoration in that area of their heart and life.

This is why I believe God will go out of His way more to reach the homosexual community and the sexually broken than almost any other group. He sees what we cannot see, and He is the only righteous Judge. He sees the one who was never accepted into a family. He sees the one who never experienced a safe family. He sees the one who was sexually attacked, rather than protected, from within their family. He sees the years of rejection and the years of abuse that the sexually promiscuous have experienced. For them, He is a compassionate Father and not some dictator of rules. His rules still apply, and yes, not following them will still bring consequences and heartache. But God's heart is that they not experience eternal separation from Him brought on by sin committed against them when they were too young to choose. Satan would like to believe that he merely needs to mess with a young boy or young girl's sexuality in order to insure they spend eternity in hell—but God, being great in love, mercy, and

---

25. See, for example, http://www.orthodoxytoday.org/articles/
DaileyHomosexualAbuse.php; Marie, E. Tomeo, et al., "Comparative Data of
Childhood and Adolescence Molestation in Heterosexual and Homosexual Persons,"
Archives of Sexual Behavior 30 (2001): 539.

compassion will look for every way possible to triumph over Satan's plan and provide mercy. That's why He has provided this huge mercy clause that states, *"Whoever calls on the name of the Lord will be saved"* (Romans 10:13).

God wants His rules to be followed so that it will go well with you. He isn't an obsessed, rules-keeping Pharisee, but rather a loving Father who took time to think through the DNA of every person on the planet and prescribe a path of restoration and hope. If you could ever carry a banner that reads "God hates homosexuals," you have zero idea of who He is and,

Stay off of the Mountain of Family if you're there just to be the Pharisee who knows the rules and points them out.

most important, *how* He is. He is the Good Shepherd who will leave the ninety-nine sheep that are accounted for and go after the one that is lost. (It's interesting that the homosexual percentage in America is not much different from that.) God will always go the extra mile to extend grace to those who are lost because of sins committed against them. That's why I say God wouldn't consider a homosexual as a greater sinner than an adulterer; in most cases, the homosexual will first have been a victim. The sin may seem more unnatural, but the sinner would still be allotted more understanding grace. God really does know what each of us has gone through, and though His standard still remains, He has compassion on the broken and wounded.

Stay off of the Mountain of Family if you're there just to be the Pharisee who knows the rules and points them out. I fear that many ministries aimed at families are in fact just that—they're there to pat the backs of the rule-keepers and to wave a finger at the rule-breakers, while ignoring the storylines that are involved. God cares for His kids even more than He cares about His rules. To ignore that is to miss out on everything He is and has ever been about. He sent His Son to reach out to the rule-breakers. Jesus said, *"I did not come to call the righteous, but sinners, to repentance"* (Matthew 9:13).

God didn't come for those who thought they were executing life and their spirituality in a perfect fashion. Again, He cares for His sons and daughters even more than He cares for the moral fiber of society. Yes, His ways are the best ways, but among those best ways is His mercy clause, which will always trump our sin and brokenness, if we let it.

How Can I Be Set Free from Homosexuality if I Want to Be?

First of all, please note how I worded the question. This is not a homophobic section, nor a section on how sinful homosexuality is; rather, it's simply a section where I can offer some thoughts to those who struggle with their homosexuality and want to be free. Whether you think homosexuality is all right or not, I assume that all of us must be supportive of at least the freedom to choose to be free of those desires. Hopefully, whoever might quote that statement will do the fair thing of including, at minimum, this entire section of the book, and hopefully the whole chapter.

I've experienced many years as a pastor and minister, which has allowed me to speak to many Christians who've struggled with homosexuality. I've even spoken to pastors and leaders who've wept as they told me about their struggles to be free from homosexual feelings. I say that so you understand that I'm not naive or simplistic as to the monumental task that it can be to overcome homosexual desires. Great lovers of God and His ways struggle with these feelings and truly wish they didn't. What I will share will apply to many who have struggled with homosexuality.

Five Stages into Homosexuality: Relationship, Reaction, Rejection, Rebellion, and Radicalization

I believe there are basically five stages of descent into homosexual behavior that all begin with the letter *R*. Please know that I'm not pretending to know all there is to know about this topic, nor that every person who is in a homosexual lifestyle fits perfectly into my generalization. We aren't all exactly the same, but the enemy is fairly simple and consistent with his approach, which is why I am taking the liberty to present a potential scenario of how many people become entrenched in homosexuality and, more important, how freedom can be accessed.

The descent into homosexuality usually begins in the Relationship stage, which takes place in the context of your interaction with your parents and God. Somewhere early on, a seed is planted in you that tempts you to believe a lie that says, "I'm not wanted."

Next is the Reaction stage where you begin to react to the dynamics of those relationships. Reaction typically occurs from a challenge that arises in the relationship with your parents. For some, the father could be absent—in essence or in reality—and/or abusive. Or in some other significant way, there is often an unhealthy relationship with one or both of the parents. In the Reaction stage of this downward spiral, you find yourself coming to grips with the sense that "something is wrong." An individual may feel some initial anger, and there may also be some early pushing back against one parent or both parents. This all usually takes place when you're so young that most of it plays out subconsciously. Perhaps you're aware that guardian angels are assigned to each of us the moment we are conceived, but did you know that Satan also assigns demons to harass us? Most certainly, for those who struggle with the lie of homosexuality, the demons assigned to you are whispering, "You aren't wanted, and something is definitely wrong." That lie can literally begin when you're still in your mother's womb.

The third step toward homosexuality is the Rejection stage. During this time, you've already taken serious inventory of yourself, and your conclusion is, "I'm different." Some will actually go straight into this stage if they were sexually assaulted, abused, or touched inappropriately in any way—even if it was by another child. The more serious the assault, and the more it has been repeated, the more this stage can become hardwired in you. If this has been a life reality for years, then the rejection can become a demonic stronghold. In the Rejection stage, you begin to believe that you are of little value. Demons are again whispering the whole time, "You're not wanted." Sometimes they're telling you the truth about rejection that you're actually experiencing, and sometimes they're trying to convince you of something that isn't real but is rather just a misperception. However, if they convince you that you aren't wanted, then the rejection begins to be harmful to your mind, your spirit, and your sexuality. We must realize that demons can even convince children who are completely loved that they've been rejected; therefore, they especially have a lot of ammunition to use against you if there actually is any reality to it, or if you perceive your only value to be sexual. Whether you are a child or an adult, when you feel like your sexuality is your sole value to the people who are supposed to love you, you essentially feel worthless.

As rejection progresses further and further, confusion and anger can become attached to it. You go from becoming a rejectee to becoming a rejecter yourself. It becomes your mechanism to protect your heart from more pain. Subconsciously, one of the first things you reject is your own sexuality. Your initial experiences with sex are so traumatic that you attempt to shut off that part of who you are. This lockdown of your sexuality causes your natural sexual bent to go awry. You are a sexual being trying to reject your own sexuality, so it pops up on the other side of the tracks, so to speak. Furthermore, all sexual intercourse and activity involves a spirit exchange with the other person; so, if you've been abused by someone who's homosexual, then your spirit has received what's in their spirit. Again, this is just a brief, generalized explanation of some of the possible dynamics that take place—usually on a subconscious level.

The fourth stage into homosexuality is the Rebellion stage. This is where you choose to stop being a victim. Because you feel you can't trust anyone else's way of doing things, including God's, your operating mind-set becomes, "I'm going to do things my way." This isn't the kind of rebellion that you think of as being from an evil motive but rather from an instinct to protect yourself. The Bible says that rebellion is like the sin of witchcraft. In witchcraft, you come under demonic influence and begin to relate to the wrong supernatural power. Unfortunately, the "doing things my way" kind of thinking begins to build on your previous mind-set, which says, "Something is wrong. I'm different, and I'm not wanted." Because you're young and incapable of properly processing all that's happened to you, you're now extremely susceptible to a demonic suggestion to protect yourself by rebelling. In the previous stage, you were rejecting your own sexuality; in this stage, the demons begin to attempt to convince you of a new lie as they whisper to you, "You are gay." The first time you hear it, you shake it off angrily, but then as the whispers increase, you begin to think it makes sense. If you were molested, you now believe that this is the reason you were targeted sexually, perhaps even blaming yourself for it. At this point, if you haven't yet experimented sexually, the demons still use these mind-sets of "Something is wrong. I'm different, and I'm not wanted" to begin working on your mind and spirit. At the same time, your internal anger is exponentially increasing. Your rebellion may arise against any and all authorities because no authorities have protected you from this complicated mess of thoughts and emotions. You're against all standards because the status quo has been vicious to you—either in reality or in your mind. Demons work with reality, but they are also experts at working through our agreement with their lies. Again, they can even trick greatly loved and accepted kids into believing that they're not loved or accepted.

Last, the fifth stage—Radicalization—comes in, building on top of the previous ones. In this stage, the internal pain and anger from the rebellion has affected you much like witchcraft would. In either one of these two stages, you may begin making inner vows about who you are *not*. These inner vows have the power to lock you down indefinitely in the direction of your vow. For example, you may think, "I hate my dad/mom and never want to see or be like him/her." As you find your voice, you may also make inner vows against God because you blame Him for not protecting you from the pain of rejection or abuse. In the Radicalization stage, you begin to take additional inventory of who you think you are—and, of course, the inventory is against the backdrop of feeling, "Something is wrong. I'm different. I'm not wanted." Now suddenly you hear, "You are gay." Therefore, you believe and accept that you are gay.

> *It seems most children growing up today are exposed to these demonic lies.*

In this phase, you agree with what the demons have been telling you and what life's tough realities seem to have confirmed to you. Since you now agree with the lie, you make a leap into an identity of being gay. If you progress into choosing to act on this identity, then you're probably now fully opening yourself up to the homosexual lifestyle. The longer you engage in it, and the more partners you have, the more entrenched your radicalized new identity becomes.

I should make it clear that, in an almost unprecedented way, it seems most children growing up today are exposed to these same demonic lies—so don't assume you or your children are homosexual simply because the thought has crossed your mind or their mind. As I said, demons will seek your agreement with the lie, even if there's nothing to work with. But the good news is, through Christ, you have authority over that lie. You can also teach your children how to reject the lie and how to use the authority God has given them over demons.

I realize that many who struggle with homosexuality may not identify with these stages exactly as I have presented them. There are always exceptions to things we generalize, but for those who may identify with all or some of these five stages into homosexuality, remember that there is always hope and a way out.

Five Stages Out of Homosexuality: Repentance, Radiation, Restoration, Reward, and Relationship

The stages out of homosexuality are similar to the stages leading into it. Each also begins with the letter R. The first one is the Repentance stage. This is the first huge step toward wholeness, and it starts with a choice—not a feeling. This is about choosing to trust God instead of yourself and your way of reasoning about your own sexuality. Repentance is not so much about saying you're sorry, but rather about embracing a new way of thinking. Repentance is saying, "I choose to believe I am wanted and loved by God; therefore, I choose His way instead of mine." You may have gotten so far into a gay lifestyle that you actually enjoy the sexual pleasure and your new identity. Yet, in the same way we learn to make a decision for the sake of our health—like when we stop eating certain delicious foods that are bad for us—you, too, must make the difficult decision to leave what is harmful to you. Repentance is a decision that, through God's help, can become easier and easier. Although I acknowledge the following example is trivial in comparison, it may be helpful. I mentioned earlier that I had to give up donuts and coffee for health reasons. I wasn't delivered from liking donuts and coffee. I had to *choose* to stop eating them. It still sounds like something pleasurable to me, but every day it loses more and more of its ability to seduce me. Honestly, after abstaining for months, I rarely think about eating them, and then only briefly when I'm exposed to either one. The key to your freedom is in your choice to come into alignment with the rules of the One who designed you and designed how sexuality works best. You are halfway to freedom just by arriving at this place of surrender.

The second progressive step toward freedom is the Radiation stage. In a medical context, radiation therapy is the use of high-energy rays to damage cancer cells and stop them from growing and spreading. In this stage, your "radiation" treatment comes from soaking in the presence of God and receiving His amazing love into the core of who you are, as often and as much as possible. You've already won His heart simply by being His son or daughter, but you gained access to His power that makes you whole by your willingness to embrace *His* way. His desire is to radiate you with as much hope, truth, and love as you can handle. The radiation of His love and presence not only begins to damage the cells of the enemy's lies, but it also quickens and strengthens your spirit. The goal in this stage is not to achieve perfection, so that you never have a wayward thought, but simply to let Him in. You can do this by seeking Him in every way you know how—by listening to and participating in worship that you enjoy, by attending meetings with other Christians that give you life and encouragement, by spending time with friends who will support your desire to be whole and free, and by writing and reading truth statements about who you are in and to God. You're no longer a "Something is wrong" person, but rather a "Wow, God is good and His ways are good" person. You no longer subscribe to "I am different" from the vantage point of feeling like you're damaged goods; instead, now you think and say, "*I am fearfully and wonderfully made*" (Psalm 139:14 KJV). Now you truly believe that even if you don't feel it, you're accepted and wanted. Because of that new reality, you are able to say with your whole heart, "I choose God's way." Then, of course, you're ultimately able to exchange the "I am gay" identity tag for "I was willing to be transformed by God, and I have now allowed Him to transform me into who He designed me to be." The desired result isn't to become anti-homosexual. It's to become pro-God.

I expect that some who are reading this may be stuck in the rationale that says we should accept ourselves the way we were born. But again, just because someone is born with certain desires or even birth defects doesn't mean we are rejecting that person if we try to change them. It simply means we are rejecting the reality they appear to be stuck in as we suggest a way to improve their quality of life. Like a good parent, God always offers us a way out of something that He knows is harmful to us. Just because God allows circumstances in our lives that cause us heartache doesn't mean He's okay with those circumstances or desires for us to remain in them. For those who have struggled with the particular issue of homosexuality, I bet if you are able to recall the first moments that you felt sexual feelings for someone of the same sex, you instinctively had a negative feeling attached to it. We are all made in God's image, and that negative feeling you had was most likely something He wired into you. Think about this: Even children who are born without the ability to walk are aware, when they see others walking, that they were meant to walk.

> *Like a good parent, God always offers us a way out.*

The fact that they can't walk or may have to learn to walk through a much more difficult process than others shouldn't squelch that voice inside that tells them they were born to walk, too. We were all born with various things that need changing and improving. Why would we settle for less than God's best for us just because it may seem difficult or even impossible?

Everyone's experience of the divine radiation therapy is different. Some will immediately be so supernaturally charged by God's love and presence that they'll realize they never, or rarely, have thoughts or desires toward their past lifestyle. Others may find it an extended process, depending on how relationally tied in they are to other partners. The important thing to remember is not to stop your radiation therapy until the lie you believed and lived under no longer has power over you. If you have to do it for the rest of your life, that's okay—all you're doing is getting more hooked on God, and that never has a downside! In your radiation sessions with God, renounce soul attachments with every person you can remember having had improper sexual and emotional interaction with. The Holy Spirit will lead you through that process, especially if there have been too many to remember. The important thing to know is that God is greater than your sin and your broken-ness. His grace can bring you back from anywhere and anything.

The next *R* on your path to sexual wholeness is the Restoration stage. In this phase, your desires begin to match up with your declarations of wholeness. At first, you may have only momentary flashes of attraction to the opposite sex, but these will increase more and more until your sexuality shifts completely. As this process continues, you may even find yourself considering all kinds of new and exciting possibilities, including marrying someone of the opposite sex, if that's what God has for you. We know many people who have experienced this level of healing and were able to enter into the joy of being a part of a healthy, traditional family. They are such a beautiful testimony of God's power to restore. Whether you get married or not, your motto during this stage is, *"Behold, all things have become new"* (2 Corinthians 5:17)!

The Reward stage is next. Again, every stage is built upon the previous ones. Repentance, Radiation, and Restoration lead to Reward. You start with, "I really am wanted; therefore, I choose God's way." You progress to "I am fearfully and wonderfully made." You then incorporate "Behold, all things are new!" One aspect of the Reward stage is the heavenly reward you'll receive for your courageous and overcoming walk here on earth, but there are earthly rewards for you, as well. King David spoke of seeing *"the goodness of the LORD in the land of the living"* (Psalm 27:13). When you show the courage, resolve, and love of God to choose His way, even when your feelings don't immediately support your choice, this really touches His heart. He will move heaven and earth to see you rewarded here in the land of the living. His rewards are specifically designed to touch such a key place in your heart that your love for Him grows deeper and deeper. You'll no longer do things just because they are the right thing to do, but you'll be able to feel the pleasure of your heavenly Father as you align with Him.

This will take you, as never before, back into the fifth and final Relationship stage—the stage in which the enemy first brought his assault. Ever since your Repentance stage, a level of truly healthy relationship had begun, but this is now a stage where you no longer just accept by faith that God loves and accepts you, and that you can trust Him. You'll now be able to enjoy your relationship with God because you thoroughly know and experience His love and acceptance, with only momentary lapses. Additionally, part of your whole recovery journey will be connecting with spiritual brothers and sisters who will love and accept you unconditionally, encourage you, pray for you, prod you on, and provide the practical, healthy peer pressure you need to keep choosing the right thing. Continuing to choose the right thing is of utmost importance. When we are learning to overcome anything in our lives, and especially this issue, it's critical that we not overvalue our feelings. Feelings are rarely the truth. You could say that feelings make great employees but horrible bosses. This is particularly true when any kind of abuse or trauma has rendered them even less dependable. You want feelings in your vehicle, so to speak, but you don't want them driving. As you fully embrace this final Relationship stage, you'll begin to live a life so full of freedom and victory that your very life declares, "Exceedingly, abundantly above what I asked or thought!" (See Ephesians 3:20.)

> *The time period of 2015–2050 will see thousands upon thousands of gays, lesbians, and other sexually broken people come into wholeness.*

As a last thought on how to overcome homosexuality, let's look at one more *R* that will serve you well to remember. Relapse is possible at any point in the healing stage, but God in His goodness has provided the *R* of Repentance to instantly put you back on the journey to recovering all that has been stolen from you. The goal is not just to learn how to manage your sexuality. The goal is to get to the place where all aspects of your psyche that were damaged by abuse, abandonment, or lies can now come into relational wholeness. This can happen, this does happen, and this will be a common testimony in the coming years.

The time period of 2015–2050 will see thousands upon thousands of gays, lesbians, and other sexually broken people come into wholeness. As the atmosphere of revival breaks out in many places, the presence of the Holy Spirit will be so strong, and many will be touched so powerfully by Him that they will go through the five stages of recovery almost instantly. Many will be supernaturally delivered from their sexual brokenness in just one encounter with God. A greater measure of the burning love of God is about to be poured out upon the planet, and with it will come the same kind of once-and-for-all freedom Jesus brought. Mary Magdalene, the prostitute, had one encounter with the One who is the embodiment of love. She never relapsed, because the deepest core of who she was had been touched, and she never forgot it. This will be a common testimony in the coming Renaissance. Strippers, porn stars, porn addicts, prostitutes, sex slaves, sex traffickers, and pimps will all be pursued by the Holy Spirit's burning fire of love. They will have great testimonies, and out of their ranks will come great champions of the kingdom of God. God will be revealed as the One who is greater than any sexual brokenness. Many of the future great leaders on the Mountain of Family are presently in the very prisons of brokenness that God will enable them to set others free from. Likewise, the very wound that the enemy inflicted on you could become your platform for ministry.

As a reminder, the five steps of descent *into* homosexuality are:

1. Relationship stage: "I'm not wanted."

2. Reaction stage: "Something is wrong."

3. Rejection stage: "I'm different."

4. Rebellion stage: "I'm going to do things my way."

5. Radicalization stage: "I am gay."

The five steps *out of* homosexuality are:

1. Repentance stage: "I am wanted."

2. Radiation stage: "I choose God's way."

3. Restoration stage: "I am fearfully and wonderfully made."

4. Reward stage: "Behold, all things are new!"

5. Relationship stage: "Exceedingly, abundantly above what I asked or thought."

The Legalization of Gay Marriage

As I've traveled around the world, I've spoken to many friends in other nations who are very concerned about the legal advances that allow gays to legally marry. As is the case in the United States, this issue is often seen as an assault against the institution of family. There is great fear and concern associated with the shifting landscape of public opinion toward gays being permitted to marry. Personally, I'm much less inclined to be concerned. Allow me to explain.

The Assault Against the Family Is Not from Gay Marriages

First of all, a big reality check: The most definitive and credible report on the gay population of America was released in July 2014 by the CDC in conjunction with the National Health Statistics Report. This survey was done on behalf of the government specifically for the healthcare industry. The following data is taken from a survey of the American population in 2013 and was conducted with great attention to privacy:[26]

+ 96.6 percent identified themselves as straight

+ 1.6 percent identified themselves as gay or lesbian

+ 0.7 percent identified themselves as bisexual

---

26. Brian W. Ward, Ph.D., et al., "Sexual Orientation and Health Among U.S. Adults: National Health Interview Survey, 2013," *National Health Statistics Report* 77 (July 15, 2014), http://www.cdc.gov/nchs/data/nhsr/nhsr077.pdf.

♦ 1.1 percent identified themselves as something else or did not answer

So, first of all, let's gain some perspective. Only 2.3 percent of Americans identify themselves as gay, lesbian, or bisexual. Obviously, the public perception of the percentage of gays is much greater than that. In 2011, Gallup released the results of a poll of the perceived percentage of gays in America. The average answer was above 24.6 percent.[27] That's perception, as opposed to reality. Due to the aggressive "gay agenda," the perception is that we are becoming an increasingly gay society, but the reality is that the facts just don't bear that out. Gays are more strategically organized than ever, but they certainly don't pose an imminent threat to the institution of the family. Furthermore, even statistics that are markedly friendly toward gays confirm the CDC numbers that show only 1 percent of all households in America are gay/lesbian (around 600,000 couples). And note that of this one percent, only some desire to have legally sanctioned marriages.

This statistic begs a few questions. Just how does allowing this less than 1 percent of the population to get married assault the rest of American families? And how does this constitute an attack on marriage? Are we not scapegoating, instead of just owning up to our own problems as heterosexuals? If a law were passed that forced all homosexuals to be banned to a faraway island, would that fix marriages? Would we stop fighting over finances, sex, chores, and other matters simply because gays are gone? Would we stop viewing pornography if homosexuals weren't around? As I said, I have counseled many couples over the years, and none have stated that the problem in their marriage had anything to do with the "gay agenda."

Can we please stop pointing the finger at easy targets and go ahead and deal with our own brokenness and neediness? Can we keep the real numbers that are at play in perspective? Yes, some gays are exerting a lot of influence, and the radical edge of the homosexual community clearly has an advancing agenda—but if anything, even that

27. See Lymari Morales, "U.S. Adults Estimate That 25% of Americans Are Gay or Lesbian," Gallup (May 27, 2011), http://www.gallup.com/poll/147824/Adults-Estimate-Americans-Gay-Lesbian.aspx.

reality should encourage us about what would be possible if we were more unified, more strategic, and more intentional with our strategy of love. If less than 3 percent who are in unison can shift our culture and laws, then we can only imagine what changes could take place if only 10 percent of the Christian population properly united in bringing God's solutions and better ways of doing everything. What could happen if we were motivated by love, unafraid of how we might be affected by others, and convinced that God was ready to help us fix every problem in society?

Positioned as Healers

Recently, I was in a hotel talking with a high-ranking political friend of mine from another nation. He asked me what he should do about the advancing radical gay agenda that was seeking to legalize marriage in his nation. He was very concerned and shared with me that he had recently participated in an anti-gay marriage parade in conjunction with pastors and other Christians. I responded in a manner similar to what I stated above—that I personally didn't think it was that big a deal if gay marriages were allowed or not. Of course, that surprised him, as it may still surprise you. Let me explain further.

What could happen if we were motivated by love, unafraid and convinced?

I believe God's heart toward homosexuals is love. Their core wound is rejection, and their great need is for acceptance. Again, most homosexuals have been molested or abandoned in some way. I told my friend that we must find a way to stop perpetuating the feeling of rejection that they receive from the church—especially if we honestly believe that it's the only possible institution that can spiritually connect them to the transforming power and unconditional love of God. I suggested that, as a politician, he initiate legislation that simply stated care and concern for homosexuals, as well as their rights not to be bullied or otherwise mistreated. Of course, this would be something that's already guaranteed to all citizens, but at least it would make a statement of love and acceptance from a Christian politician. My friend was quite taken aback, but he listened to everything I said.

The next day, we met for breakfast, and as soon as we sat down, my friend excitedly said, "You'll never guess what happened this morning!" He explained how earlier that morning, he'd gone down to the hotel business center to handle some e-mails, and a young man was there working next to him. The man initiated conversation that caused my friend to easily recognize that he was gay. Remembering our conversation from the previous night, my friend decided that he would do all he could in that brief conversation not to say anything that might make the young man feel rejected or judged in any way.

After some dialogue, the gay young man learned that my friend was attending a Christian conference (where I was the keynote speaker). Upon learning this, he commented, "You all [Christians] pretty much hate us, don't you?" Sensing his rejection, my friend said, "No, we don't hate you; we love you." The young man pressed him with various questions, looking for the rejection that he was expecting—but my friend refused to give him any answers that could be perceived as rejection. Finally, the young man said, "But sir, at the end of the day, do you actually believe that homosexual sex is wrong?" My friend was finally faced with a direct question that was seemingly going to lead to an answer that would communicate a lack of acceptance to this young man, yet he beautifully yielded to the Holy Spirit and responded, "Well, you tell me about *your* experience. How do you feel after you have sex with a man?" The young man paused and then softly said, "I feel bad. We all feel bad. We all know it's wrong." This ultimately led to a very sweet time of prayer. As the young man wept, my friend was able to lead him into a relationship with Jesus.

When he met with me for breakfast, my friend was still in shock about what had just transpired. Like most Christians, he originally thought the need was for him to convince homosexuals that what they were doing was wrong. He suddenly realized that when he brought unconditional love and acceptance to the young man, it gave the Holy Spirit access to him—and the Holy Spirit is the only One who can properly convict us of our sin, setting us free from its effects without shaming us.

I share this story because there's so much to learn from it. Once we decide to lose the fear of the "gay agenda," we can be positioned as healers on the Mountain of Family. My friend is a top politician, but he also considers himself to be someone who is passionate about families. Although his motives were right, his previous inspiration to prove his love for families was to run to the familiar anti-gay battlefronts. Now he has learned how to actually heal the wounded and brokenhearted. If we are going to learn the same lesson, we must let go of the fear of appearing to condone or approve of sin. God knows you well enough to know your heart, even if others may not—and wouldn't you agree that the homosexual community definitely already knows that Christians believe homosexuality is wrong? Just because you unconditionally love and accept those who are gay or lesbian doesn't mean you are giving them permission to sin. It means you realize your responsibility and privilege is to love them and have a friendship with them, allowing them access to the God of love and to the love of God that is in you. Without it, how can they ever have an opportunity to be free and whole?

I realize that there are other concerns and issues, such as whether gay marriage should be legalized. Among other considerations, this issue has financial repercussions for the state. However, I still must say that if we'll lose the fear of being taken over by less than 3 percent of the population, then we really can be much better ambassadors for the King of Kings. The next generation of kingdom kids will show up on this mountain and bring God's heart and solutions to it even better than we will. They'll discover how to restrict the collateral damage that arises from laws that are friendly toward gays, while still providing acceptance and love to a community whose number one need is the love and acceptance of the Father. May that concern be greater than our fears.

The Abortion Dilemma

Another major issue on the Mountain of Family is abortion, which of course is an extremely hot and divisive topic. The Roe v. Wade Supreme Court decision in 1973 legalizing abortion drew attention to the topic of abortion as never before, and the pro-choice versus pro-life battle has raged intensely ever since.

Winning the Battle over Hearts and Minds

While Roe v. Wade hasn't been reversed, there are many signs that the hearts and minds of society on this issue are slowly being won over. For example, the CDC reported that abortion numbers have decreased from around 1.4 million in 1990 to around 800,000 in 2013.[28] This is a significant drop, since the national population has greatly increased since then. Additionally, there are reports that show two-thirds of all abortion clinics have closed since 1990. This, too, is encouraging.

Though much effort and cost have gone into attempts to reverse Roe v. Wade, it's quite clear that the recent downward trends in abortion are not related to changes in the *law* but rather because *hearts and minds* are indeed being won over. Recent medical studies proving that pre-born babies have the capacity to feel pain have created another shift in public opinion against abortion. Society is in a tender moment regarding the rights of individuals. People will no longer tolerate bullying, discrimination, or abuse against anyone. Should the battle be won to prove that unborn babies are also individuals who have emotions and feel pain, I believe society will make yet another strong adjustment toward life.

28. See "Abortion Surveillance—United States, 1990," Center for Disease Control and Prevention (December 17, 1993), http://www.cdc.gov/mmwr/preview/mmwrhtml/00031585.htm; "Abortion Surveillance—United States, 2011," Center for Disease Control and Prevention (November 28, 2014), http://www.cdc.gov/mmwr/preview/mmwrhtml/ss6311a1.htm?s_cid=ss6311a1_e.

Staying Away from the Wrong Battlefronts

One of the reasons we've been so slow to win this battle is that we've allowed ourselves to be drawn into the wrong battlefronts. As long as the argument is framed as one between pro-choice and pro-life, we'll continue to find strong polarization and slower gains. Agreeing to fight at that battlefront allows the real moral issues to remain obscured. Being pro-choice and being pro-life are both good *ideals*, and that's why there will always be strong support for both. Presently, American men are almost evenly divided between these two options. Perhaps surprising to many, 49 percent of women are pro-choice,[29] even though females are clearly much more relationally sensitive as a gender. To not explore this factor and address the underlying heart issue is a significant oversight.

Understanding the Fuel Behind the Pro-choice Side

Though it's extremely easy to demonize those who are pro-choice as being immoral—"How can you be against *life?*"—we really must be aware of and understand some of the history behind this movement. A gender battle seems to be brewing under the surface, which must also be considered. Margaret Sanger (1879–1966) was essentially the founder of Planned Parenthood and is a hero to many women in America, despite her unpardonable, Nazi-like support for eugenics and its ensuing influence in her efforts to make birth control available for blacks and other minorities whom she considered "less fit" for reproduction. For example, she wrote that Australian aborigines were "just a step higher than the chimpanzee."[30]

Today, Margaret Sanger is greatly vilified by the pro-life crowd for being the founder of what became Planned Parenthood. Her advocacy

---

29. See "48% are Pro-Choice, 44% are Pro-Life," Rasmussen Reports (July 6, 2014), http://www.rasmussenreports.com/public_content/politics/current_events/abortion/48_are_pro_choice_44_pro_life.
30. Margaret Sanger, "What Every Girl Should Know—Part II," Margaret Sanger Project, https://www.nyu.edu/projects/sanger/webedition/app/documents/show.php?sangerDoc=304923.xml.

of eugenics, along with abortion rates that reveal a much higher level among blacks, have caused her to become the poster child for what's considered to be wrong with the foundations of the pro-abortion movement. However, not only did Margaret Sanger not found pro-abortion ideals, but she was strongly against them. In her book *Woman and the New Race*, she wrote, "While there are cases where even law recognizes an abortion is justifiable if recommended by a physician, I assert that the hundreds of thousands of abortions performed in America each year are a disgrace to civilization."[31]

> *Not only did Margaret Sanger not found pro-abortion ideals, but she was strongly against them.*

Yes, this is why actually knowing history is important. The de facto founder of the modern abortion engine called Planned Parenthood considered abortions to be a disgrace to civilization. Furthermore, she wasn't against abortions just because they were dangerous to the mother (which was one of her reasons), but also because she believed that life started at conception and that an abortion was actually the taking of a life. Isn't it amazing that this lightening rod pro-abortion figure was actually extremely clear on her complete rejection of abortion?

Margaret Sanger is, in fact, the founder of modern-day birth control, and that was her primary advocacy. She believed in birth control as a cure for the multitude of abortions already taking place in society, well before Roe v. Wade. Note that she acknowledged there were hundreds of thousands of abortions each year, decades before abortion became legal. The voices that imply that abortions were rare before 1973 are factually wrong. The clandestine nature

31. Margaret Sanger, *Women and the New Race*, http://www.bartleby.com/1013/10. html.

of abortions at that time makes statistical certainty impossible, but Margaret Sanger seemed to be in the know about American reproductive behavior.

As we look back at the underlying gender war in America, we see that Sanger was a very important historical figure. She is wrongfully connected to abortions on demand, but she was, in her own way, pro-choice. She fought tremendous battles in relation to women's reproductive rights, and she was even jailed over supporting the right of women to limit their number of children. For centuries, it had been very common for women to have many children, and it was also very common for women to die in childbirth. While the rate of death by childbirth is still a jarring 1 percent today (about 275,000 maternity deaths per year worldwide), for centuries the rate was closer to ten times that—and possibly as high as twenty. Sanger's own mother went through eighteen pregnancies, with eleven live births in twenty-two years, before dying at age forty-nine. This was a rather common reality of the day, and it greatly motivated Sanger in her lifework.

Accordingly, to understand some of the fuel behind the pro-choice movement, you must understand that neither the church nor men have a great record of caring for women and their bodies. Generally, if it were up to the church or men, women would ideally still be "barefoot and pregnant." The great reformer Martin Luther expressed this as a matter of a woman's value. To read his writings is to know that not only was he anti-Semitic, but he was also anti-woman (a chauvinist, if you prefer that terminology). His version of reform didn't involve valuing a woman's place in society. However, we don't need to pick on Luther, as women have not been properly valued by either the church or men since the days of Jesus—though Christ Himself modeled the opposite.

Margaret Sanger was a relentless campaigner for a woman's right to self-determinism as it relates to having or not having children. The foundational tenets of her efforts toward birth control options were the following:

We hold that children should be

(1) Conceived in love;

(2) Born of the mother's conscious desire;

(3) And only under conditions which render possible the heritage of health.

Therefore we hold that every woman must possess the power and freedom to prevent conception except when these conditions can be satisfied.[32]

Surely, we wouldn't argue with the first two points; and although we may have questions about the third point, we certainly must recognize that Sanger was sympathetic to the mistreatment and neglect women commonly experienced in the good ole days that many yearn for America to go back to—a day when women were not properly valued, cared for, listened to, and protected, when men expected them to have as many babies as their bodies could manage before giving out. Every pregnancy risked a woman's life, yet it was against the law to distribute contraceptives or even literature on how to reduce births. Sanger fought fiercely for a woman's right of sovereignty over her own body. I must say that at least some of the honor she garners today is deserved. Women deserve to be the primary determinants of when and if they will have children. Even in modern

> *Women deserve to be the primary determinants of when and if they will have children.*

32. Margaret Sanger, "The Birth Control Movement in 1923," The Margaret Sanger Project, https://www.nyu.edu/projects/sanger/webedition/app/documents/show.php?sangerDoc=300368.xml.

society, pregnancy still exacts a serious toll on women's bodies and poses enough of a risk to their lives that it should be their decision.

So, when the abortion battle is framed over a woman's right to choose, we bump into a societal gender-wound that somebody should repent for on behalf of the callous men of yesterday and today. Here is my part:

> Ladies, on behalf of chauvinistic and woman-oppressing men of history, I repent for how we have not properly honored you over the generations. I ask forgiveness for the ways we have led you to believe that your only value was under our guidance, under our service, at our beck and call for sex, at our beck and call for giving us more children, and at our beck and call for your opinions and thoughts. Please forgive us for not properly valuing your body, your life, your aches and pains, your emotions, and your hormonal changes, as well as for all the ways we have implied that you need to "shush" in society. You definitely have the right to be the primary consideration in everything that happens to and in your body. It is your body, and neither men nor society should be able to dictate to you matters having to do with your reproduction. You are special, loved, valuable, and cherished, and your voice must be heard in matters of life and society.

Finding Better Battlefronts

There's no doubt that demonic influence is involved in the proliferation of abortion. The devil comes to steal, kill, and destroy (see John 10:10), and abortion is, in fact, a very practical way in which he accomplishes that. He has been behind the murder of millions of unborn babies because he hates humans and would love to see us become extinct. Yet, when we take the fight that's actually against *him* and show up at the battlefront of a woman's choice—telling women that they don't have the right to determine matters that men and the church have imposed on them for millennia—then we have gone to a battlefront where it's difficult to gain critical mass, even while having a moral upper hand. At this battlefront, the devil is able to stir up enough past gender wrongs and grievances that moral clarity eludes those who are under his fog. New approaches are required.

One new approach I advocate is that of simply appealing to women. Forget trying to appeal to men. How many husbands know that it's wisdom to *appeal* to their wife rather than try to tell her what to do? The same wisdom applies societally. It requires us to exercise this thing called humility, instead of running around with the moral superiority card. Much of the abortion dilemma is not just about valuing life. It's about valuing women. What if we acknowledged a woman's right to make a decision over that which is still in her body—even though we realize that taking that life is killing a human being? What if we led with that foot and then pushed for other concessions that assisted her in making the best choice within her right to choose?

I propose a new pro-informed choice platform on the abortion matter. This is where we would acknowledge a woman's right to choose, but we would campaign for stipulations to be met before she makes that choice.

Stipulation #1: A woman must see a video of what an actual abortion looks like and must be told exactly what the process is. Full disclosure would be given concerning what the baby looks like and what it can feel.

Stipulation #2: A woman must see some kind of ultrasound of her unborn baby.

Stipulation #3: A woman must be advised of all the options that could be made available for her baby—for example, adoption.

Stipulation #4: A woman must be advised of the potential risks from an abortion to her own physical and emotional health.

Stipulation #5: A woman must wait seven days after receiving all of this information before getting an abortion.

The problem is not one of choice. I have no problem with a woman's prerogative to choose. The problem is the lack of an informed choice. I am fully convinced that more than 90 percent of all abortions would cease if a woman seeking an abortion were required to watch a video depicting the process. In my view, only a very troubled woman, perhaps one who is capable of murder, could still proceed with an abortion. Abortions become easier when a woman either doesn't know what's really going on or chooses to be in denial. The state does have a responsibility to at least let her know exactly what she's doing. Only when a woman thinks of what's in her womb as merely unviable tissue and isn't confronted with the reality of what she carries, can she easily follow through with an abortion.

> *The problem is not one of choice. The problem is the lack of an informed choice.*

There are, of course, secondary moral issues in the abortion dilemma. The answer to moral issue number one is clear: The life of a human being shouldn't be ended by another human being. But there are other moral issues. Do unwanted babies have the moral right to be in families where they're wanted? What if an abortion would save the life of a mother—is it still morally wrong? If the argument for abortion under such a scenario is, "You're playing God with someone's life," the reality is that you're doing so anyway, if it's truly an either-or scenario.

Other questions include: Is it morally acceptable to bring into this world an unborn baby that has no brain waves? No eyes? No limbs? A painful, progressive, degenerative disease? Where is the line to be drawn? Would you agree that these are at least difficult considerations if you are not a dyed-in-the-wool Pharisee? Where is the cut-off point of intervention? It is because of these difficult questions that I trust a potential mom above all other options, including state mandates, as long as she has been given full disclosure of all the facts. A mom will instinctively know better than anyone. Of course, the hope is that the mother would be able to lean on the child's father for strength and advice, but I would trust her and vote that she be given pro-informed-choice, regardless.

You see, part of the problem is that, at times, we can forget how complicated life can be, and we prefer simplistic black-and-white answers. Take this example: What if you were a fourteen-year-old girl who had been impregnated by her alcoholic stepfather, and you had no state support structure to assist you, so you had to remain in his home? What if you knew that bringing this child into the house could subject the child to similar abuse by the same father? Would you agree that this is a tough decision for a young lady to have to wrestle through, wondering if she can handle bringing a baby into that environment? Can we maybe at least cool off our pro-life jets and pull back just a moment to reconsider the battlefront and decide if we are showing up with wisdom? I'm not saying such a girl should have an abortion. I am saying only that it's a very tough decision either way and that, at the very least, a caring and understanding heart on our part is in order. It really is possible to be right about a moral issue but totally wrong about one's approach to it. We need to show up on the abortion battleground knowing and wisely understanding the correct battlefronts. I know many people are making adjustments in this regard, and that must and will continue. The battle is ultimately not a legal one but one that's over hearts and minds.

The Renaissance Army on the Mountain of Family

In the coming days, months, and years, an army of lovers of God and life will arise on the Mountain of Family. They will bring God-inspired ideas and approaches that will reach the hearts and minds of society in a clear, impactful way. All of the family matters we have discussed are connected to one another, and holistic solutions will be forthcoming that show a profound understanding of this reality.

Obviously, the abortion dilemma begins with sex outside of marriage, although there are exceptions, of course. To ignore that fact in the abortion battle is not helpful. Sex outside of marriage also generally has a root cause, and that, too, must be addressed. God will provide wisdom and real answers for those called to the Mountain of Family as the Renaissance moves forward. His arising sons and daughters must first give themselves to understanding the importance of carrying God's heart of mercy, compassion, and love to all His broken and wounded children. The members of this rising army won't just be moralizers; they will be empathizers. Finger-pointing could never be considered a correct portrayal of how Jesus would respond to people if He were walking the earth today. He pointed His finger at only one group, and that was at the finger-pointing Pharisees. We must do better than they did—and we will. Renaissance is coming to the Mountain of Family as we advance and grow in favor and influence and learn to bring the Father's acceptance to those who have experienced so much rejection in His name.

Eight

RENAISSANCE ON THE
MOUNTAIN OF GOVERNMENT

In every nation I travel to, I hear the common complaint that there's so much corruption in government. In some countries, the evils and corruption in government are so profound and systemic that hardly a day goes by without the citizens of those nations feeling the torment of their corrupt leadership. In fact, I recently read a report that more people had been killed by their own government (directly and indirectly) in the last year than by all the wars between nations. This is truly tragic and a major reason why the sons and daughters of the King of Kings must now arise on this mountain and allow their presence to be felt. We must stop focusing on the giants in the promised land and fully enter into it with the presence and solutions of God.

Over the next thirty-five years, the Era of Renaissance will hit this supremely important Mountain of Government. By 2050, there will be at least fifty nations that will have a primarily righteous government in place, and the people of those nations will be in prosperity and rejoicing because of that reality. This dynamic is spoken of in Proverbs 29:2: *"When the righteous are in authority, the people rejoice; but when a wicked man rules, the people groan."* This Scripture also confirms to us the idea that the righteous are supposed to be in authority, which is something that many people in the body of Christ have been opposed to for faulty doctrinal reasons. There has been a resistance to contend for a place that could improve society because it would set back the expectation of Jesus' imminent return to earth. As a result, we've abdicated authority and sent panic e-mails to one another.

> *By 2050, there will be at least fifty nations that will have a primarily righteous government in place.*

The good news is that we are awakening from this poor-eschatology-induced slumber. We will soon have a worldwide love-army of the righteous who seek to bring heaven's reform onto the Mountain of Government. Every nation will require a different strategy of advancement, depending on how entrenched the enemy already is in that country. In nations that have no real freedom, there are no official governmental positions that can be sought after; instead, there must simply be a reliance on favor and influence to bring about positive reform. Remember this: Joseph, Daniel, and Nehemiah all had immense governmental authority, and yet all were in essence slaves who gained favor. There can be no such thing as hopelessness toward any government, because God will make a way even when there seems to be no way. Also, remember the taking of Jericho, where the key for Israel was to simply show up with the expectation that *God* would be the difference-maker? This will be the case in the future as God will make a way for His righteous kids, not only in democracies but also in dictatorships of every kind. He is decidedly greater than any form of government, and as His kids head for this mountain with the kingdom of God as their priority, He will send the armies of heaven to make a way. Believe it, and live the reality of it.

Over the last several years, I've had many friends become excited about the Seven Mountain message, and they've run toward the Mountain of Government expecting God to do the impossible. Some of them are now positioned in key places in their nations, and some were surprised to find out that the landscape of government and politics was much more dangerous than they'd previously thought. We are learning that the kids of the King must be prepared to persistently approach government and keep coming in waves. Our post in the governmental arena has been abandoned for centuries (in some cases, such a post never existed); therefore, we cannot expect unreasonable results after just a couple of years of action. We must be prepared to take the time to fill thousands of positions in every nation that we desire to see turned around in a significant way. If we understand beforehand the effort and time it will take, it can save us from a lot of frustration.

What Does Renaissance Look Like in Government?

As we ask this important question, we want to remember that our point of reference is God and heaven. We are contending for what Jesus Himself instructed us to pray: *"On earth as it is in heaven"* (Matthew 6:10). As we ponder that desired outcome, it will lead us to the Holy Spirit for wisdom and grace on how to proceed. He will instruct us based on what is revealed in the Scriptures and based on what He speaks to us as His strategy and voice for today. We have governmental leaders in our biblical history such as Joseph, Moses, Joshua, David, Daniel, and Esther who all gave us excellent examples on earth of how government works in heaven. Someone called by God to this mountain will be courageous, righteous, wise, servant-hearted, and humble. These qualities will be in contrast to what generally rules on this mountain: cowardice, foolishness, pride, and greed.

Renaissance looks like the face of God shining through His children now being the light of the world through government. As this Era of Renaissance advances, the expectation that public servants be courageous, righteous, wise, servant-hearted, and humble will increase. The bar has been set so low in government because of the lack of involvement of righteous people. The standard will be raised by the infusion of sons and daughters of God who are seeking to advance His kingdom. In many nations, it will become the norm that good people fill positions of authority. And the trickle-down effect on the citizens will be significant. Believe it, and expedite the process.

The Primary Assignment: Bring Transparency

In simple terms, the problem in government is corruption; therefore, step one to stemming that problem is transparency and accountability. We'd like to say that the need is for more honest leaders, but the reality is that, in many nations, honest leaders can't make it very far because of the corruption in the voting process. I've advised righteous candidates in several nations where the political spectrum is so corrupt that, in essence, no significant election could be won unless the candidate participated in the corruption. My advice has been, at this stage of the battle, these candidates may need to forgo attempting to win elections and instead look to do all in their power to bring full transparency to the electoral process. Without it, elections will continue to be stolen from good people. We know that the devil comes to steal, kill, and destroy, and he does these things in the midst of elections, as well.

It's of little value for a nation to officially be a democracy when the electoral process itself is absolutely tainted and rigged. This is the reality of many, if not most, of the world's democracies. For many of those called to the Mountain of Government, bringing transparency to the electoral process has to be the assignment of highest priority. The whole point of democracy is that it be a government chosen by the people. Instead, what's happening is that an electoral charade is being put on by the economic powerbrokers of the nation in which the results of elections have, by and large, already been decided before the people ever vote. The electoral system in these corrupt countries has several procedural points where it's no longer under public scrutiny; it's at that level where the vote-rigging is occurring. An initial primary assignment for God's kingdom kids on this mountain is therefore to implement an electoral system that has no blind spots that make room for corruption and has a public eye on every electoral step, including the counting of votes.

> *Bringing transparency to the electoral process has to be the assignment of highest priority.*

My suggestion has been to work on the infusion of transparency sometime after an election when the electoral engine is at a lull. What's needed is the formation of a Citizens for Transparency in Government Commission, or a Public Anti-Corruption Task Force. This should be a group formed by kingdom-minded individuals that can identify the loopholes in the electoral process where there may be the potential for corruption. Such a citizens' group wouldn't carry a partisan agenda; its sole goal would be to eliminate corruption in elections. We've been so eager to contend for winning elections that we haven't had the patience to take on this assignment first. Jesus said, "*You are the light of the world*" (Matthew 5:14). We must first bring that light to the electoral process. A citizens' initiative will work only if it is conducted transparently, openly. In regard to an upcoming presidential election, the assignment must be complete before the halfway point of the current presidential term, because by then the forces of power are back on the job, beginning to attempt to control the outcome. But remember, God is greater than mafias and strongholds.

A Citizens for Transparency in Government Commission could be run from an Internet domain and count heavily on social media to advance its goal of transparency in the electoral process. The home Web page could also serve as a sounding board for the public and a place where people could report governmental fraud or political corruption at any level. Here it would function not only as an election objective but as an ongoing anticorruption effort. The business community could help with funding this social media platform, as it would be in their best interest if they were able to function on a level playing field. Such a home page could function in a way similar to what a trip advisory page does for the travel industry where one can look up a hotel online and view guests' complaints and the managers' response to those complaints. There would be a need for more oversight than with a trip advisor page, but that would be the idea.

For example, a citizen could post a complaint of corruption in regard to a specific politician, which would then be pointed out to that politician. The political leader would then have an opportunity online to respond to the complaint. At some point in the process, the Citizens' Commission would make their ruling on the matter, based on verifiable evidence they're receiving. Everyone could view the initial complaint, the politician's response, and the commission's opinion. This wouldn't bring legal accountability, but it would bring significant public peer pressure toward operating honestly. It would be a battle, but it would be one that the public would join forces in because the site would exist for the sole purpose of removing corruption in government, and no other partisan objective would be accepted. Nonpartisanship would be guaranteed by the site's commitment to free access for anyone to report anything.

Full transparency and accountability in government would weed out those who desire political positions primarily for the power or money it would give them access to. Right now, in many supposed democracies around the world, the known shortcut for becoming a millionaire is to do what it takes to win a significant election. Many democratic governments run no differently from the mafia. The system itself is conducive to a mafia-type personality. Bringing the light of transparency into government would have an endgame result of the removal of anyone who truly doesn't have serving the public interest in mind but has come to raid the national kitty.

Now, in most countries, if only an individual or two attempted to bring this kind of accountability to government, it would put their lives at risk. For this reason, a national or international social-media-based transparency platform must be developed that has no key names or well-known people running it. It must be a grassroots public movement. There are already electoral transparency agencies, but they all presently come with an agenda of their own, as well as the ability to be tainted. This is why we need to have people involved in such an operation who have character and to whom the kingdom of God is a priority. It's a very important initiative for the Mountain of Government because it essentially lays the groundwork for good men and good women to run as candidates and to win elections. God sovereignly works and moves even with corrupt elected officials in place, but we must begin to be the salt and light of the world in these practical structural systems. What we don't salt with our integrity will trample us. (See Matthew 5:13.)

I'm anticipating that some nation will develop the initial model of this vision, and then, once an effective model has been developed, it will go global. In truth, there are many politicians who wish their own systems were less corrupt, but they don't have the courage to face the political suicide they'd certainly risk by speaking out on the matter. Many governmental leaders are double-minded—they want to help their citizens, but they also want the power and the money at any cost. A cleaner political landscape will allow them to break free from their own double-mindedness and give in to the redemptive side of their leadership gift.

What Do We Do When It's a Dictatorship?

The above solution is intended for nations with some semblance of the democratic process in their governance. The question many have is, "What should we do when there seems to be no pathway to participation on the Mountain of Government?" Joseph, Daniel, Nehemiah, and Esther all had to function within dictatorships. Elections aren't the only way to arrive at a place of political or governmental influence. Because God can orchestrate so many variables, one needs only to watch for the doors He opens, and then go through them. In the future, many great national turnarounds will take place by the influence of countless modern-day Josephs, Daniels, Nehemiahs, and Esthers.

I believe I've seen that at least fourteen current nations will no longer exist by the year 2050.

From extra-biblical sources, we're told that Joseph was the de facto ruler of Egypt for eighty years. We know that he was thirty when he came to power (see Genesis 41:46) and that he lived to be 110 years old (see Genesis 50:26), so the biblical account supports this probability. Daniel was a de facto ruler for many decades, as well. Both of these men undoubtedly were able to position many friends in key positions throughout their governments. I'm saying this so that we will remember that elections are not the only way in which servants of God can come into power. Whatever form of government exists in your nation, if you have a call from God to be on that mountain, then He will open a door for you. Ultimately, heaven views the men or women who stand in the gap on a mountain as the top authority representing heaven's interests.

When Is It Proper to Resist a Government?

This question, significant now, will become even more significant in the future. I see in part and prophesy in part, but I believe I've seen that at least fourteen current nations will no longer exist by the year 2050. Obviously, this implies instability and upheaval in those nations. If you are a kingdom believer with influence in one of those nations, it will require a lot of wisdom to know how to proceed. The simple answer is, "Be led by the Holy Spirit." The general rule is never to take up arms against our own government. However, there could be a time when there are exceptions—for example, when a nation's government is no longer led by elected officials who were chosen by the citizens but is actually controlled by a terrorist organization that's killing its own citizens. When things reach this stage, I see no clear guiding principle, and only a directive from God will do. Peaceful resistance is the general principle, but there can be situations that leave no peaceful choice.

I am currently aware of a government in South America that has significant popular backing yet probably stole the last election. There seems to be a substantial amount of high-level corruption in its administration. This government is also accused of certain targeted assassinations and unjust imprisonments. However, at this point, it doesn't appear to qualify as a terrorist organization; therefore, I don't believe taking up arms would be God's way of dealing with the situation. Many of these types of situations must be dealt with primarily through prayer and Christian unity, anticipating God's supernatural intervention.

The United States Government: The Burden of Being a Lead Nation

There are certain governmental realities that are primarily or only applicable to the United States. Right now, America has clearly been ordained by God to be the lead nation of the world. This role and call will continue for some time, and possibly indefinitely, because the United States was formed as a gift from God to the nations of the world. One has only to think of where the world would be without this nation in order to understand that. Honestly, most of us are probably incapable of properly assessing that reality. It requires a thorough knowledge of history, plus an ability to know many behind-the-scenes scenarios that aren't known to the general public. Only in eternity will we understand how greatly the United States was used to circumvent world domination plans that were inspired by demonic forces; there are a few instances, however, that are immediately apparent. For example, without the United States, a large portion of the world might have been forced to speak German. If Hitler's full agenda had advanced, as it no doubt would have without the contribution of U.S. military power, there might be only white people on the planet. After Hitler, Communism was poised to take over the world, and it might have done so if the United States hadn't intervened and resisted. More recently, it seems quite possible that only the United States has had the firepower and resolve to stop extreme Islam from global domination.

Never has a nation had so much power but showed so much restraint.

Although, in general, Americans seem to despise their own government (Congress and the Senate often have a disapproval rating of more than 75 percent, and presidents usually have an approval rating of less than 50 percent), and although much of the world resents her power and leadership, there has never been a more righteous leading nation in the history of the world. Never has a nation had so much power but showed so much restraint. No other nation has ever defeated countries in war—at great cost in lives and money—and then assisted in rebuilding them. Germany and Japan are two very powerful independent nations today, whereas they could have been forced to become part of the United States. While the world said that America was in Iraq to take over the nation because of its oil fields, the United States actually gave the country back to the Iraqi people (some might say prematurely) and left the oil fields alone. Every other lead nation of history would, in fact, have taken over their oil fields. I believe that because the United States showed restraint, even while desperately needing oil ourselves, the Lord allowed incredible discoveries of oil to take place in America. These discoveries, along with new energy technologies being developed, assure that we won't be needing any foreign oil in the future.

Whenever a world disaster takes place, it's usually the United States that first and foremost arrives with charitable help. America serves as a Good Samaritan to the world. In Jesus' lifetime, the Samaritans were a despised people to the Jews, yet He challenged their poor reputation by telling the story of the Good Samaritan who came to the aid of a Jewish man who had been robbed and beaten. The United States is resented for its primary role in the nations, yet she continues to be a Good Samaritan to the very ones who despise her.

Yes, America has done many things the wrong way in her lead role among the nations. The CIA has overreached into countries and been on the wrong side of righteousness, yet America is still valued and loved by God for the level of righteousness that she *has* exhibited among the nations. At times, America has overly intervened in other nations, and at other times she hasn't intervened enough. This is the burden of being a lead nation. There is great responsibility and accountability—both for acting and for not acting quickly enough. The country of Chile may have had too much of the United States' intervention. Rwanda is a glaring example of a place and time where we critically delayed in bringing help. America has championed political, social, and personal freedoms among and around the nations, and yet our culture of freedom has also allowed pornography and decadent movies to invade the planet—eroding morals and promoting the unbalanced freedom of licentiousness. It's not easy to lead as a nation, especially if people whose integrity is compromised are in leadership positions in the government. For America to truly be who and what she is called to be, the occupants of our governmental positions must be upgraded. This will be America's reality for the next thirty-five years, as every subsequent election will carry an upgrade of integrity into government. Believe it, and participate in it.

The Five Primary Roles for the American Government in the World

As America advances God's agenda on earth, she becomes entitled to further mercy and grace from God, despite her many sins and weaknesses. There are the five primary assignments that the American government has been given by God:

1. World Freedom
2. World Security
3. World Economy
4. World Human Rights
5. World Melting Pot

These five assignments were essentially hardwired into our Constitution because the Holy Spirit moved on our founding fathers centuries ago, so that America might fulfill her God-given assignment in the twenty-first century. This assignment she will fulfill, though she will do so imperfectly. Even very anointed men and women of God run their churches and ministries imperfectly, so America won't be judged for being imperfect but will be given grace for championing His causes on earth.

1. World Freedom

"*Where the Spirit of the Lord is, there is liberty* [freedom]" (2 Corinthians 3:17). Freedom is a fundamental aspect of who God is and of the environment He best loves to operate in. It's the atmosphere of heaven. Again, America has been the champion of personal freedoms around the world, and this will continue to be one of her core assignments. America leads clumsily at times because she's still trying to sort out what to do when varying freedoms clash and collide. How do you allow freedom to one person or group when that freedom imposes on the freedom of another person or group? For example, the freedom of religion clause allows someone to host a church meeting in their home, yet if they're worshipping loudly at midnight, this encroaches on a neighbor's right to peace and quiet. Both cannot fully exert their desired and rightful freedom but will need to find some measure of compromise.

> *If we want Christianity to be respected in other nations where other religions are dominant, then we must model respect for those religions here in our own land.*

Another good example is prayer in the public schools, an issue we looked at in the chapter on the Mountain of Education. We Christians have been bellyaching for years about "prayer being taken out of the schools," when in reality only state-sponsored prayers have been removed. If the government were to act fairly, it would need to allow every religious group represented to have an official prayer slot. This would be the only way to value everyone's freedom of religion and not just the majority's. Although this wasn't a challenge when other religions were scarcely represented in this nation, it certainly is now that we've become a melting pot for many religions. This is an important test of our freedom because we're modeling something for the world. If we want Christianity to be respected in other nations where other religions are dominant, then we must model respect for those religions here in our own land, as well.

Freedom of religion is a right we must tirelessly model and support. One of the ways we are to do that is by limiting our economic ties and benefits to nations who don't incorporate this value. When we're willing to do this, we will demonstrate a primary allegiance to values above economic gain. The good news is that we have a God who will make up the difference for us in other ways.

Freedom of speech is also a high priority. The Internet, including social media, now assures that a multitude of voices have a place and outlet for expression. The few nations that don't allow free access to social media are in some way oppressors of free speech. I believe we are justified in withholding economically from those nations that violate this basic freedom. Social media does need some policing because demonic forces have also learned how to use it to advance evil. This is another example of how freedom must be tempered at times with wisdom that understands restraint.

Economic freedom is another important freedom that America must continue to model around the world. We generally call this economic freedom "capitalism," but raw capitalism is freedom without the wisdom of restraint; unrestricted capitalism would allow all sorts of harmful monopolies that would oppress the average consumer. Even with our current antitrust laws and actions, many monopolies exist and thrive. Again, it isn't easy to be a leader of freedom, but lead we must. The world is a better place today because of America's leadership, yet there's much room for improvement.

2. World Security

Whether we like it or not, there is a need for America to be a policeman of some sort to the world. We've always preferred to mind our own business, but for the most part, we haven't been able to because of the call upon us. This call will only increase in the future, so if you have any significant role in the United States government in the future, you must be aware of this fact. When you're the lead nation in the world, under-involvement is as dangerous as over-involvement. Our current president, Barack Obama, has discovered this intense reality for himself. Based on all of his preelection rhetoric, President Obama came across as a pacifist who didn't want any American troops on foreign soil. Yet when he stepped into the presidential role, that became a much tougher call for him. We have many well-meaning people who protest for peace at every turn but can't seem to understand that when you have the firepower to stop genocide in a foreign nation, you must do so, even if it requires war. Sometimes, the greatest means of peacemaking on the planet is to show enough early firepower that warmongers lose the desire to remain at war. No one wants to see nuclear bombs used, but the threat of nuclear bombs has been one of the best incentives for peace. When you have the world's greatest military power, you must incentivize the world's terrorists and rogue nations to prefer peace. Because of this reality, we must continue to have the greatest military might on the planet, while continuing to show great restraint.

> *Perhaps our primary security assignment is the nation of Israel.*

As I wrote earlier, perhaps our primary security assignment is the nation of Israel. To the degree that we fail on this assignment, we will find our own national security compromised. Almost every one of our national disasters or calamities has come on the heels of the United States abandoning the security of Israel in some measure. For relevant and thorough reading on this topic, I again recommend John McTernan's book *As America Has Done to Israel.* This is a critical concept that anyone involved in government must understand.

3. World Economy

Part of the assignment of the United States government is to protect and foster the world economy. Many Christians are ambivalent about this, knowing that greed and mammon are wrong but not understanding the fact that God is never behind the destruction of the world economy. Satan has always been the one who steals, kills, and destroys. God is our Father who heals, gives, and provides. God isn't trying to make the world suffer so much that people finally come to Jesus. He wants to be so extravagantly kind that they choose a relationship with Jesus. (See Romans 2:4.) He needs His kids on the planet as partners in order to be able to properly show love and kindness to the world, but this is His core heart. God loves to give. God loves to provide. One of His biblical names is *Jehovah-Jireh*, which means "the Lord is Provision." David expressed how God was his Provider when he wrote, "*The* LORD *is my shepherd; I shall not want* [lack]" (Psalm 23:1).

Some time ago, I was asking the Lord about the world liquidity problem and if there was enough money for everybody. What I heard Him say to my heart has really stuck with me. He said, "Do you know how ridiculous that is—the very idea that the world could lack resources. The whole earth is filled with My glory. The whole earth is filled with My [material] gold. Despite the mismanagement of what I've provided, the whole earth is still filled with My resources. It's simply not being properly validated, and for that reason there's lack." He then began speaking to me about the matter of gold and pointing out how there's much more of that precious metal to be discovered. He explained that if we'll follow the biblical secret that the kingdom of God is like a treasure hidden in a field (see Matthew 13:44), then we'll access much greater wealth. I was shown that treasure must be valued as such, even when it's still hidden in the field, so to speak—and that if we'll do that today, the world's liquidity would skyrocket.

Presently, gold is valued only after it has been removed from the earth and purified. Fort Knox is an underground storage facility that we use for the nation's gold. We remove gold from the earth, purify it, and then store it back in the ground. However, we could create a new asset base if we began to equally value treasure once it's discovered, even while it's still underground. There are presently advanced technologies for detecting gold that identify both the type and the purity of it, as well as its depth. This technology is capable of proving that there are major veins of gold in the ground yet to be mined. A new valuation of gold that hasn't been extracted could be initiated—allowing it to be considered a treasure even while it is still underground. It could have, for example, 25 percent of the value that extracted gold has, and we could benefit from it without having to remove it. This would allow for environmental protection of mining areas while still making it possible for the gold to be considered an asset and a credit to the landowner's account. In the United States, 28 percent of all land belongs to the U.S. government (concentrated in the West),[33] so there would still be plenty of resources for all. We would think of our existing underground veins of unearthed gold as "naturally occurring Fort Knoxes." There would be no need to actually harvest those veins unless there was a world shortage, which is highly unlikely because gold isn't consumable. Once a land area had been approved as having a hidden-treasure value, it would no longer be eligible for harvesting. This would protect the overall price of gold.

Part of the logic here is a motivation to keep a level playing field, which is just common sense. Most other assets and resources are already considered valuable before they're harvested. For instance, oil is

---

33. See "Federal Land Ownership: Overview and Data," Congressional Research Service (February 8, 2012), https://fas.org/sgp/crs/misc/R42346.pdf.

valued based on its in-ground value. The world price of oil is based on underground reserves, even though the oil has to be extracted and refined before it's globally viable. We just need to apply the same standard to gold and other treasures that are mined. Gold trumps oil because it isn't a consumable resource, and for that reason it should be valued in whatever form it's discovered, when its value can be scientifically ascertained.

Furthermore, that's how the futures market works with goods like pigs. Value is established today over a projection of how many pigs will be available in the future. That's why it's called the "futures" market. In the futures market, pigs that aren't even born yet are valued based on a projection. Literally trillions of dollars are released into stocks and trading based on this projection—and not just with pigs but with the entire futures market. If technology provides clear proof of the type and amount of gold that's in the ground, then it's even more reliable than the futures market, which is always subject to potential disasters brought on by drought, flooding, or other variables.

The world is in economic difficulty because of its inability to properly recognize treasures.

We are literally sitting on trillions of dollars' worth of assets in hidden treasures that we're not accounting for. If this were to change, it could be an instrument to reduce world poverty and fund the harvest in the Era of Renaissance. At a minimum, this should be applicable for the United States, which holds the world currency and needs to remain financially strong in order for the world to progress. With this new valorization of unearthed gold, the U.S. government would be justified in printing billions and even trillions of dollars—based on the fact that these would actually be asset-based printings. We've already been printing billions with no asset base, so to modify our proceedings in order to strengthen our economy would surely bring a positive response from the rest of the world who financially depend on us.

I believe it's a prophetic parable that the world is in economic difficulty because of its inability to properly recognize treasures. This is also a problem in the church in that we haven't yet discovered the hidden treasures that are in our own members. Many Christians often feel useless and of little kingdom value because their leaders in the church haven't made known to them their value—which brings us back to my earlier point about gaining Caleb-vision, or the ability to see and value treasures. It is Caleb-vision that literally permits you to enter into promised land territory.

4. World Human Rights

There is some overlap here with the assignment to bring freedom, but it is part of the United States' designed call to be a model for human rights, as well as an exporter and validator of human rights globally. Our basic human rights stance is written in the United States Declaration of Independence: "We hold these truths to be self-evident, that all men are created equal, that they are endowed by their Creator with certain unalienable Rights, that among these are Life, Liberty and the pursuit of Happiness." The United States has been the greatest exporter of human rights to the world, despite coming very late to the table in valuing the rights of anyone who was not white and male. It took us a couple hundred years to manifest in full what our forefathers advanced verbally.

In the coming years, America will be a stalwart defender of human rights and will raise its voice around the globe to decry every form of slavery and the demeaning of women as property. A courageous government will arise that will refuse to interact economically with those who don't allow women to have equal rights with men in society. This policy will serve primarily as a global attention-getter and will allow the next level of proper emancipation for women to take place. America carries an important leadership role in the world that she must not back off from. There will, of course, be many additional human rights issues than what I have mentioned. My intent is not to be exhaustive on any of my points but merely to give some examples.

5. World Melting Pot

America has become the "melting pot" of the world, and this assignment reflects a major call of God to her to be a principal instrument in breaking down the demonic stronghold of racism in the world. Becoming a melting pot has brought with it many, many challenges that this nation is still working out—challenges that our founding fathers never would have dreamed of. The diverse races bring their particular cultures and religions into a common geographical area. Because we are not quite sure how to assimilate all those who desire to be included in this melting pot called America, we have gone from "Bring us your tired, your poor, your huddled masses yearning to breathe free" (a portion of the wording on the Statue of Liberty) to border guards, tall fences, and a heated national debate on how to better protect our borders.

Immigration presents many complex issues that we will need to address and find solutions for; however, I think it is in order for us as a nation to have a softening stance toward the "huddled masses" and that this will take place. The white majority will become a thing of the past, and new paradigms will emerge. I believe the Lord showed me that the United States can easily hold and provide for three billion people, and that it actually has the resource capacity to sustain thirty billion people—particularly if all the "hidden treasures" are found and valued.

There are, of course, many other resources besides gold to be discovered and valued, and as we find a reasonable way to reopen our doors to those "huddled masses," it will be God Himself who prospers us. For security reasons, we definitely need to have an orderly process to opening our doors to the masses, but this is possible. Furthermore, we need a better plan for citizen assimilation so that those who do immigrate and become naturalized citizens will have greater common ground with other Americans. The ideal "melting pot" concept is not just that we have Chinatowns, Little Italy's, Little Havana's, and so on, all over the place, but that we interface more as cultures and peoples— and incorporate new things from each other that promote racial and cultural harmony around the globe. We are the world's test laboratory for racial healing. It has happened and is happening to some extent, but I am confident that we can do even better.

In the near future, the government will seek a way not to close its borders but to open them with wisdom. There is a spiritual parable being played out here, as well; God desires us always to be an open-arms nation, even when it puts us at greater risk. He has already protected us from multiple attempts against our national security and our national economy, and as we properly care for the world, He will continue to protect us. Protectionism thinking along many fronts may make natural sense, but it doesn't make spiritual sense. Ultimately, protectionism is simply an expression of an orphan spirit that believes it must control all outcomes. The United States was God's idea, and His protection, provision, and covering over us as a nation is not contingent on our perfection but on our fulfilling our basic national assignments.

Renaissance in the Prison System

Another of the reform priorities that's on God's heart for the Mountain of Government has everything to do with jails, prisons, punishment, and rehabilitation. In Matthew 25:32–46, we read about God's separation of the sheep nations from the goat nations at the end of time. One of the determinants of a nation being accepted or rejected is the matter of how it cares for those in prison. In that Scripture passage, Jesus identified Himself with those in prison, saying that the treatment of those prisoners was equivalent to the treatment of Himself. He said, *"Inasmuch as you did it to one of the least of these…, you did it to Me"* (Matthew 25:40). We should strongly heed this consideration as we seek to receive His heart for reforming society. Nowhere is reform more needed, and nowhere will we see more available kingdom solutions, than in the prison system. Our Papa's heart is close to the imprisoned, no matter what the offense or failure. Just imagine if one of your own sons or daughters were in jail—perhaps you would reach out to that child the most, even if he or she had been the worst-behaved of all your children.

> *Nowhere is reform more needed, and nowhere will we see more available kingdom solutions, than in the prison system.*

Presently, our penal system has many systemic injustices. A strong prison reform movement will begin, starting with the human rights of inmates. God will be greatly involved in supporting, endorsing, and advancing this movement. The way a nation treats its prisoners is ultimately an indicator of the quality of the basic human rights of that nation. For example, one serious issue in prisons is the sexual assault of inmates by other inmates. We now have enough surveillance technology that we should be able to effect a zero tolerance policy for sexual assault against either females or males in any correctional facility, from juvenile detention centers to maximum security prisons. The practice of having inmates shower at the same time in common showers is an incubator for sexual assaults. The emotional damage to an individual suffering sexual assault is incalculable, and we seem to forget the fact that, except for those who are on death row or have life sentences, almost all others will be released back into society at some point.

In many cases, the imprisonment of individuals is like locking up society's common cold, turning it into a flu epidemic, and then releasing it back into society. We really must shift the prison system from being a punishment center to a rehabilitation center—and no one is rehabilitated by enduring further depravities and greater instances of demeaning. Yes, people need an appropriate consequence for their illegal choices, but that consequence must be geared toward rehabilitation; otherwise, it's ultimately destructive both for that individual and for society.

When rehabilitation becomes the ultimate goal for a civilized nation's prisoners, then all aspects of the penal approach begin to shift and change. The focus is no longer just about making a criminal suffer and pay; instead, forward thinking is involved. Presently, a concern for all human rights is growing around the world and will soon invade the prison systems as never before. Many fine people and ministries have already been working faithfully for many years with prisoners, but the systemic help must go to another level. We're doing pretty well at visiting prisoners, thus technically fulfilling Jesus' words, but I believe His point was that He cares about prisoners, and He was imploring us to do the same. If we truly care about someone, we will be concerned about all aspects of their quality of life. Simply giving a prisoner token visitation while they serve time in a degrading system isn't enough. Prisoners are clearly in need of emotional healing because most will have suffered from some kind of crime, trauma, or abuse themselves. Again, they should pay their debt to society for their crime, but as that's happening, there must be a conscientious effort to rehabilitate them for future reintegration into society. Their potential reintegration must be a prevailing consideration from day one, as even many who are serving life sentences will have appeals, hearings, and possible reversal of convictions that can make them candidates for release later.

In the coming days, believers in Jesus will carry a primary impetus for bringing the kingdom of God into the penal system at every systemic level. Much of our latent societal racism is seen in our prison systems. Imagine what societal healing could take place if, for instance, a group of primarily white evangelicals spent time, money, and effort contending for the ethical treatment of minority prisoners. Almost every single African-American family in the United States will be affected by an immediate family member or relative who is imprisoned, on probation, or on parole. This is based on the fact that nearly one in twelve black males age 25–54 are in prison,[34] and—according to today's societal trends—one in three black males born today are likely to be imprisoned at some point in their lives.[35] There is no doubt in my mind that there's a racial element to this sad reality. Many young black men, as well as many Latino young men, are in trouble because of their involvement with illegal drugs and, in general, are serving too severe a sentence for their crime. According to the NAACP:

- 5 times as many Whites are using drugs as African Americans, yet African Americans are sent to prison for drug offenses at 10 times the rate of Whites.

- African Americans represent 12% of the total population of drug users, but 38% of those arrested for drug offenses, and 59% of those in state prison for a drug offense."[36]

When candidates campaign as being "tough on crime," this is almost always a reference to drug crimes that black males are perpetrating. Campaigns are always pointing at the crime occurring on our inner city streets rather than the crimes in our white neighborhoods and boardrooms, or anywhere else. We must admit that there really is a systemic racist root to much of this discrimination. We may personally say and truly believe we aren't racist, but when our systems show evidence that is otherwise, we have to acknowledge it in order to change it. For someone who is on the receiving end of racism, they don't care if it's coming from an individual or from a system—it still affects their lives in a tangible way and constantly conveys to them that they hold a "less-than" status.

---

34. http://www.nytimes.com/interactive/2015/04/20/upshot/missing-black-men.html?_r=0&abt=0002&abg=1.
35. http://www.naacp.org/pages/criminal-justice-fact-sheet.
36. Ibid.

The young black male has a tougher time getting hired than any other demographic because he's often perceived as being prone to crime—thanks to the dynamic I'm about to explain. The unemployment rate for young black males is about three times higher than the average rate.[37] There are many predominantly black neighborhoods without enough jobs, so an alternative economy becomes necessary for survival—and, of course, this is almost always an illegal activity. Drugs are the clandestine economy of choice. Sooner or later, a young man gets arrested for his crime and is thrown into prison. Upon completing his prison term, he returns to a society that already didn't want to hire him before he had a criminal record. Now he's even less likely to get a job, and so, almost by default, he returns to his alternative economy.

> *Somehow, we have to interrupt the cycle.*

Soon, he's arrested again, and this time he gets the book thrown at him as a repeat offender and has to stay even longer in a punishment center (notice that I didn't say rehabilitation center). The cycle continues and intensifies into a complex, systemic issue that clamors for a humane solution beyond simplistic blame-shifting. Whoever works on God-solutions and reform in this area will find themselves at the forefront of God's heart and will receive His supernatural help.

What would some of those solutions potentially look like? First of all, a major change in drug sentencing guidelines is needed. They are, and I'm generalizing here, overall too severe for something that's a national and worldwide problem. Our inner city families are being devastated in the long-term by the severe drug sentencing policies that are in place because of how these policies contribute to the overall societal

---

37. See Bryce Covert, "Eight Charts That Prove Obama's Right," Think Progress (February 27, 2014), http://thinkprogress.org/economy/2014/02/27/3338521/obama-black-men-charts/.

drug problem. We may simplistically think, *Yay, we're getting a drug dealer off the streets!* However, the truth is that we're also almost always ensuring that this young drug dealer will have no positive future. Somehow, we have to interrupt the cycle by addressing root issues earlier in the process. Yes, every young person needs to take responsibility for their own behavior, but perhaps we can shape their future behavior by giving them some consideration and concrete help.

I want to acknowledge that more and more young African-Americans are slowly finding a way out of the street life, with over a million now in college each year—but this often requires extraordinary resolve because of the challenging realities many are born into. There are currently about a million incarcerated black males.[38] On any given day in 2005, one in four African-American men age 20–29 were in prison, jail, or on probation or parole, usually over the drugs/alternative economy issue.[39] So, while there has been some good progress, going after a systemic breakdown can assist with the restoration and renaissance of many of the communities in the inner city.

I was a pastor for many years, and I've seen the heartbreak and shame of many moms when they've asked for prayer for their sons or other relatives, and this has stirred my heart to better understand the root issues. It's so easy to point a finger at those who make bad decisions about drugs, without really understanding how difficult it is to make necessary bold decisions toward right living when you're stuck in neighborhood environments like these. I don't want to overstate this point, but I truly feel the profound significance of the racial wound—a wound that could perhaps be healed with just a little bit more care and compassion in the context of drug-related criminal sentencing.

I believe that, as the sons and daughters of the King arise in their rightful places of government, they will begin to connect to Papa's heart as it relates to those in prison. Latinos face many similar racial attitudes and also find their life possibilities compromised over

38. http://www.naacp.org/pages/criminal-justice-fact-sheet.
39. See "The African-American Male: A Distressing Rap Sheet National Data," Diverse Issues in Higher Education (February 25, 2005), http://diverseeducation.com/article/4372/.

drug arrests at a young age. At age fifty, many Latinos and blacks find themselves unable to participate in societal life through voting because they followed the crowd at age eighteen or twenty. We must discover a path in which they could regain their electoral participation, because such a path would be both just and merciful. Ultimately, virtually all who find themselves in prison are in a place of brokenness—and the Lord is close to the broken and downtrodden. Should we not follow His lead?

> *We must begin to care more for societal reform than just making criminals suffer degradation and hopelessness.*

I believe God-inspired programs that reach kids early in their interaction with the criminal justice system are forthcoming and will help turn things around for many. New laws and new ways of doing things will take place throughout the entire penal system. Some people who have little understanding will complain because, in the future, many will go into prison and come out educated, trained in a career, emotionally healed, and clearly better off than when they entered. This will create a twisted narrative that some political candidates will seek to leverage by saying, "We have to quit rewarding our criminals with free education and career training." The truth is, we must begin to care more for societal reform and improvement than just making criminals mercilessly suffer degradation and hopelessness. The eye-for-an-eye moral code that exists in our legal system is Judeo-Christian, but it's "Old Testament Christianity" and not the New Testament Christianity that was clearly communicated and modeled by Jesus Christ—a Christianity that's based in, and infused with, grace.

As a society, we have begun to shift, and will continue to shift, toward compassion for lawbreakers rather than vitriol against them. This is not about patronizing, condoning, or enabling sin. It's about giving second chances. There will be an aspect of societal renaissance that will be birthed out of the good that spills over from our prison systems. Those who begin to be prison system reformers will find themselves greatly appreciated and rewarded by God. Sometimes, more of the reward will come later, but He will reward those who contend for healing, wholeness, and hope for those who have failed and need another chance. For God so loved the world that He gave His only Son, that whoever believes in Him would get another chance, and another, and another. Yes, He's a God of justice, but His mercy is always looking to reach even those who've been apprehended by His justice. Mercy triumphs over judgment every time. (See James 2:13.)

Lobbyist Reform

As almost anyone in government is quick to point out, this, too, is an area that needs serious attention. We'll definitely have to access God's solutions for this issue as we move forward in Renaissance. Some people jokingly call lobbyists the fourth branch of government because of their influence. Lobbyists are people hired by major corporations or major interests to present their cases before key politicians, hoping to ultimately alter or maintain laws in their favor. That aspect of what they do is actually not so troubling, as there's really nothing wrong with having a spokesperson for one's economic (or other) interests. The real problem occurs when money is attached to these requests.

There are many ways in which such an exchange of money might occur. A lobbyist might even present a straightforward bribe of a whole lot of cash, asking a politician to vote on their behalf or to legally draw up roadblocks for a competitor. Whenever unethical or illegal practices such as this occur, government is corrupted. The issue of dishonest lobbying is a major problem in most democratic nations on the planet, as democracies have not yet figured out how to eliminate or even weaken the corrupting influence of big business and special interests. In fact, it's the greatest weakness of the theoretical ideal of democracy because most nations just become democratic facades that are dominated by big money and special interest groups.

> *As the sons and daughters of the King arise in government, they will receive very practical systemic solutions from God.*

The special interest groups are generally much more connected to politicians, even months and years before their vote or influence is needed. In the United States, it now takes in the vicinity of a billion dollars to win a national presidential election. Up and down the electoral spectrum, almost every political position has a price tag attached to it. If you want to contend for the Senate in a particular state, it will cost a certain amount. If you want to contend for Congress, you will need to raise a certain amount. If you want to be the mayor of a city, such and such is the going rate for a successful campaign. The entire democratic process has become corrupted by those who provide campaign finances. Even if the campaign financing is conducted aboveboard, it's expected that, down the road, when the lobbyist shows up on behalf of his client, the politician should remember to return the financial favor. Truly, this is a difficult political reality, even for people of character, because the democratic electoral process is run by campaign funds.

This is an Achilles' heel to our form of free, representational government, and it's why many have suggested a new election path for candidates in which the federal government provides matching funds for candidates who have obtained a certain number of signatures of support. This concept hasn't yet been made fully viable, but some version of it seems to be a potential solution moving forward. Between the aforementioned concept of increased transparency and accountability for elected leaders, and this new way of campaign funding, there really is a solution for systemic electoral corruption. Undoubtedly, some corruption will always remain, but it would be a good goal for us to greatly reduce the on-ramps for corruption and then count on better people being in positions to change the governmental culture. As the sons and daughters of the King arise in government, they will receive very practical systemic solutions from God that will reset the political environment. It's a righteousness that's worth contending for because, without this salt of righteousness, the governments of this world will continue to trample their citizens. Until democratic processes become stripped of the ability of lobbying groups to put a candidate in or out, they're essentially no better than dictatorships because the will of the people is still being bypassed. Remember though, no matter how big a giant is, God always has a way to take him out. God is always looking for a modern David to arise with that conviction and understanding.

Reforms Everywhere Will Bring Renaissance to Government

It would be impossible to exhaustively look at all areas of government that need reform. Suffice it to say that, across the board of the political spectrum, there will be reform. Immigration reform is clearly a huge area begging for superior wisdom from heaven on how to balance competing needs, freedoms, and interests. I believe that by 2020, we will have a wise immigration plan ready to be implemented. IRS reform is another urgent need; kingdom solutions are quickly in order, or it will simply have to be disbanded. Healthcare reform is perhaps needed more than ever as "Obamacare" has succeeded in making healthcare more affordable for some but hasn't addressed a myriad of other dysfunctions in healthcare itself and has possibly overreached in an illegally intrusive way into the private sector.

The good news is that, if you've been called by God to the Mountain of Government, there are multiple opportunities for where and how to bring kingdom influence to bear. The kingdom is not just a Christian ideology; it always comes with God's better ways of doing things that, if we correctly approach and reveal, will be celebrated by all. We need God's better ways of doing things at a federal level, a state level, and a city/town level. It all starts with our showing up in whatever areas He gives us as open doors. At this stage of Seven Mountain advancement, winning elections is a relatively minor achievement. Reforming systemic corrupted agencies, structures, and practices is of more immediate value. Yes, sometimes a big election win will greatly accelerate that process, but we have to be prepared to think beyond winning elections.

The best is yet to come in American government. By 2020, we will have a real stronghold of righteousness in play that will progressively and positively affect government in this nation—and the world as a whole. By the year 2030, we will be manifesting the highest level of governance ever known. Believe it, and support your rising sons and daughters as they ascend this mountain.

Nine

RENAISSANCE ON THE MOUNTAIN OF ECONOMY

In the previous chapter on the Mountain of Government, we noted how big business and special interest groups are behind the power-brokering in that important area of societal influence. The well-known adage "follow the money" reminds us where to look when we want to ascertain the source of influence on any of the mountains of society. The Mountain of Economy (or Business) is one of the main spheres where the Era of Renaissance is going to leave its greatest mark. Believing sons and daughters of the King will begin to value their assignments on this mountain, which, up to now, hasn't typically been the case.

Spiritual people didn't prioritize business in the old, expiring paradigm that has dominated the church for centuries. If you were considered to be truly spiritual, then you gave up business to pursue church and ministry opportunities—and that made you feel like you were more on the front lines with God. Again, this is a paradigm that's quickly expiring. God's people with vision are realizing as never before that if we want to see society reformed, spiritually mature individuals must be willing to position themselves on the Mountain of Economy. Jesus taught about the dangers of the love of money, and the church got the wrong idea and gave up on having money altogether so as not to be in spiritual danger. The reality is, Jesus also said, *"You are the light of the world"* (Matthew 5:14). Those who know how to properly steward great finances can become some of the greatest expounders and expanders of cultural and societal light.

Over the next twenty years, there will be an explosion of kingdom multimillionaires all over the globe.

Right now in Hollywood, many believers who have anywhere from good to great movies ready to produce are practically begging for someone to finance their movies. Kingdom financiers are as scarce as can be because this isn't terrain that has been prioritized as spiritual. Similarly, many honest and capable candidates for high office in many nations are also virtually having to beg for money because we simply don't have the big money that's required for political campaigns. I could go mountain by mountain and make a connection between our lack of significant influence there and the lack of kingdom financiers. This is all going to change, and it starts with learning to value the Mountain of Economy as an important spiritual inheritance.

Over the next twenty years, there will be an explosion of kingdom multimillionaires all over the globe. There are literally going to be millions of these kingdom financiers raised up who will be extremely key to the whole process of societal reform and the Era of Renaissance. These new "ministers of finance," through their new way of doing business, will bring about a new atmosphere on the Mountain of Economy. Old assumptions of what it takes to be successful in business will be erased, or at least seriously upgraded, as this new knowledge of God's way of providing invades the business community. The fear/greed model of bottom-line-only thinking will take a serious hit, as success story after success story of new ways of doing business infuses the marketplace.

The Old Economic Model for Success

The existing model for economic success is more about being, or trying to be, a Type A personality who overexerts, overworks, and knows how to leverage every opportunity and every relationship to get ahead—the behavior you learn from most how-to-succeed books. This person sleeps only six hours or less a day, and every appointment and interaction is intentional and part of a wealth-building strategy. They have learned how to dot every business "i" and cross every business "t," becoming the ultimate capitalist.

Now it's true that, if you could have this type of personality and follow this model of intentionality, you'd have a good chance of becoming wealthy. However, that model isn't sustainable for most people and makes it very difficult to actually be successful. Being successful is different from merely getting rich. Because becoming rich requires so much overdrive, one's relationships tend to suffer in every direction, beginning with one's relationship with God. A person who operates in this way may be able to technically check off the spiritual duties on their list—attending church, tithing, and adhering to other principle-based behaviors—but will truly find it almost impossible to live out a relaxed, peaceful, and intimate friendship with God. God desires that kind of friendship with each of us, no matter our specific calling.

Honestly, this Type A model is also presently what seems to dominate the ministerial circuit and most mega-church pulpits. It does bear fruit, but it comes with a heavy price of relationship attrition. I believe there's a better way.

The New Economic Model for Success

The coming ministers of finance will either not have a Type A personality or will have learned to dial it down. Much of what gets referred to as Type A is really nothing more than an inspired orphan spirit. It can seem to be natural wiring, but in actuality it's drivenness that's brought on by the subconscious or conscious conviction that God has left us to figure things out on our own—so we do just that. At different times and seasons, we all can feel challenged and wonder how involved God truly is in all the details of our lives. When we live from that spiritually isolated place, we will overexert, overwork, and be driven to leverage everything. We will take on an incessant agenda and end up connecting primarily to others who also function according to such an agenda. More than being something dastardly evil, this kind of life is so much less than what God has for us.

Seven Marks of the Coming Ministers of Wealth

The coming ministers of wealth will be noted for seven distinctive marks. They will be worshippers, prophetic, reformers, hopeful, generous, humble, and friends with God. Although most of these seven marks have significant overlap, it's worth exploring them individually.

1. Ministers of Wealth Must Be Worshippers

Worship and adoration is the ultimate pathway to transitioning from an orphan spirit to a spirit of sonship. When worshipping God is important to you and comes from your heart, it means you truly get His greatness, His sovereignty, and His parental obligation and joy over your life as His son or daughter. This compels you to worship Him even more. When it becomes easier to worship than to leverage, you really are getting on the right track. Some of the most amazing business and technological breakthroughs have been coming to people while they have been in the midst of worshipping God. They didn't worship Him so that He would give them

The best way to deal with the weeds of fear and greed is to frequently and intentionally run to God's presence and exalt Him.

secrets, but it just happened. Similar reports will be given by believers time after time after time in the coming years, and many books will be written with this phenomenon as a core story. It will be a central aspect of the coming Renaissance in business, and worship and praise meetings will begin to spring up in the corporate world and become very popular. Thus, the best way to deal with the weeds of fear and greed is to frequently and intentionally run to God's presence and exalt Him.

2. Ministers of Wealth Must Be Prophetic

"Prophetic" means you value hearing from God. Many Christian businessmen are primarily principled in their approach to the Lord. They faithfully read their Bibles on the side and then follow biblical principles as they run their businesses and lives. Again, this approach isn't evil; it's just less than what God has for you. It's like living on canned food when a buffet of steak and seafood is available in the next room. Being prophetic is not something you are either wired or not wired to be. Being prophetic is a choice you make. You decide that not only did God speak valuable things thousands of years ago that we can apply to our lives, but He also speaks valuable things to each of us today. The prophetic and provision were always tied together in Scripture, and they continue to be tied together today. Most of Elijah's and Elisha's miracles were economic, and many of them affected entire nations.

There are many resources available to help you learn how to discern God's voice in your life, including our own "Growing in the Prophetic" DVD series with accompanying workbook. The key starting point for it all is your choice to be prophetic and to value His voice every day. If you do that from your heart, you'll begin to hear things even without being formally trained. Ultimately, it's God's great joy to share hidden treasures with you. Cyrus, in the Bible, is often seen as the ultimate minister of wealth. In Isaiah 45:3, the Lord prophetically told him, "*I will give you the treasures of darkness and hidden riches of secret places.*" I have prophetic, worshipping friends who have actually discovered oil, gold, new technologies, and breakthrough business ideas—all because they so valued God's ability to speak today concerning the affairs of men. "[God] *is a rewarder of those who diligently seek Him*" (Hebrews 11:6). Sometimes, that reward is more than just something spiritual.

3. Ministers of Wealth Must Be Reformers

Being a reformer is about embracing God's storyline for this day and age, as well as your assignment within that narrative. Reformers know that God is great, practical, and available enough not just to save souls but also to heal and restore society. When you're a reformer, you're like David in the sense that you would faint if you didn't believe that you would see the goodness of God in the land of the living. (See Psalm 27:13.) Reformers don't believe that the only hope for the world is Jesus' return one day, but rather that Christ in us provides real and living hope and solutions for every area of society. Owning this practical narrative is a must if you're to become one of His designated ministers of wealth in the Era of Renaissance. I believe I've heard from the Lord that, for Rosh Hashanah 2015, the first wave consisting of a million ministers of wealth will be released and empowered by angels to accelerate the reformation of society. All of these ministers will have the seven distinguishing marks that I'm presenting here.

4. Ministers of Wealth Must Be Hopeful

This distinguishing mark of the coming ministers of wealth is closely connected to and overlaps with the previous one. You cannot commit yourself to being a reformer apart from being a carrier of hope. Hope is one of the abiding values of 1 Corinthians 13, along with faith and love. The hope level you can grow to while on earth will even determine your eternal assignments. Being hopeful is an invitation to live from God's narrative and storyline. Hopefulness comes from having a root system in one's life that's deeply planted in the greatness and kindness of God.

As we discussed earlier, if you overly study the giants in the land, you won't be hopeful. If you become an expert on darkness and dark things, you'll find it difficult to have a hopeful perspective on most things. If you spend time studying witches, warlocks, demons, principalities, the occult, Freemasonry, the Illuminati, the Beast, the Antichrist, the False Prophet, the Tribulation, and so on, you'll not only lack hope but you'll also be in danger of being an exporter of hopelessness to the body of Christ, while perhaps thinking that you're helping.

You'll be a puny tree if your roots of hope don't go down deep into the goodness and expanded knowledge of God.

David was the one famous giant-killer in the Bible, and he knew almost nothing about the giant he easily took down. He was an expert in God. Hope comes from studying God, His heart, His passions, His narrative. As a believer, you're called to be a tree of righteousness. (See Isaiah 61:3.) Love is the water table that must be accessed, but hope is the root system that taps into it, and faith is the visible tree itself. You'll be a puny tree if your roots of hope don't go down deep into the goodness and expanded knowledge of God. In the coming years, every economic-related crisis that comes to planet Earth will have an antidote or solution in the rising sons and daughters of God—in particular, the ministers of wealth that He will be releasing. I believe that the great archangel over the Mountain of Economy will be released on Rosh Hashanah 2015, and he'll be looking for hopeful people whom he can assist.

5. Ministers of Wealth Must Be Generous

It would seem to go without saying that, if you're called to be a kingdom financier, you must be generous. A key aspect of generosity is one's own trust in God. This allows generosity to not simply be token but extravagant. By that, I mean God is going to call His finance ministers to live off of the same zero digit He is providing for them. He wants billionaires to give billions and millionaires to give millions—and if you're in the early stages of your calling, He wants "thousandaires" to give thousands. Many who get credit for being generous are actually playing it so safe that their seeds for true financial breakthrough and greatness are sitting dormant in their own bank accounts or stock options. True generosity touches your heart of compassion, but it also tests your trust-muscle. It's quite easy to be a billionaire and give away hundreds of thousands. It requires a bit more trust to give millions. A fully strengthened, trust-in-God muscle allows a billionaire to generously give billions. This isn't about putting guilt on anyone. It's about knowing what is required to actually become one of God's Renaissance and harvest financiers.

Papa God appreciates and blesses all economic compassion, but He has a path of acceleration available for those who fully embrace the call to be a minister of wealth. Many of the current faithful "thousandaires" will become the future kingdom billionaires. Generosity is about being a giving person before your big break-through. Many people have promised they will give great things to God and others once they get their breakthrough, but meanwhile they are essentially hoarding their present wealth. Financial hoarding is a disease brought on by an orphan spirit that sons and daughters of the King have no business having.

6. Ministers of Wealth Must Be Humble

First Timothy 6:17 says, *"Command those who are rich in this present age not to be haughty, nor to trust in uncertain riches, but in the living God, who gives us richly all things to enjoy."* There's a reason for this specific command. Becoming haughty is seemingly a direct effect of having at-tained wealth. Throughout my years in ministry, I've observed that the first tendency of someone who's experiencing financial breakthrough is to become haughty or a bit arrogant. Men, in particular, so closely view their identity through their success grid that it can be a struggle for them to maintain humility when they're more financially blessed than others. The power that comes with being a financier is immense and intoxicating. When you're wealthy, even great spiritual leaders will practically beg you to provide them with more financial resources. It requires a great deal of grace to overcome the dynamics of privilege related to financial breakthrough. Always be aware that "[God] *resists the proud but gives grace to the humble"* (James 4:6).

Many potential high-level kingdom financiers have remained at their initial level of breakthrough because they didn't pass the humility test. Of course, they can work to change that at any time. Repentance is a beautiful restorer of new possibilities. Wealth, along with humil-ity, is a clear indicator that one walks as a son or daughter of God, and not as an orphan who's prone to take too much credit and thus be wrongfully arrogant. Clothe yourself in the wonderful fragrance of humility, and you'll attract not only greater provision but also a greater amount of the priceless presence of God.

7. Ministers of Wealth Must Be Friends with God

The end result of carrying the first six distinguishing marks is to be a friend of God. Very few high achievers in life are, in fact, friends of God. Again, this is because most high achievers attained their exalted level of accomplishment through sheer grit, determination, drive, hard work, and personal sweat. A lack of dependence on God on the way up makes it hard to properly value Him once you've arrived at that economic status. This is true for all areas of life, not just for business. Many famous ministers struggle with the same thing. They are so aware of how hard they worked and struggled and leveraged in order to become famous/successful that their own conscience doesn't see God's friendship as being all that key. This is why it's so important not just *to get* a breakthrough, but *how* you get that breakthrough. Orphans count on their own hard work. Sons count on their inheritance as an overflow of relationship. Generally speaking, you'll have to walk with God as a son/daughter for some time before you experience the friendship stage, similar to a natural parent/child relationship.

Abraham and David are two noteworthy individuals of the Bible because of the relational equity they gained with God. The Scriptures call Abraham God's friend. (See 2 Chronicles 20:7; James 2:23.) God promised Abraham unending blessings on his descendants because of their friendship. David was called a man after God's own heart (see 1 Samuel 13:14; Acts 13:22), and we see in him, as well, a man who so touched God's heart with his personal zeal for Him, that God made him unending promises over the city of Jerusalem that David loved. To this day, Israel and Jerusalem are important in the economy of God because of these two men who became His friends. Abraham and David were, not coincidentally, two of the richest men in the Bible. By calculating the amount of gold that Scripture tells us David possessed, he clearly would have been a present-day multibillionaire. The wealth that he left to his son Solomon blew away the Queen of Sheba, who had thought of herself as being the epitome of wealth. Abraham was also a man noted for his wealth; as it increased, it caused him to need a new land of inheritance to contain it all. When one becomes a friend of God, one is told secrets of God. Among these secrets are the revealing of treasures, and that's particularly the case when the assignment upon one's life is to be a kingdom minister of wealth. Learning to be-

Attaining a friendship with God is, much more to be desired than even being a minister of wealth.

come friends with God starts with simply enjoying being with Him and loving to please Him, growing into higher and higher levels of interaction. Attaining a friendship with God is, of course, much more to be desired than even being a minister of wealth; it is truly the equivalent of being a multitrillionaire in life.

So, the new model for success on the Mountain of Economy is a relational one. It will always be about growing in God, which means growing in love—because God Himself is love. If we simplified the formula for success all the way down to its basic essence, it's love. God wants lovers advancing His kingdom. He wants them to be lovers of Him, of each other, of their spouses, of their families, of His church, of His kingdom, and of the world. Lovers of God with vision will receive empowerment from Him to be able to be reproducers of this love in society. In the future, when we think business, we need to think love. Kingdom business is always about the advancement of love in a tangible way.

Jesus' 5-Step "Miracle-grow" Formula for Provision

Now, in general, I'm against the idea of using spiritual formulas. However, Jesus Himself modeled His proven method for provision so thoroughly in His ministry that we must learn from His example.

In order to find this "miracle-grow" formula for financial provision, let's look at four very well-known stories that reveal Jesus as Provider. Although they may be quite familiar to you, there's significant new revelation to be gained from each story. We will be looking at these five steps of Jesus' miracle-grow formula for provision:

Step 1: Identify your need, bring it to Jesus, and then wait for His answer.

Step 2: See what you do have.

Step 3: Find out what Jesus' special instructions are.

Step 4: Move forward with counterintuitive obedience, even when there doesn't appear to be enough provision.

Step 5: Watch the miracle bloom!

The Feeding of the 5,000

First, let's look at the account of the feeding of the 5,000 and connect it to Jesus' miracle-grow formula.

And Jesus, when He came out, saw a great multitude and was moved with compassion for them, because they were like sheep not having a shepherd. So He began to teach them many things. When the day was now far spent, His disciples came to Him and said, "This is a deserted place, and already the hour is late. Send them away, that they may go into the surrounding country and villages and buy themselves bread; for they have nothing to eat. But He answered and said to them, "You give them something to eat." And they said to Him, "Shall we go and buy two hundred denarii worth of bread and give them something to eat?" But He said to them, "How many loaves do you have? Go and see." And when they found out they said, "Five, and two fish." Then He commanded them to make all sit down in groups on the green grass. So they sat down in ranks, in hundreds and in fifties. And when He had taken the five loaves and the two fish, He looked up to heaven, blessed and broke the loaves, and gave them to His disciples to set before them; and the two fish He divided among them all. So they all ate and were filled. And they took up twelve baskets full of fragments and of the fish. Now those who had eaten the loaves were about five thousand men. (Mark 6:34–43)

Step 1: Identify Your Need

Step 1 toward the miracle of provision was identifying the need for food and bringing the problem to Jesus. The disciples came to Jesus with their concern and basically said, "Hey, Jesus, You've been preaching to them all day, and the people are hungry." They were likely the most concerned about their own hunger, but we'll give them the benefit of the doubt. Though identifying the need seems like an obvious step, it's one of the most overlooked steps in the process of receiving supernatural provision. We often prefer to try and figure things out ourselves, and in that process, we experience much more worry and anxiety than is necessary. The disciples had initiated dialogue among themselves about the need, and obviously even did their best to figure out what to do. They ultimately did the wisest thing they could have done—they brought Jesus into the conversation and were silent until He spoke.

We often prefer to try and figure things out ourselves.

You have to love Jesus' initial response to the disciples. They had a shirk-the-responsibility solution of sending the crowd home so that they could eat. But Jesus' first answer was, ***"You give them something to eat"*** (Mark 6:37). I have to believe this answer reflected some of the playfulness of Jesus. Not only were the disciples not going to be able to dismiss the conference and feed their own hunger by making a run to Peter's favorite seafood buffet, but Jesus was implying that they needed to stay and somehow feed this whole crowd themselves. So they laid out the need before Jesus in a more explicit fashion. "Jesus, it would take two hundred denarii to feed this crowd, and we don't have it." That was the equivalent of approximately two hundred days of wages for an average workingman in that day.

Step 2: See What You Have

With that, Jesus moved forward to Step 2 of His miracle-grow formula for provision. Like the disciples, we are always telling Jesus what we don't have, and He always wants to know what we do have. So, He asked the disciples, "What do you have?" followed by the command, "*Go and see.*" His question, followed by His specific instruction, gives us further insight. Provision is always preceded by being able to see. It takes the ability to see in order to determine what we do have. We can be so focused on what we don't have that we miss what we do have. It requires some of the Caleb-vision we discussed earlier. The miracle of the multiplied bread and fish existed in what was already available but was not yet recognized or activated. There's so much more to explore in that, as well.

The disciples then walked through the crowd and discovered that one boy had five little loaves of bread and two fish. There are two amazing things about that: First, the fact that a mother would have the foresight to know that this unplanned conference with Jesus would extend all day. Second, and maybe most remarkable, was that it was late in the day, and the boy hadn't consumed his meal yet. The disciples showed a significant ability to see by not ignoring the insultingly low level of existing provision and taking it to Jesus anyway. They probably had a sense that a lesson was coming, because that's what life with Jesus was like—and, as we know, "*Jesus Christ is the same yesterday, today, and forever*" (Hebrews 13:8). He's still doing this kind of stuff. He's still quite interested in educating us in His ways of doing things. Essentially, this formula is about seeing His way of doing things.

Step 3: Find Out Jesus' Special Instructions

Jesus was now ready for Step 3, as He always works with what there is and not with what there isn't. It was time for His special instructions. Special instructions from Jesus entail the orchestration of the miracle stage. Jesus loves a good story. He loves a good setup. He loves drama, and He also loves co-labor and participation from us. He wasn't just doing "the Jesus show." Jesus wanted His disciples doing the supernatural work with Him. He was staging a miracle. That's why He originally said, "You feed them." He didn't want them off the hook of participation, even if He planned to be the One doing the heavy lifting.

So, Jesus' special instructions involved the disciples. He commanded them to have everyone sit down in orderly groups on the green grass, which required another great step of faith for the disciples. They must have said to the people, "We're go-

Show the faith His disciples did, stick with His crazy plan, and perhaps you'll see the same miraculous results that they did!

ing to feed you now, and it will help with distribution if you sit in groups." One can only guess at the concerned whispers among the disciples as they orchestrated this arrangement among fifteen thousand people or more (including women and children). Either Jesus was going to hit a home run, or this was going to be the most embarrassing day of their lives. Has a similar situation ever happened to you? Well, if it does, show the faith His disciples did, stick with His crazy plan, and perhaps you'll see the same miraculous results that they did!

Step 4: Move Forward with Counterintuitive Obedience

In Step 4, Jesus looked to heaven, blessed the bread, and began breaking it. Here's where the disciples' counterintuitive obedience came into play. I believe that when Jesus looked to heaven, He was looking to see what the Father was doing. The Bible tells us that Jesus did only what He saw the Father doing. (See, for example, John 5:19.) So, Jesus offered thanks for the small provision and proceeded to start with what was ridiculously not enough. I heard somewhere recently that, if you're waiting for God to lay out a nonstop string of green lights before you'll take the route He has for you, then you'll never get started. You must take each green light He gives you, one at a time, and continue to move forward with each individual green light. This is what Jesus modeled for us.

Meanwhile, the disciples were still intricately involved in this miracle of provision. They're the ones who were assigned to take the bread and fish to all the groups. Pretty early in the process, they must've realized something special was happening to the bread when it was in Jesus' hands. There, too, is a great lesson—something special happens to our provision when we put it in Jesus' hands. Now, this process went on for some time because the crowd was so large. Perhaps, in the early stages, the disciples were tempted to wonder if the miracle of the moment was going to last until they were all fed. Maybe they'd fed the first five hundred when Thomas, who was prone to doubting, whispered to them, "This is all fine and dandy so far, but feeding five hundred men is not the same as feeding five thousand. I'm projecting that if He used up a third of the bread getting us this far, the last two-thirds will only feed fifteen hundred people." This was logical thinking, but when you try to project an outcome based on logical thinking, you can short-circuit a miracle. This is something I've personally had to learn over and over again. God will be in the process of taking care of all of our family and ministry needs, but I'll still be tempted to logically project whether or not this same level of provision will work three months down the line. In my logical projecting, I fall into the fear of entering into financial trouble. If God is supernaturally taking care of you to begin with, then let Him figure out how to adjust what He's pouring out at the time you need it. This lesson is, of course, only for those interested in accessing a supernatural level in their finances. It takes courage and counterintuitive obedience to contend for financial miracles.

Step 5: Watch the Miracle Bloom!

Step 5 of Jesus' miracle-grow for provision was now in full bloom—the miracle was happening! Thousands and thousands of people were eating to their heart's content. They weren't just getting a snack but a full meal deal. When that young boy's mother cooked his bread and fish, little did she know that—whatever ingredients she put in her bread and whatever spices she put on her fish—they were going to be the flavor of the day for over fifteen thousand people. If her bread was stale, everyone's bread would be stale. But if it were fresh, everyone's bread would be fresh. If her fish was too salty, everyone's fish was going to be too salty. Jesus didn't change the essence of what was offered to Him—only the amount. That, too, is something to chew on.

Jesus added a final touch that we're still learning from today. He has always been the exceedingly-abundantly-above-all-that-we-ask-or-think kind of God. (See Ephesians 3:20.) Jesus told the disciples to go collect *the leftovers*. We read that they came back with twelve baskets full of leftover fragments of bread and fish. Wow! What a statement! "Boys, not only can I feed fifteen-thousand-plus people with five loaves and two fish, but I can provide even more leftovers than what I started with."

A couple of questions beg to be asked here. Question number one for me is, "Where did they get the twelve baskets? Who brings empty baskets to a spontaneous gathering with Jesus?" Well, I believe that the baskets belonged to the disciples. I think that when the day started, Jesus said, "Guys, I need each of you to bring an empty basket with you today." Perhaps they'd been wondering all day when it would become evident why He'd asked them to bring baskets. Maybe the baskets were what each of the disciples had to use to carry the bread as Jesus broke it. As that miracle began to happen, perhaps they nodded to each other and said, "Oh! This is why He told us to bring the baskets." But there was more. I think the reason there were only twelve baskets of leftovers was that there were only twelve disciples involved in the miracle.

Question number two is, "What did they do with the extra food?" Jesus was very specific and detailed with everything, but He didn't give a reason for the leftovers. Everybody within sight had already been fed. I think the poignant point He was making is that He's not just the God of enough. He's the God of more than enough. Abundance and superfluity is His essence. He loves to provide us with what is running over, pressed down, and shaken together (see Luke 6:38) when He's allowed to be intricately and intentionally involved in the process. This isn't the reward of simply being a Christian. It's the outcome of intentionally inviting Him into the practical processes of provision.

The Catch of Many Large Fish

After these things Jesus showed Himself again to the disciples at the Sea of Tiberias, and in this way He showed Himself: Simon Peter, Thomas called the Twin, Nathanael of Cana in Galilee, the sons of Zebedee, and two others of His disciples were together. Simon Peter said to them, "I am going fishing." They said to him, "We are going with you also." They went out and immediately got into the boat, and that night they caught nothing. But when the morning had now come, Jesus stood on the shore; yet the disciples did not know that it was Jesus. Then Jesus said to them, "Children, have you any food?" They answered Him, "No." And He said to them, "Cast the net on the right side of the boat, and you will find some." So they cast, and now they were not able to draw it in because of the multitude of fish. Therefore that disciple whom Jesus loved said to Peter, "It is the Lord!" Now when Simon Peter heard that it was the Lord, he put on his outer garment (for he had removed it), and plunged into the sea. But the other disciples came in the little boat (for they were not far from land, but about two hundred cubits), dragging the net with fish. Then, as soon as they had come to land, they saw a fire of coals there, and fish laid on it, and bread. Jesus said to them, "Bring some of the fish which you have just caught." Simon Peter went up and dragged the net to land, full of large fish, one hundred and fifty-three; and although there were so many, the net was not broken. Jesus said to them, "Come and eat breakfast." Yet none of the disciples dared ask Him, "Who are You?"—knowing that it was the Lord. Jesus then came and took the bread and gave it to them, and likewise the fish. This is now the third time Jesus showed Himself to His disciples after He was raised from the dead. (John 21:1–14)

Let's look at this story in a new light, as it relates to Jesus' five-step miracle-grow formula for provision.

Step 1: Identify Your Need

Remember, Step 1 is to identify the need, bring it to Jesus, and then wait for His answer. The disciples had gone out fishing the night before. Fishing was their livelihood, not just the hobby it might be for many of us today. Jesus had already died on the cross and been resurrected, and the disciples had been commissioned in their apostolic assignment. Their normal pattern was to fish at night and then take the fish to market the next day to sell so they could provide for their families. But on this particular night, these professional fishermen were having a hard time. They were catching nothing in their area of expertise—while using all of their expertise. Most likely, frustration and panic began to set in during the early morning hours. Though the disciples were slow to recognize it, Jesus was suddenly in the picture. Even when we can't see or recognize Jesus, He's always in the picture when we need provision, especially when we've been commissioned into our kingdom assignment.

As the disciples got closer to Jesus, He asked them, "Children, do you have any food?" He knew that what they were doing was both directly and indirectly putting food on their table. The disciples answered Him with a simple, "No, we're not catching anything." Step 1 was complete: The need had been identified, and, even though they didn't know it, Jesus was now involved.

Step 2: See What You Have

Step 2 in Jesus' miracle-grow formula is once again seen in how He refused to focus on what they didn't have. He saw that they did have a net, a boat, and some fishing skills—even if they weren't working at the moment. He let them know He wanted to use what they already had. He didn't shout, "Abracadabra!" and make provision appear out of thin air. Nor did He say, "Leave your boat and your nets, because I need you to become bankers in order for Me to be able to provide for you." He asked them to use what they already had. Even if what you've been doing hasn't been working, He still wants to know what you do have, as opposed to what you don't have. *What* you have isn't important, only that you have *something*.

> *What you have isn't important, only that you have something.*

When meek and insecure Moses was called by God to lead all of Israel out of Egypt, he asked God, in effect, "How will I do this? I'll be laughed at." God asked him, "What's in your hand?" Moses answered, "My stick." God said, "We'll work with that." (See Exodus 4:1–5.) That stick ended up being quite powerful; with it, Moses performed many signs and wonders, including the parting of the Red Sea. His stick ultimately became called "the rod of God." (See, for example, Exodus 4:20.) When you work with God, it isn't important that you have something impressive to begin with. He actually prefers working with what seems to be small and foolish—making it into something of value and renown.

Step 3: Find Out Jesus' Special Instructions

Now the boys were ready for Step 3—receiving Jesus' special instructions to cast the net on the right side of the boat. This was truly an unusual command. They were professional fishermen who already knew everything about fishing in the Sea of Galilee. They'd been fishing all night and hadn't missed a spot. Yet, when they heard, "Cast the net on the right side of the boat," the boys shifted to the other side of the boat and prepared to cast the net once again.

Step 4: Move Forward with Counterintuitive Obedience

Step 4 quickly followed as they obeyed, even though casting their net hadn't worked all night. Jesus used the same disciples, the same fishing hole, the same boat, and the same net, but this time required just a small, counterintuitive act of obedience. The kingdom of God generally advances contrary to what we would intuitively expect. This is why Jesus said, "Repent, the kingdom of God is at hand," as He showed authority over every demon and disease. They were a left-brained, mind-of-reason society, and He was telling them they'd better make a shift from left-brained to right-brained processing if they wanted to get what He was about. The word for *repent* was a military word meaning to make a 180-degree turn. Even after Jesus died and was resurrected, He continued to teach this to His disciples so they would never forget that the supernatural isn't subject to man's reasoning or restrictions. Everything Jesus did or taught seemed counterintuitive. He said, among other things, "If you want to be the greatest, then become a servant of all. If you want to become wealthy, then give. If you want to go up, you must go down." The miracle is rarely in the logical.

Step 5: Watch the Miracle Bloom!

To the amazement of the disciples, Step 5 was complete as the net overflowed with fish. The net was so full that they couldn't pull it up into the boat and ended up having to drag it to shore, where they counted a record 153 large fish, the weight of which miraculously hadn't broken the net. Evidently, this size of a catch would have provided these men with weeks or months of income. Once again, God isn't just the God of enough but the God of more than enough! When you have a need, choose to involve Jesus, and then receive and obey His special and sometimes illogical instructions; it can position you for a supernatural release of provision. These lessons that Jesus demonstrated are invaluable for us today.

The Coin in the Fish's Mouth

> *When they had come to Capernaum, those who received the temple tax came to Peter and said, "Does your Teacher not pay the temple tax?" He said, "Yes." And when he had come into the house, Jesus anticipated him, saying, "What do you think, Simon? From whom do the kings of the earth take customs or taxes, from their sons or from strangers?" Peter said to Him, "From strangers." Jesus said to him, "Then the sons are free. Nevertheless, lest we offend them, go to the sea, cast in a hook, and take the fish that comes up first. And when you have opened its mouth, you will find a piece of money; take that and give it to them for Me and you."*
>
> (Matthew 17:24–27)

Let's take a quick look at the five steps to provision demonstrated in this account. Peter basically needed to pay his taxes, and when he was approached about it, he immediately initiated Step 1 by taking that need to Jesus. I love the fact that, as Scripture states, *"Jesus anticipated him."* He already knew Peter was coming to Him, but He didn't intervene until He was invited into the situation. In Step 2, Jesus identified the fact that, although Peter didn't have the money for taxes, what he did have were the ability and equipment to fish. Peter then received a rather strange instruction to literally cast a hook into the sea for the money, fulfilling Step 3. I say it's strange because Jesus was always very specific with these things. Notice that He didn't tell Peter to cast a baited hook into the sea, simply a hook. Now that's some unusual fishing. Jesus was again messing with Peter's fishing expertise. Wisely, Peter chose to defer to the Expert on everything.

> *Jesus was messing with Peter's fishing expertise.*

Jesus then told Peter that the first fish he caught would be the one with the coin. Of course, Peter followed Step 4, counterintuitive obedience; sure enough, he caught the fish, which must have had an appetite for shiny things. The other fish with no coins in them leave the hook alone because it has no bait; however, this fish loves shiny things, and because of that it becomes the source of provision for Peter's taxes. Many commentaries say that the coin was a Greek *stater*, which was the exact amount to pay the temple tax for two people. Jesus had already explained why it was ridiculous that they should pay taxes because of who He was, but that they would go ahead and pay this tax so as not to offend people. Apparently, when Jesus is paying the IRS, He limits the provision to exactly what is needed, and no extra—though the principle continues to ring true that He is the God of more than enough. With one cast, Peter caught twice the amount of provision than what he needed for himself. Perhaps, in heaven, Peter playfully brags about Step 5 as the time when He paid Jesus' taxes for Him.

As a final thought, remember that the supernatural veins of provision generally run outside of the natural veins of provision. Man can teach you how to find the natural veins, but Jesus can teach you how to cast to the right where the really staggering catch awaits you.

Turning Water into Wine

> On the third day there was a wedding in Cana of Galilee, and the
> mother of Jesus was there. Now both Jesus and His disciples were
> invited to the wedding. And when they ran out of wine, the mother
> of Jesus said to Him, "They have no wine." Jesus said to her, "Wom-
> an, what does your concern have to do with Me? My hour has not
> yet come." His mother said to the servants, "Whatever He says to
> you, do it." Now there were set there six waterpots of stone, accord-
> ing to the manner of purification of the Jews, containing twenty or
> thirty gallons apiece. Jesus said to them, "Fill the waterpots with
> water." And they filled them up to the brim. And He said to them,
> "Draw some out now, and take it to the master of the feast." And
> they took it. When the master of the feast had tasted the water
> that was made wine, and did not know where it came from (but
> the servants who had drawn the water knew), the master of the
> feast called the bridegroom. And he said to him, "Every man at
> the beginning sets out the good wine, and when the guests have well
> drunk, then the inferior. You have kept the good wine until now!"
>
> (John 2:1–10)

This final example is perhaps my favorite of these four stories because it reveals so much about Jesus. This was Jesus' first public miracle,
and it offers a very important lesson for those called to the Mountain
of Economy. In Step 1 of the miracle-grow formula for provision, Jesus'
mother, Mary, identifies the pressing need. They are attending a wedding with many guests when she hears that the wine has run out way
too early. Because she understands what a huge social embarrassment
this is for the family, she brings the need to Jesus. All she needed to
say was, "They have no wine." This tells us so much about their relationship and how well Mary knew her Son. I imagine Jesus had bailed
her out multiple times before when she'd run out of something in the
kitchen. Surely, He'd managed to produce an extra cup of flour she'd
needed at some point, seemingly out of nowhere—so she knew He
could do it again. Mary must also have known His heart and that He

was a sentimental softie. Jesus immediately protested, reminding her that it wasn't time for Him to start His public miracles. Apparently, they had discussed when and what the scenario would be, and this wasn't it. The Son of God wasn't planning to start His life of signs and wonders at a wedding by simply saving a family from embarrassment and potentially helping tipsy people get totally drunk. That would be so improper. Or would it? If you didn't know it, this is real wine we're talking about. They didn't serve grape juice at weddings back then.

Despite Jesus' protests, Mary knew she'd touched His heart, so she told the servants, "Do whatever He tells you." Evidently, Mary already understood how Step 2 worked—that Jesus wouldn't be limited by the reality of what they didn't have but would use what they did have. Perhaps it was she who instructed the servants to bring six water-pots of stone that were used for ceremonial purification, which held between twenty and thirty gallons of water each. Setting the stage for His miracle-grow for provision, Jesus gave His Step 3 special instructions to the servants to fill the waterpots with water. He then said to them, "Now draw some out and go take it to the master of the feast." Within the obedience to His special instructions came the miracle of provision, contrary to what anyone might have intuitively thought in the moment. When the master of the feast tasted the water that had turned to wine, he was so blown away by its excellence that he commended the bridegroom for what he assumed had been a brilliant plan of saving the best for last. Instead of being socially embarrassed for their wine snafu, this family was acclaimed for their extravagant celebration. Like so many other times, Jesus fulfilled Step 5 of a miracle in full bloom!

As always, this miracle came with over-the-top abundance.

As always, this miracle came with over-the-top abundance. Did the already satiated guests really need another

120–180 gallons of top-grade wine? What's the deal with Jesus not turning it into grape juice or apple juice instead? Ah, so much we still have to learn about Jesus. He is so not religious. He literally changed His divinely appointed schedule for ministry kick-off because His heart was touched by the fact that a family needed to be able to successfully celebrate their son's wedding. It would've been a major social faux pas had Jesus not rescued the party—He actually cared about the family not being embarrassed! Although He's clearly against people getting drunk, He thought it was even more important to help this family. Wow, I love this Guy!

Know That God Always Provides

These four biblical examples of "Jesus' 5-step 'Miracle-grow' Formula for Provision" are designed to leave us with a working model. But, even more than that, they should cause us to further fall in love with who Jesus is. What's revealed to us about the person of Jesus through these stories is as important as the formula we gain from them. Of these four miracles of provision that Jesus performed, only one of them had something to do with His ministry. He fed over five thousand people at His spur-of-the-moment conference. When He provided large fish for Peter and the other boys, He was providing for their personal family needs. Do we realize that God not only funds ministry but also delights in funding our family's needs? He knows what we have need of and only looks for us to bring matters to Him, with the intent to obey His special instructions. Are you aware that you can ask God to supernaturally help you with your taxes, as He did for Peter? What a God! In the story of how Jesus turned the water into wine, we also see how important celebrations are to God. He cares about our weddings, anniversaries, birthdays, holidays, family reunions, and vacations. Can you imagine a God who provides supernaturally for Christmas presents (even though Christmas has some pagan origins mixed in with it)? That's who He is. He isn't all about religious rule-keeping—He's all about adding His supernatural touch to our lives.

Much more could be written about the coming changes on the Mountain of Economy. So many discoveries, strategies, inventions, and technological advances are coming. I could also report on many current examples, but the biggest news will be the new knowledge of God that will be displayed in every area of culture. We've got to be able to show that the historic Jesus of the Bible is still active in the real world and in our real lives, particularly if we have an assignment as one of His ministers of wealth. We need to know what He's like in order to access what He has—and we need to know what He's like so that we can meet needs in the way He would. He is totally extravagant, compassionate, sentimental, and abundant. That's why it's so wrong to pursue abundance outside of Him.

> *God is always greater than the challenge.*

There's no glory to poverty. Yes, peoples' hearts can be more moldable when they're poor, but God knows a heart hasn't truly been tested until it has the experience of abundance. The devil is the one who makes us poor. Jesus offers us abundant life and life in abundance. If we really believe that we're to contend for *"on earth as it is in heaven,"* we have to know there's no poverty in heaven. If poverty were a virtue, it would exist in heaven. Moving into abundance begins with recognizing the fact that lack is an actual need that you can take to God. Not only will He willingly provide for you, but an increase of His presence in your life is also part of the package deal. There's nothing more exciting than to be partnering with God in receiving and disbursing His abundance. This is the great call on the Mountain of Economy and one that millions will respond to in this Era of Renaissance. No matter what happens to world economies in these next thirty-five years, there will be no shortages for those who've learned to access Jesus' miracle-grow formula for provision—it's the one safety net that tops all others. No matter what currency collapses or what precious metal devalues, there's always more in God. The new knowledge of God to be released from this mountain to the world is that He is always greater than the need—He is always greater than the challenge. He is ever so kind and generous. Start from this foundation, and all things are possible.

Ten

RENAISSANCE ON THE MOUNTAIN OF MEDIA

And they overcame him by the blood of the Lamb and by the word of their testimony, and they did not love their lives to the death.
—Revelation 12:11

As I introduce the Mountain of Media, it may seem strange to begin with this verse, yet its fulfillment is intimately connected with your assignment if you're called to impact this area of culture. The word "*testimony*" in the above verse is a Greek word that means "record, report, or witness." This verse tells us that ultimately we defeat Satan both by what Jesus did on the cross and by broadcasting the correct report or narrative of heaven.

Habakkuk 2:14 says, "*The earth will be filled with the knowledge of the glory of the Lord, as the waters cover the sea.*" Again, the endgame is when the knowledge of God and His ways fill the earth. It's not just that His glory itself will fill the earth, but there will also be knowledge, or understanding, of His glory and goodness in the whole earth. He wants the truth about His glory to be reported and recorded. As that happens, the enemy and his lies about God will be demolished. God is executing an amazing storyline on earth, and He wants that testimony to be the ultimate witness and evidence against Satan both now and at the judgment seat.

A large part of Satan's strategy for advancing his kingdom is to take over the airwaves of media. He's the ultimate counterfeiter of God's ways, so he too counts on his testimonies getting out in order to advance his agenda of hopelessness. Often, as believers, we fall into being unwitting participants in passing along his false storyline. We forget that we must advance with testimonies of God's goodness and kindness. We get stuck thinking that our role is to warn people about every encroaching danger and every conceivable conspiracy of the enemy. We don't mean to, but we're getting Satan's message out, and it accomplishes exactly what he wants it to—releasing discouragement, dismay, and hopelessness. Like the ten spies, we find ourselves giving a "reality check" to the body of Christ, erroneously thinking it's been helpful to warn others.

In June 2013, the Lord spoke to me, saying, "I'm looking for a Pollyanna bride." This surprised me. I'd been prophetically speaking of the good things God was going to do in the future, and I found myself frequently almost apologizing by adding, "And I'm not just being a Pollyanna." Being a "Pollyanna" is an expression used to describe someone who's thought to be excessively sunny and optimistic, even when the occasion seems to call for the opposite. One day, the Lord said, "What's wrong with Pollyanna? Actually, I'm looking for a Pollyanna bride."

The Rise of the "Pollyannas"

Pollyanna was the central character in a 1960 Disney film that was based on a best-selling 1913 novel by Eleanor Porter. In the story, Pollyanna is a young orphan who comes to live with her wealthy but stern Aunt Polly. There, she goes about enacting her philosophy of life taught to her by her father. He had taught her to play the Glad Game. The game consisted of finding something to be glad about in every situation—sort of like the original "Pollyanna," Paul the apostle, who made many Pollyannaish statements. For example:

> *I have learned in whatever state I am, to be content.*
> (Philippians 4:11)

> *In everything give thanks.*   (1 Thessalonians 5:18)

> *Giving thanks always for all things.*   (Ephesians 5:20)

> *Rejoice always.*   (1 Thessalonians 5:16)

What kind of naive nut is this Paul guy? In whatever state? In everything? For all things? Rejoice always? That sure would get on the nerves of some of us more balanced realists.

In the original Pollyanna story, the heroine transforms her aunt's dispirited New England hometown into a pleasant place as she practices and teaches her game (or, rather, philosophy) to everyone she meets. Pollyanna's robust optimism is given a real test when she's hit by a car and loses the use of her legs. Her joy becomes challenged as, day after day, she has a harder and harder time finding the glad-angle to her pain and discomfort. At this time, the townspeople into whose lives she had diligently sowed her philosophy begin calling and visiting to tell Pollyanna how her instruction of finding something good in every challenge changed their lives for the good, encouraging her to get back on track with her own philosophy. She decides to begin by being thankful that at least she still *had* legs. Ultimately, the story ends happily when Pollyanna regains the use of her legs and learns to walk again.

The Pollyanna story was such a hit that, for years and even decades, it inspired people to live out the Pollyanna principle of finding the glad-angle in everything. Parker Brothers created a board game called "The Glad Game" that was popular for over fifty years. In addition to that, Glad Houses and Glad Clubs formed all over the nation, in a brief explosion of popularity, for people to gather together to find things to be thankful about. They would testify of any good news, even when everything wasn't a bed of roses. Little did society realize that they were actually connecting to a powerful spiritual principle and a golden key for advancing the kingdom of God.

Paul the apostle further developed this philosophy of life that's relevant to the Mountain of Media when he made this statement:

> *Finally, brethren, whatever things are true, whatever things are noble, whatever things are just, whatever things are pure, whatever things are lovely, whatever things are of good report, if there is any virtue and if there is anything praiseworthy—meditate on these things.*
>
> (Philippians 4:8)

Paul's guiding philosophy was to only be involved in the testimony of good things. If there's any virtue or anything praiseworthy, meditate on it—or, to take it one step further, report on it. This practice and discipline is a golden key of life for everyone, but especially if you're called to the Mountain of Media. You must understand this verse as a guiding precept for what you do with your platform. This may seem obvious to some, but unfortunately many who get involved in a media platform believe that it's primarily for informing and warning of the enemy's advances. Remember that when you do that, you're actually testifying of the devil. When you do that, you're saving him the need to do so for himself. We've given some of his best testimonials and probably a good bit of playback material for hell, as well. The demons get excited when we speak of their greatness. They relish the notion of causing us fear or concern. They do a dance when we broadcast the statistics of their advancements.

All kingdom assignments to the Mountain of Media involve advancing news that is true, noble, just, pure, lovely, and of good report. This is actually possible, even when you must report on a tragedy or disaster. It may not

The demons get excited when we speak of their greatness.

be the easiest perspective to find, but it will be available as a treasure to be discovered in a field of dirt. A good example from a few years ago was when the deadly earthquake struck Haiti. It was catastrophic and obviously needed to be reported. However, early on in the process, a news channel began to highlight the treasure that was in the midst of the disaster. They shared stories of heroic rescues and of people coming together to worship and praise God. Somehow. they found hour after hour of news reports that spoke of heroism and hope—stories of Israeli medical mission teams arriving, babies being delivered, and critical surgeries being performed. Ultimately, this channel was instrumental in motivating many to donate toward rebuilding Haiti, as well as stirring many to go there and help. A disaster is always an opportunity to extract the silver lining that God is always offering. It doesn't need to be done in a religious way, but simply in a truthful way. Replaying a tragedy over and over is not truthful because, in reality, it happened only once. When we watch it and relive it again and again, it allows the trauma of the event to gain a second life—bringing further devastation and fear. Never forget that it's Satan who always steals, kills, and destroys. God is always giving, healing, and restoring. We must make sure our media appearance registers that reality.

The new social network opportunities have created a massive rearrangement of the Mountain of Media. Just a generation ago, it might have primarily been radio that theoretically kept everyone informed about what was going on in the world. The manipulative ability of the news media was profound because there was almost no easy way to verify the credibility of what was being reported. When I was kid, whatever ABC, CBS, and NBC news said became the reality of the day. Even local newspapers, another option for information, relied primarily on one or two sources. Today, there are multiple, multiple streams of news reporting. We still have radio, TV, and newspapers, but Twitter, Instagram, and Facebook posts are more likely sources for what's considered credible news. TV news will now often defer and report on what's trending on Twitter, and so forth. This major shift has served to decentralize the power of media as never before. Every single one of us now has a chance to play some role on the Mountain of Media. If you have a social network account with a decent following, then you're an influencer on this mountain. To the degree you understand your call and assignment here, your ministry can have great impact. This really is a ministry platform and should be thought of in that way. However, be sure to screen your posts through the Philippians 4:8 lens, or you may just find yourself advancing the enemy's agenda. We need to stop encouraging him in every way we can.

Magnify God, Even When It's Hard to See Him

Oh, magnify the Lord with me, and let us exalt His name together. I sought the Lord, and He...delivered me from all of my fears. They looked to Him and were radiant.   (Psalm 34:3–5)

In this passage, we see again the key to advancing the kingdom from the Mountain of Media. We must magnify Him; and, by doing so, we are delivered from all of our fears, and our faces can be radiant. In the natural, you use a magnifying glass to be able to better see what is either hard to see or is invisible to the naked eye. Whenever there's a tragedy or a disaster, God and His goodness can be hard to see. It requires intentionally "magnifying" Him in order to see Him. Someone whose assignment is the Mountain of Media is, in essence, an evangelist called to discern and communicate the good news from whatever is presently taking place. The more dire the news of the day, the more evangelistic anointing is required to properly see and disclose whatever redemptive silver-lining event is also taking place. It's not about ignoring unavoidable bad news, but rather being able to see the hidden face of God that's always there—even, for example, in a fiery furnace. (See Daniel 3:24–25.) We must learn to disclose the truth about how good, kind, and compassionate He is from whatever platform we have.

> *If your voice is generally hopeful, then you're promoting the agenda and atmosphere of heaven.*

Media becomes the means by which we promote either heaven or hell, and I don't mean that in a directly religious way. If your influence through media is always about complaining, exposing, or warning, then you're essentially promoting hell's perspective. If your influence or voice is generally hopeful, Pollyannaish, or otherwise redemptive, then you're promoting the agenda and atmosphere of heaven. Heaven advances on earth under a spirit of good news, and hell advances under a torrent of bad news. Once you get this matter clear, then your assignment becomes clear. A media army of those who recognize the battlefield and mission will be the mark of the coming Renaissance on the Mountain of Media. Right now, I would guess that 90 percent of

Christians who have a media platform of some significance are either wasting that platform or literally advancing the enemy's agenda. This will begin to change dramatically in the coming years as we shift from kingdom defensiveness to kingdom offensiveness.

A primary reason for our lack of kingdom success on this mountain is that most ministries with a media platform have built their ministry on fearmongering. Scaring people into giving to your cause so that you can save the day is, to a large extent, the modus operandi for too many ministries. It certainly does grow an audience and raise resources. For example, pro-family ministries often meet their budget by sending out letters, e-mails, and other social media appeals warning of all the ways the enemy is advancing against families—solidifying the need for your financial support. Anti-abortion ministries likewise raise funds by telling of all the enemy's advances in abortion and why you must support the ministry's efforts. This goes on around the ministry circuit in almost all directions. Fear and misery love company, so an audience and a financial base are easily created by trumpeting bad news.

This tactic is generally so effective that most ministries are hesitant to share any wholesale positive national trend or good news because it might send a signal to donors that they can back off from their giving. For instance, as discussed earlier, over two-thirds of all abortion clinics have shut down since 1990, and abortion rates are down to almost half of what they were in 1990. Yet rarely does any ministry prioritize getting that message out because they feel the need to justify their spot on the battlefield. Presently, Christians love to gravitate toward bad news, mainly because it's the path of least resistance. If we care about the bad news we're hearing and then e-mail that information to someone else, it somehow makes us feel like we did something about the problem, when in reality all we did was aggravate it. Personal prayer requests are not in this category, so I'm not trying to stop true prayer support that's needed for special situations.

I have a following of sorts on social media, and every time I have a very hopeful prophetic message to give, I know that it will elicit mostly critical comments. I'm never being blasted by satanists or atheists but by very religious, longtime believers. They tend to be quite prideful, know-it-all, and particularly in tune with a holy God who's always about to come and judge everything and everybody for not being holy enough. Honestly, this is a systemic illness or addiction that's been in American Christianity from its inception. Every generation since the original Pilgrims in the 1600s has been warning society about the coming judgment of God. Ultimately, it's a sad indictment on how we see God. Fortunately, our God-view is going to begin to be radically healed during this Era of Renaissance. Those who understand their assignment on the Mountain of Media will be very important in this endeavor. They'll be entrusted with advancing the knowledge of the glory of God on earth. With the exception of where media overlaps with the Mountain of Religion, this expansion of His knowledge will be advanced best in a nonreligious way. Promoting the King's values will ultimately lead people to the King of those values, and it isn't necessary to always feel the need to make that connection for them in an obvious way. By simply championing love, forgiveness, compassion, justice, and kindness, you're properly and effectively promoting your King. His ways lead to Him. The glory of His ways will fill all the earth, and to the degree that you have a media platform, you have an opportunity to contend for the fame of our God on earth.

The Renaissance Media Army, 2020–2030

I believe that by 2020, there will be an impressive army of God's kids who will understand their role and their opportunity through the various media platforms that will be available. This army will be instrumental in changing society's negative soundtrack, which seems to dominate the atmosphere. Probably even more important, they'll begin to neutralize the profound negativism and testifying of the devil that currently issues from so many Christians. What dominates in media becomes, as it were, the soundtrack to all else that's

Media provides the soundtrack for society.

taking place. Even as a movie has a soundtrack that's key to its success or failure, media provides the soundtrack for society itself, thus influencing its chances for success or failure. To see society transformed, we've got to march to a transforming new melody. This must happen—and it will happen.

The Renaissance will hit a turbo of sorts by 2025, and the rise of this Renaissance media army will be tremendously important to that acceleration. Even as David had to arise and shut the negative, intimidating mouth of Goliath, so too this Davidic media army will arise and change the narrative. They will understand that we overcome the enemy by the word of our testimony and will therefore search out testimonies everywhere. They will find every creative way to brag about heaven, about the attributes of heaven, and about the fruit of the Spirit that are displayed in practical ways here on earth. This is a big assignment, and the sons and daughters of the King will be up for it. By 2030, this will be perhaps the most efficient force on all of the mountains, and they'll provide the drumbeat for the overall arising army of lovers of God. The atmospheric shift will be dramatic.

Becoming God's Spokesman

You will stand in My presence. And if you speak noble words, rather than worthless ones, you will be My spokesman.
(Jeremiah 15:19 HCSB)

Anyone who has a significant call on the Mountain of Media must recognize that being a spokesman for God is your privileged assignment. To some degree, we're all invited to be His spokesmen, and, to some extent, we're all to carry the word of our own testimony that contains the platform for what we speak. But, if you specifically have a divine assignment to significantly impact media, it will be because you've become a steward of noble communication, rather than a promoter of worthless communication.

Other Bible translations of Jeremiah 15:19 speak of being able to take the precious out of the vile. (See NKJV, KJV.) Your effectiveness on this Mountain of Media isn't determined by your ability to mobilize social networks, produce a television show, edit a newspaper, direct a radio program, or perform some other skill of leveraging media. You can be a Christian with a huge following, yet still be making almost no kingdom advancement because you misunderstand what your assignment is. Whether it's your Facebook page, your newspaper, your television show, your newsletter, or whatever—you must be able to be someone who can separate the precious from the vile and the noble from the worthless.

The original Hebrew word for "*precious*" means valuable, brightness, clear, costly, excellent, precious, reputation, and honorable women (how interesting). The word for "*vile*" means to shake, to quake, to be morally loose, worthless, or prodigal. You don't want to champion that which is shaking, but rather that which is valuable. Furthermore, our assignment through media is mainly to be done in a covert manner and not in an overt way. Overt proselytizing basically takes place only on the Mountain of Religion. On every other mountain, the kingdom advances through God's ways displayed in an atmosphere of freedom that then brings attention to Him within the hearts of those who experience the blessing that comes with those ways. The kingdom way of doing things always has the best outcomes, though it often requires us to exercise patience until those outcomes are fully manifest.

The long-term Renaissance that will take place on the Mountain of Media will ultimately have to do with even unbelievers and secular institutions realizing that noble communication is the new standard for how news and reporting is most profitable. God's ways are the better ways of doing things, and among His outcomes are extended credibility and financial viability for those who commit to doing things His way. This new standard-bearing for media will eventually go institutional, as the new guidelines for media that advance through educational institutions will intentionally embrace the goals of noble and valuable reporting. It will be generally understood that reporters have an inherent responsibility to advance precious and hopeful things, as opposed to being instruments of terror or scandal. This is the present status quo in media, but it will greatly change in the coming years as God's hope-filled media army arises with understanding and intentionality in their kingdom assignment.

> *We can each do our part just by what we communicate in our next Facebook post, e-mail, Instagram, or Tweet.*

This noble assignment is available for engagement even today, and we can each do our part just by what we communicate in our next Facebook post, e-mail, Instagram, or Tweet.

Hope is the endangered commodity of the age, and every child of the King should be in the business of manufacturing and reproducing it. In the coming years, this Mountain of Media will be the great releaser of hope—as opposed to being the great releaser of fear. As Christians, we'll finally stop releasing fear ourselves through our irresponsible use of media. The ministries built on promulgating fear will either change or lose their financial base. It will be a better day. I don't mean to cheer against them, as many of them are as sincere as the ten spies were in their giant-magnifying mission in the Promised Land. Yet, it's just as wrong and just as faulty a mission today as it was then. We will ultimately know that we're winning the battle against the enemy on this mountain when the world itself is more hopeful than fearful. So, media army of God, arise with hope in your wings and release the soundtrack of good news through every outlet that you have. Let hope arise!

Eleven

RENAISSANCE ON THE MOUNTAIN OF CELEBRATION/ARTS

During the Era of Renaissance through 2050, no other mountain will go through a more extreme makeover than the Mountain of Celebration/Arts (including entertainment and sports). Of all the Seven Mountains on earth, the Mountain of Celebration/Arts looks perhaps the least like its counterpart in heaven and will therefore draw our attention in a dramatic way over the next thirty-five years as it radically changes. This mountain in heaven is in a perpetual explosion of creativity that continually releases joy and awe there. In fact, there's so much joy and awe that it really has to be reclassified as glory. The Mountain of Celebration/Arts is specifically designed to release glory, which will be the case not just in heaven, but also here on earth. Wave after wave of glory will be released to and from this mountain, and that glory will testify of a God who is exponentially greater than the world has even imagined.

Hollywood Is Going to Drop an "L"

I've been saying for some time that Hollywood is going to become "Holywood." This isn't simply over-the-top, wishful thinking but a future reality. There'll be an upcoming season where Hollywood will be ahead of the church in properly understanding and reflecting God, His love, and His story. In fact, the church will begin to take note and follow Hollywood's lead during that season. When this Renaissance Era fully hits Hollywood, the "l" that's going to be dropped symbolically stands for lust and licentiousness. This progression will take place because it'll no longer be profitable and desirable to champion movies and art that pander to the lowest common denominator. In the coming days, over 90 percent of these types of movies will be box office flops.

When I speak of Hollywood, I'm not only referring to geographical Hollywood but also to all that's represented in the arts and entertainment industry. One of the ways that God is shaking and overhauling geographical Hollywood is by decentralizing its power base through alternative Hollywood hubs that are developing in places such as Atlanta, Nashville, Dallas, Seattle, and elsewhere. Famed director Steven Spielberg has been widely quoted for his statements about the extreme changes that are taking place in the industry. He has said that Hollywood is in full implosion and that the rules of the game have never been less clear. This dynamic is something God Himself is doing. I believe He's released angels to assist in breaking up all mafia in Hollywood that hasn't made room for His agenda and His sons and daughters who are prepared to represent His heart and creativity. God showed me that a great archangel was released in 2010. As uncompromising sons and daughters of the King arise in Hollywood, they'll begin to encounter the favor of this great archangel whose assignment is the restoration of God's glory to this desecrated area of culture.

For years, Hollywood has run to the beat of Jezebel (which is simply Satan's personification in this industry) and her supporting cast of demons. This is already beginning to change, but we're not yet at even 2 percent of the influence we will have there shortly. This is significant because, in 2014, Hollywood was again stunned at the success of Christian and faith-based movies such as *Heaven Is For Real, God's Not Dead, Son of God, Noah,* and others. At the center of it all, Hollywood runs by numbers, and they've only recently discovered that the best and safest return on investment comes from a well-produced, faith-based movie. This trend will increase, but at some point soon, the movies that are full of God's actual glory will rearrange the landscape of all that is Hollywood.

Soon, the movies that are full of God's actual glory will rearrange the landscape of Hollywood.

There's an aspect of moviemaking that's kind of like the fast-food industry. If delicious, good food is not readily available, we tend to opt for cheap junk food. But when good fare is made available, junk food is no longer tempting. Generally speaking, Hollywood has literally run out of ideas other than the junk food equivalent of movies. However, since they're charging steak dinner prices for those movies, it will be a great game changer when real quality movies come to the forefront.

Four Types of Christians Currently in Hollywood

My wife and I now live very near Hollywood and engage with people in the industry on a regular basis. We've found that we don't actually lack Christians in Hollywood, but we lack kingdom believers who have an expanded idea of what their mission and assignment is. Many Hollywood stars began as Christians but lost their way because of the unique challenges that the atmosphere of this industry brings. I'm going to generalize, but I believe there are currently four different types of Christians in Hollywood who are unfortunately contributing to the existing spiritually dark landscape. The purpose for identifying these types is to, first of all, help those who have participated in any way to recognize it, repent, and then shift into their correct role and assignment. The good news is that each of these types are just one encounter with God away from shifting into bringing the light that they were created to shine.

#1: The Compromising Christian

Compromise is a systemic problem throughout Hollywood. The reasons for it are easy to see, as you can be blackballed in the industry for carrying your Christian light too enthusiastically. Furthermore, Jezebel's basic way of advancing in Hollywood is through a step-by-step, patient process of seduction. For those who really want to be glory-carriers on this mountain, you cannot do so while bowing down to its demonic principality. Just as Daniel could not bow to Nebuchadnezzar's image and still have authority, the same is true for you. If you're getting drunk or using any kind of illegal drug or mood-altering/mind-altering substance, don't think you can possibly carry His favor or authority into Hollywood without getting thrown off the mountain. Yes, you can still love and pray for people, but your light will be a dim flashlight instead of a bright spotlight. The same is true if you're compromising sexually in any way, such as having sex outside of marriage, or are stuck in the same cycle of dysfunctional relationships that is normal for Hollywood. Your light cannot be of the same essence as the darkness and still be considered light.

Though I'm against excessively pointing out the giants in the land, I must emphasize that Bacchus is perhaps the most empowered demonic principality in Hollywood. Bacchus was the name of the ancient god of wine and alcohol, and this principality is totally connected to all the excesses of Hollywood. He empowers homosexual behavior, licentious behavior, and all illicit sexual behavior, and he is essentially being bowed down to daily by the masses working in Hollywood. Innocent-sounding cocktail parties are the norm for every occasion in Hollywood, but they are, in actuality, gates for entering into submission to a ruling demonic power. I suspect that more than 95 percent of all the compromising in Hollywood

> *Your light cannot be of the same essence as the darkness and still be considered light.*

is directly connected to the consumption of alcohol. Because of this reality, anyone who's seeking to carry God's influence in Hollywood should consider completely abstaining from alcohol or at least having a firm, intentional guideline for alcohol, such as a one- or two-drink maximum, depending on how you're affected by it.

Though caution about drinking alcohol should be considered anywhere, it's especially so in Hollywood because of the power of the demon associated with its excess. Obviously, wine or alcohol itself isn't the problem, but the culture created around its use in Hollywood has made it a severe problem. If you're a Christian in Hollywood who wants to carry authority and light for the kingdom of heaven, and yet you find yourself always in a position of compromise, consider cutting out alcohol altogether. You may just find that your tendency toward compromise in all areas is greatly reduced. The bottom line is to understand that the door that alcohol opens for you is full of things that kill your destiny, disempower the impact you were created to have, and destroy your life. Is it worth missing out on what others are doing in order to protect what's really at stake? I think so. In fact, in doing so, you will literally help to completely change the status quo for this entire area of culture.

One more note on the problem of Christians in Hollywood who are in positions of compromise: You must be aware that the enemy is out to defile you in every way that he can. One of the ways he does that is by affecting your speech. For example, the f-word has become an extremely common word in society today, perhaps beyond anything recent generations have seen. Many believers have also entered into easily using this and other words that, despite the cultural desensitization and disassociation from their meaning, are still inappropriate. Remember that in Ephesians 5:4, Paul told us explicitly to avoid coarse language and filthiness. Of course, you have the freedom to use whatever language you choose, including the f-word, but be aware that you immediately degrade your spiritual authority when you do. Even society acknowledges the f-word as one of the filthiest. If you wouldn't use certain language in heaven, don't use it on earth. Consider this: If you're working in Hollywood to bring about change and to help make the world a better place, but your version of change looks and sounds just like the existing culture, then what are you really doing?

#2: The Doomsday Christian

A doomsday Christian in Hollywood is just as troubling and unhelpful as a compromising Christian. This is the believer who is narratively challenged. If they could get their movies funded and produced, they would be doing merely a rehash of the typical Christian narrative: Everyone should get saved now because Jesus is about to rapture His people at any moment and bring horrible judgment on the rest of the world. This storyline does perhaps bring some people to salvation, but it doesn't advance the kingdom of God on earth. Scripture is clear in Acts 3:21 that Jesus is not coming back any day now but will do so only when some significant advancement of the kingdom of God has taken place on the earth. We haven't come close to seeing that take place yet. Presently, the only reason we even think it's possible that He's coming soon is that we have almost no idea how little of the kingdom plan we've actually advanced. By 2050, we'll understand more clearly why Jesus couldn't have come sooner without sabotaging His own storyline.

Besides the many believers in Hollywood who would only try to advance a premature rapture narrative, there are many others who have overstudied the demonic realm that influences Hollywood. Sadly, they have almost no hope that Hollywood will ever be transformed apart from severe judgment and almost complete demolition. There's no doubt about it—Hollywood is infested with witchcraft, idolatry, demons, and the Illuminati. Yet all of that put together is nothing compared to that which will be arising from the household of God. What God is about to raise up in Hollywood far exceeds any demonic ability to resist it. He will have sons and daughters who deeply love Him and one other, who love the world passionately, and who fearlessly and creatively display what His kingdom looks like on this mountain. These will be people of hope who speak of a better future, not just in eternity but here on earth. Like David, they will believe in and contend for seeing the goodness of God in the land of the living, and they will back it up with their hard work and excellence in both skill and character.

#3: The Narcissistic Christian

Those who are narcissistic are preoccupied with themselves and their own agendas. The Hollywood culture is teeming with narcissism because the very idea of being famous or being a star is quite a self-absorbing goal. Apart from a Seven Mountain understanding of their kingdom role in Hollywood, many Christians see their pursuit of the entertainment business as a chase after their personal dream, which they hope God will help them with. Such a mind-set sets the table for their becoming as narcissistic as the culture they're entering into. If you enter this industry without seeing it through the grid of a kingdom assignment and mission, you have almost no hope of being anything other than an ineffective, narcissistic Christian—so interested in being a star that you'll do almost anything it takes to make it happen (which opens wide the door to compromise). Self-absorbed believers see everything through a perspective of, "What's in it for me?" They become quite skilled at leveraging every relationship and every situation for their own goals and gain.

Self-absorbed believers see everything through a perspective of, "What's in it for me?"

When you meet someone like this, it's easy to look in their eyes and see that, to them, you're not a person anymore but rather a potential connection to be leveraged. Being overly self-centered and self-driven is, in itself, anti-kingdom; therefore, you must take intentional steps to ensure that you don't lose your Christlike identity. You must purposefully choose to be even more caring toward others than you are for yourself, and more trusting in God than in yourself or others around you. If you truly desire to represent God's heart in this arena, you must constantly ask Him to show you what the interests of the kingdom are in every meeting and scenario you're a part of. Thus, the main cure for this disease is kingdom-mindedness. As you process things through a kingdom-first paradigm, you inoculate yourself from the narcissistic virus of the Hollywood culture. Living according to a countercultural, kingdom-first perspective is almost impossible if you're a loner Christian, so be sure to find a tribe of fellow believers who mutually help one another to stay strong, balanced, and full of life.

#4: The Legalistic Christian

The legalistic Christian is at the opposite side of the spectrum from the compromising Christian. The legalistic Christian is so religious and sterile that they were probably meant to function on the Mountain of Religion and not on the Mountain of Celebration/Arts. Those who come under this category are trying to be light in the same way the Pharisees were trying to be light—showing a radical commitment to external behaviors but missing the heart of it all. For example, a legalistic Christian won't take a part in a movie if it has a four-letter word in it, even if the movie overall carries a redemptive message. They are concentrating so hard on avoiding being tainted that there's almost no chance of their engaging with the culture and transmitting anything of value.

I've heard it said that the path of life inevitably has deep ditches on both sides. In Hollywood, the ditch on one side is compromise, and the ditch on the other side is legalism. We have to know how to come into a place like Jesus did. He entered into the real world and didn't start championing values and principles, but instead modeled practical love and concern. A prostitute named Mary Magdalene followed Him because evidently He'd been in the area where prostitutes were. He was accused of being friends with alcoholics ("winebibbers") because He actually hung out with them and became their Friend. He came down to their level, but He didn't *become* their level. He didn't get drunk with them in order to reach them or to make them want to be around Him, but neither did He chase them off with His personal lofty standards. Legalists want heathens to be judged by our standards, whereas Jesus was always more concerned that the lost felt loved and valued by Him. Legalists judge while Jesus loves. It's that simple. Fear of judgment ourselves, which ultimately stems from a wrong perspective of God's heart toward us, causes us to focus on making sure we never look like we are condoning sin. Yet remember, there's no fear in love. (See 1 John 4:8.) I believe God is aware of our personal stance on sin and gives us permission to stay focused on the love part. We need believers who will learn how to navigate what the path of life and love looks like in Hollywood. Will you be one who bravely accepts that mission?

The Coming "Thermostatic" Christians in Hollywood

With this backdrop of the unhelpful Christian presence in Hollywood, join me in declaring that there will be an army of rising men and women on this Mountain of Celebration/Arts who will not compromise, be legalistic, or get stuck in a doomsday narrative or narcissistic thinking. These gifted, called, and empowered ones will come into Hollywood not as thermometers but as thermostats.

A thermometer enables you to measure temperature, while a thermostat enables you to set the temperature to a desired level. As you know, you can use a thermometer to check if you have a fever. It can do nothing about a fever, one way or the other, but it can definitely tell you if you have one. A thermostat regulates the temperature of a house or building. If it's too cold or hot outside, the thermostat works in conjunction with a power source to produce hot or cold air that then dictates the temperature.

Hollywood has enough thermometer Christians. In our first year here in the Hollywood area, we've gone to meetings and heard reports on what Hollywood's atmosphere and culture are like and how they work. This is okay, as there is some value to having that knowledge, just as there is some value to a natural thermometer—but we're made for so much more. Presently, there's a beginning stage of an invasion of a new breed of "thermostatic" sons and daughters of God into Hollywood. They are lovers of God and of His presence, and they know how to carry it wherever they go. They are an army of hope-filled, love-driven creatives who experientially know that greater is He who is in them than he who is in Hollywood. The spiritual battle over Hollywood is intense and therefore requires a unique kind of kingdom mind-set in order to function in that atmosphere and displace the darkness.

In order to be thermostatic, you must be filled with the Holy Spirit. Without His power working in you mightily, you'll be just a thermometer. In order to be thermostatic, you must have some understanding of God's master narrative for Hollywood and for society. You can't believe that we're here only to rescue some souls and then be zapped off the

You can't believe that we're here only to rescue some souls and then be zapped off the planet before it all falls apart.

planet before it all falls apart. You must fundamentally believe that God is pulling off a greater storyline than that. Additionally, in order to be a thermostatic Christian in arts and entertainment, you must find your tribe. Those who don't this get easily picked off by the enemy. You have to associate and rise with others who also understand they're on a mission from God. Yes, it's connected to the fulfillment of the personal dreams and goals God put in you, but it goes so far beyond that. If you don't live in the big picture of the kingdom of God, you're sure to remain a thermometer.

The Rise of the Creatives

This Era of Renaissance on the Mountain of Celebration/Arts will be unlike anything the world has ever seen. Hollywood has been essentially bankrupt of creativity, and it's because, by and large, they've been disconnected from God—whose very essence is creative. Most of what masquerades as creativity is only a distortion or a contortion of true creativity. This will change as the electrifying kids of the Creator—who understand who He is, who He can be in them, and how He wants to show off in society—arise with their true creativity.

As we discussed, the four general groups of Christians that are presently in Hollywood have a very limited capability of connecting with the higher level of creativity that's available for the new breed of rising Kings' kids. Hollywood is full of impostors who are able to function in the absence of true creativity. Risk-taking, wounded people have made themselves rich and famous simply by being willing to promote themselves sexually to some degree beyond the norm. Shallow human beauty, decadent behavior, and lifeless scripts have passed as creativity; therefore, the world has a limited idea of what true creativity looks like. There's been exploration of the dark side, and, in the absence of what is real, this too poses as true creativity. Soon all will be astonished by the glory of true creativity—when the Creator's co-laboring kids finally arise to critical mass. This is already in process.

God the Compulsive Creative

I often preach about God being not just creative but compulsively creative. Usually, I get a few strange looks when I say that, until I explain. God is introduced to us in Genesis 1:1 as Creator: *"In the beginning God created the heavens and the earth."* As the story of creation unfolds, it's quite something to see our compulsive Creator at work—or maybe He's actually at play. He started by creating light, but He wasn't satisfied with just one kind of light. He made the sun, the moon, the stars, and the firmament—creating various expressions of light. Then He created water in the form of varying receptacles and outlets of rivers, oceans, streams, and fountains.

When God created vegetation, He exploded into yet another gear of creativity. He didn't just create one kind of tree and duplicate it a billion times. He made plants of every style and size, and trees of every thickness, height, and branch structure. God went over the top with His creativity when He made a variety of fruit to grow on different types of trees or bushes, in different colors, and in many different flavors. Then, one can only imagine what He was thinking when He created animals such as elephants, monkeys, giraffes, zebras, toucans, dolphins, and so on. Every time I'm at an aquarium, I'm stunned at how compulsively creative God is when I see the fish of all sizes, shapes, colors, and even demeanors. Finally, to top it all off, God made man. Today, over seven billion humans live on the planet, and yet you'll find no two alike. Even identical twins are identifiable by their subtly unique features. Not only does God not want any of us to look alike, but He doesn't even want one fingerprint reproduced. Why would He care that we each have unique fingerprints, and how did He pull off the logistics of *that?* Have you heard that not even one snowflake's design is ever repeated? Why is the Master of the universe so committed to uniqueness and individual expression? As you see, I could go on and on. Everything about God shouts and echoes His creativity.

> *He's not just an efficient, "git 'er done" kind of God.*

Why is it important to point out the compulsive creativity of our God? It's because we were made in His image and designed to reproduce that aspect of His nature here on earth. As a whole, the church has been one of the least innovative groups, and it has often been one of most boring places on the planet. Although it can be a place of peace, it usually lacks the accompaniment of joy that is an essential part of the DNA of our Creator. Remember that the Bible says, "*In Your presence is fullness of joy; at Your right hand are pleasures forevermore*" (Psalm 16:11). So far, as His image-bearers, we've ripped off the world in our expression of who He is. Often, we have not only portrayed a stern, rules-obsessed God, but also One who's void of a sense of humor or any creativity or joy that humans could relate to. Yet our God is the celebrating God who oozes creativity, joy, and humor. He loves stories. He loves telling stories with romance, adventure, twists and turns, intrigue, and decidedly very happy endings. He so loves narratives and storylines that He's created the best one of all for us on earth.

He's not just an efficient, "git 'er done" kind of God. If He were that, He would've just spoken one word that made the devil and all his minions disappear. God created Lucifer with one word, so He can make him disappear with one word. If He just needed the world to repent of their sins and acknowledge Him as Lord, He could accomplish that in ten seconds. He could shake the earth violently with a magnitude-10 earthquake while loudly booming His voice across the whole globe, "Citizens of earth, repent now!" It would work. Once, when I asked God about that idea, He explained to me that He would receive no glory from scaring the world into submission. It's not His script, because it's not the way He functions. He's a master story writer and storyteller. In God's master script, He wins based on His love and kindness, and not just by His overwhelming power. He can pull the trump card of His overwhelming power at any juncture. He's extremely patient and longsuffering and has no problem riding the wave of the seeming uncertainty that's a part of most great stories, in order to thoroughly relish the over-the-top ending He has planned.

A great ending must always have a great villain, a great romance, a great adventure, great plot twists, and even a great uncertainty leading up to the great ending. The reason we'll generally go to see a movie like that is that we have confidence in a director who will make sure we leave excited about how good triumphed over evil, how the romance played out, how the world was saved, and so on. We're wired to like this kind of story because we're made in God's image. He's the Master Director, and this story of His won't end with a whimper but with a bang that's unparalleled in history and only dreamt of in Hollywood. It's our confidence in His directing skills that allow us to enjoy the script, even when it's harrowing at times.

I'll admit that I have a problem with the books and movie series called *Left Behind*, which champion the rapture as the ultimate hope and narrative. To me, it rips off God and belittles His majestic capabilities. It's a narrative that diminishes the power of His love and overly exhibits the power of His judgment. Yes, He's definitely all-powerful—probably infinitely more powerful than we've ever realized.

The flood is the perfect example of a rare time in history when He gave vent to just a drop of His judgment capabilities—and the whole earth died, with the exception of eight people. But we must remember that He then set the rainbow in the sky, promising, "I'll never do that again, no matter how bad you get. I'll always find another way to get things done." Jesus was ultimately the "other way," and He didn't die a gruesome death, shed God's blood on earth, and send the Holy Spirit to us just so that God would have to resort to overwhelming force again. He has clearly announced that love is His greatest power, attribute, and essence—and He's going to prove it beyond our wildest imaginations. *"Love never fails"* (1 Corinthians 13:8)! Judgment can fail. Lucifer was judged, but it didn't change his heart. The world has experienced judgments, and, generally speaking, it hasn't changed hearts. Many nations have experienced severe earthquakes, hurricanes, plagues, and other judgments, yet none of them were judged into success. Only love never fails.

> *God doesn't just want people in Hollywood to get saved. He wants His narrative to invade all other narratives.*

The Era of Renaissance on the Mountain of Celebration/Arts

I've spent more time talking about God and His ways than about the upcoming changes in arts, entertainment, and sports. That is because once we understand *who* He is and especially *how* He is, it gives us a much better idea of our mission and assignment. God doesn't just want people in Hollywood to get saved. He wants His narrative to invade all other narratives. Shadows of His narrative have influenced Hollywood from its inception, which can be seen in the fact that most box office hits have carried redemptive elements and values in them. However, there's another level that's yet to take place. God wants to wow the world with His stories, His fashions, His music, His dance moves, His sporting skills, and every other conceivable demonstration of His creative joy—and He wants to do it all with His sons and daughters! It's not because He's an ego-maniac who needs attention. It's because He's so relational and wants all of us to know what He's like and enjoy relating to the real Him.

I believe God's already informed Satan of the central part of His script, saying, "Satan, you already know I can eliminate you and your lies about Me with My sheer power at any moment, but I'm going to defeat you with My kids who so know Me that they refuse to settle for anything less than the real Me and My better ways of doing everything. They will rise up on earth with all that I am in heaven. They have My very image stamped into their core, and it's only a matter of time before it comes out in all they do. Creation itself is groaning, awaiting for that core of who I am to be released through My clear-thinking sons and daughters. [See Romans 8:23.] I'm going to crush you, but I'm going to do it with My kids. They'll provide for Me what you could not—loyalty. I let you carry My beauty, My power, and My glory, but you wanted it all for yourself. They also carry My beauty, My power, and My glory, but they ultimately will not steal it from Me, as you did. You will deceive them for a while, but they'll eventually get who I am and what I want to do with them on the earth. When they fully awaken and arise, your false accusation about Me not being fair will be fully exposed, and My satisfaction and joy will be complete with My children by My side."

This manifestation of God's sons and daughters on the Mountain of Celebration/Arts has already begun and will steadily increase during this remarkable period of earth's history. It's a war with many battles, and there will be resistance, but the war will be won. Soon it will become one of the greatest joys of all for a son or daughter of the King to expand God's fame on the earth by demonstrating His greater beauty, power, and glory on this mountain where His glory will radiate as never before. Another one of the greatest joys on earth will be to have the ability to fund these unprecedented image-bearers of God. Many of the new ministers of wealth described in a previous chapter will be those assigned to be game changers in what gets funded in

Let's start

celebrating now!

Hollywood, and how it is funded. If you're one of those, you'll experience great joy as you realize what a privilege it is to be a part of funding God's master storyline of the ages. You can be a vital figure in advancing the nuanced knowledge of God into all the earth. As knowledge of Him advances, His timetable accelerates toward an even greater day of the Lord. Let's start celebrating now!

Celebration Is Important

It's difficult for many to conceive the idea of a God who celebrates while there's so much loss and suffering on the planet. We'd like to believe that in His presence there can be fullness of joy, but that He has to restrain Himself until everything changes. However, we need to realize that it's actually important that we learn to rejoice and celebrate now. Celebration is a great key for bringing the desired results of His kingdom—righteousness, peace, and joy. For all who believe in heaven, I think one of its strongest selling points is that there are no tears or sorrow there. (See Revelation 21:4.) We long for a day when we're in a place of joy, celebration, and no more crying. Yet that place already exists. Heaven is even more aware of the sad things that are taking place around the world than we are, yet heaven doesn't put celebrating on hold. Evidently, its inhabitants have some perspective that we don't that causes joy in those who can see the whole picture.

We're invited into that celebration and joy now, by faith. God is a God who simultaneously weeps with those who weep and still finds the joy in everything. It seems contradictory to us as humans, but we must yield to His complete image in us and embrace both aspects of who He is. Our entire life on earth is in some way a testing ground for future promotion. Life here is about enduring and pressing through. But, even in the midst of this reality, it's the very Mountain of Celebration/Arts that gives us a taste of courage, splendor, and glory that strengthens us to be all we are called to be in this life. We don't want to be excessively given to pleasure, but we do want to be a celebrating people whose joy overrides whatever test we're experiencing. If you have a call to this mountain, then you have the great privilege of being someone who displays the face of a celebrating God. It's not the only thing He does, but it's sewn into everything He does and everything He is. Rise up, rise up, you celebrating ones!

Twelve

GETTING IN SYNCH
WITH GOD

No matter what your race, culture, or nationality, God is restoring the destiny of your city and your nation. He is doing this *with* His kids, not independently of them. Like the conductor of a symphony orchestra, He's producing a restoration soundtrack throughout the nations of the earth—with many instruments simultaneously harmonizing under His supernatural direction. As the Age of Renaissance progresses, each nation, like the different sections of an orchestra, will contribute its own sound. One nation will be like the percussion section, one like the strings section, one like the woodwind section, and so forth. Not only that, but as each of us allows God to bring restoration through our individual lives, we will discover our ability to contribute our own unique sound to the whole, just as individual musicians come together to play in the various sections that make up the whole symphony. God is the Master Conductor, and no matter how torn and tattered your life or hopes, He's looking for reasons and even excuses to make your personal life a beautiful work of art. As your life, your city, and your nation begin to carry His glory, the awe of it all is going to fill the earth.

The years leading up to 2050 will be unprecedented in the advancement of God's majestic plan of restoration. To the degree that we understand what He's doing and cooperate with it, we will accelerate this advancement. God is not motivated or driven by earthly time frames. He's extremely patient with the fulfillment of His masterpiece plan because He's all about making it reflect maximum glory. Because of this, it's difficult for us to put exact timing and dates to specific areas of breakthrough in culture. As sons and daughters of God arise and express in a multitude of ways His correct narrative, His character, His beauty, His power, and His love, every temporal dynamic and time consideration will yield. Something that would normally take ten or even a hundred years to accomplish might take just a day. Meanwhile, certain aspects of the Era of Renaissance could take one full generation or ten generations to accomplish. Eschatology-wise, we know that we are currently in the defining "third day" of the last days, but this gives us hundreds of years of leeway. I believe that if we fully embrace God's plan, we can greatly hasten the fulfillment of His kingdom objectives on earth.

The Amazing Patience of God

Even as we seek to hasten matters, it's important for us to be reminded of the amazing patience of our God. This particular quality of God is one that we are grossly out of touch with—but its significance cannot be overemphasized. Because the church often overlooks this aspect of His character, many Christians have predicted that the United States—and even the whole world—is about to be consumed by God's "holy" judgments due to its sin. Yet, with the Lord, a day is like a thousand years, and a thousand years is like a day. (See 2 Peter 3:8.) The extent of His patience is beyond anything we can comprehend in our mental grid (sometimes, to our chagrin!). Let me explain further.

Hopefully, all of us would agree that practices like polygamy and slave-holding are totally outside the clearly expressed will of God. No minister today who would either preach in support of these practices or participate in them would be considered anything other than a heretic or a cult leader. However, we see that God's best friends in the Old Testament, Abraham and

> *The extent of His patience is beyond anything we can comprehend in our mental grid.*

David, were polygamists and seemingly slaveholders, as well. After I realized this fact, it bothered me greatly for some time. Then I asked the Lord about Abraham, saying, "Lord, You actually walked and talked with Abraham. You showed him the stars of the sky and the sand of the shore and told him that his descendants would be as numberless as they are. (See, for example, Genesis 22:17.) Since You were already talking to him, why didn't You just add, 'Hey, Abe, *one wife* only!' Wouldn't that have been wise? There might even be peace in the Middle East now if You had done that. So, why didn't You just tell him?" His clear response to me was this: "Because I was not working on that then." I inquired similarly about David. I didn't understand how or why God wouldn't just tell someone who loved to "*behold the beauty of the LORD*" (Psalm 27:4) and "ascend His holy mountain" (see

Psalm 24:3) that polygamy and slavery were not acceptable. Again, the Lord said, "I wasn't working on that then."

The Lord went on to show me that He is a very patient God and that He knows what kind of instruction is "age-appropriate" for society. I began to understand why the God of the Old Testament seemed to be different from the Father God who is revealed to us in the New Testament by Jesus. God is able to look at society itself and know what spiritual lessons are appropriate to teach people at any given time. The earlier accounts from the Old Testament present us with a God who understands He is dealing with a "two-year-old" society. Any parent who has raised kids knows that you don't sit down with your two-year-old to talk with him or her about the deep things of life. You don't discuss profound heart issues or explain all the great options in life that will be coming to him or her. Instead, with a two-year-old, you have to hand out a lot of "No's"—"No, you may not have some more ice cream"; "No, you may not stay up after your bedtime"; "No, you may not spit your food onto the floor"; "No, you may not jump off of that chair"—as well as "Don'ts"—"Don't pull your sister's hair"; "Don't run into the street in front of cars"; "Don't put your finger into the electric socket"; "Don't play with matches"—and so on, and so on. When a child is two years old, the focus is on keeping him or her alive today so that you can have those deeper conversations and relational connections in the future. So, early on, God was just trying to keep society alive; thus, all His instructions and commandments were for that purpose. Similar to how parents of young children might come across to others as very negative and rules-obsessed because they constantly need to correct and protect their children, so our perception of God from the Old Testament is often skewed because we do not properly understand that He was dealing with very childish people, spiritually speaking. None of the people who lived under the old covenant had a personal relationship with Jesus Christ, nor did they have the Holy Spirit dwelling inside them and doing the work of conviction and instruction. It is really hard to imagine such a world.

By New Testament days, God's best friends from the Old Testament would not even have qualified for church leadership! Paul the apostle laid out the new standard—any man who wished to be a church leader needed to be *"the husband of **one** wife"* (Titus 1:6). Interestingly, no new written set of laws was given in between the two Testaments, yet somehow much of society was aware that having only one wife was the standard. By this point, society had matured to about the level of a twelve-year-old. However, even Paul was still saying things like, "If you are a slave, serve your master well," and "If you own slaves, treat them right." (See Ephesians 6:5–9.) If Paul were to show up preaching that stuff now, he would be run out of town by any of 30,000-plus Christian denominations that currently exist. Furthermore, he would not be received by our society. Society itself has grown up into enough of an understanding of God's knowledge that polygamy and slavery have been almost completely rejected, a fact that I will talk more about shortly. Knowledge of God's ways is progressively filling the earth, even though many people don't realize that this knowledge comes from Him.

> *Knowledge of God's ways is progressively filling the earth, even though many people don't realize that this knowledge comes from Him.*

It is also quite apparent that sexism was still quite prevalent in New Testament times, despite the gender-inclusive example that Jesus Himself set. Mary and Martha frequently interacted with Him and were among His close friends. Yet, when the gospel recorders wrote about Jesus and His ministry, they were more likely to mention the male figures by name, while the women were referred to in general terms. They would write about what happened to Zacchaeus and

Nicodemus but then talk about *"a woman who had a flow of blood"* (Matthew 9:20) or *"a woman of Samaria"* (John 4:7). They were still figuring out that Jesus viewed women as equal to men in value and call. Even today, sexism is more likely to occur in the church than in our society. This is an example of how the knowledge of God can advance in the general culture beyond the point where it has advanced in the church.

The point of all this is to illustrate the incredible patience of God. From Genesis 2:24, the standard was laid out that a man leaves his father and mother and is joined to his (one) wife, and they become one flesh. God didn't include this standard in the Ten Commandments but waited for man to connect the dots and figure it out. Neither was slavery or sexism or racism banned in the Ten Commandments. God instructed us on these matters in other ways in the Scriptures, and He has had the patience to let us figure out what He did not specifically command. Because of the progressive "growing up" of society, it is now a reality that the average citizen on earth has an understanding of certain rights and wrongs that even God's closest pals had not yet figured out in the early days of the Old Testament.

Therefore, as we progress in these Renaissance days, it becomes imperative that we learn to synchronize what we think God should be working on in society with what He is actually working on. We can be overzealous about matters that He has not yet placed on His "Do next" list, making us out of synch with the unfolding of His grace in the world. I believe that much of the church in America is in that overzealous place right now. For instance, many believers are sure that God is barely restraining Himself from commanding fire and brimstone to fall on the gay community, because we wrongly perceive that such judgment is His next priority. I believe that He is much more concerned about the lack of unconditional love among His children than whether society gets it clear that "being gay" is wrong. The Pharisees of Jesus' day had the same clash with Jesus and His priorities for their time in history. They hated the fact that He was a "friend of sinners." (See, for example, Luke 7:34.) He wasn't just a *Minister to* sinners; He was a *Friend of* sinners. You don't become a Friend of sinners by continually telling them about their sin—and Jesus' lack of denunciation of their wrongdoing is what really bothered the Pharisees. They told Jesus, in effect, "It looks like You are condoning sin. You hang out with alcoholics, pimps, prostitutes, and other sinners—how are they going to know that what they are doing is wrong if You keep just hanging out with them and making them feel comfortable?"

It seems that, at one point, the Pharisees set up a woman to be caught "in the act" of adultery and brought her to Jesus so that He would have to make a clear declaration about His "stance on sin" (Pharisees, then and now, always want to know your stance on sin). They laid a trap for this Friend of sinners, thinking that He would have no choice but to say, "Yes, she is guilty under the law; let her be stoned." The hypocrisy of the Pharisees is of course grossly apparent in the fact that the man who had committed adultery with the woman was not also brought into the scene for condemnation. Perhaps he had been in on the setup.

Jesus refused to be pressured regarding His stance on sin because He realized that a woman's heart was at risk, and she had been publicly shamed. So, He said, "*He who is without sin among you, let him throw a stone at her first*" (John 8:7). Then He began writing something on the ground—perhaps He was writing the various sins of those who had gathered to exert their "holiness zeal." One by one, they scattered until no one was left, and Jesus said, "*Woman, where are those accusers of yours? Has no one condemned you?*" (verse 10). She answered, "*No one, Lord*" (verse 11). Jesus then followed up with a statement that was shocking, considering He was the God who actually wrote the Ten Commandments the Pharisees had wanted to stone her with: "*Neither do I condemn you; go and sin no more*" (verse 11).

Wow, do you see the patience of God in this account? He never condoned adultery; however, the most important thing was not that this woman understand that adultery was wrong. It was more important for her to see a religious leader driving off all her malicious accusers; and then, only after those accusers had been driven away, to have Him instruct her that what she had been doing was not God's will for her. Jesus first ministered unconditional love to the woman by saying, *"Neither do I condemn you."* When He finally mentioned her sin, it wasn't in a speech or a lecture. Rather, it was in the context of an empowering statement about what she was capable of doing, now that she had encountered the unconditional love of God—through the One who was God in the flesh.

God knows that a high level of love demonstrated by the children of His household must come before there can be any focus on sinful behavior in society. Pointing our finger at the adulterer or the homosexual or the abortionist is always easier for us than growing in unconditional love. That is why the church keeps opting for the former—not only is it easier, but it also makes us feel better about ourselves and our own behavior.

> *Fortunately for us, God has patience with the church, just as He has with the world.*

Fortunately for us, God has patience with the church, just as He has with the world. The fact that He demonstrates patience doesn't mean He overlooks sin, only that He addresses matters in the appropriate order for the stage that society, the church, or an individual has attained. Isn't this the way God deals with us personally? He doesn't take on all our issues at one time; rather, He patiently deals with one matter at a time. Once we successfully resolve a certain matter that God has been working on with us for many years, we almost expect Him to suddenly zap us to heaven, similar to the way He translated Enoch to heaven. But to our surprise, He then tells us, "Okay, let's move on to the next thing." Enoch apparently had "issues" for about 365 years before he was taken (see Genesis 5:23–24), so we might have some issues to work through for a while, as well. This is why sin-consciousness is never the goal and why there is a danger when we refer only to fiery evangelists of old who carried that priority. Our goal must be sensitivity to the Holy Spirit, because He is amazing at knowing what is fitting for each stage of spiritual growth—whether of individuals, nations, or the world.

For example, it is plain to me that a significant signal from heaven was received by society about five years ago when, all of a sudden, everyone seemed to know that the sex slave trade was no longer acceptable for a society at our stage of development. Now everyone is aware of the issue, and many people are doing something to remove this cancer of society, whether they are believers or not. Not only is the church on it, but Hollywood is on it, star athletes are in on it, and the government is on it. The collective consciousness of society has been triggered by this specific revelation of the knowledge of God, and it is time to deal with this horrible reality. Additionally, at some point, the connection between pornography and the sex slave trade will be conclusively established, and then society will start rejecting pornography on a wide scale.

Evils such as slavery and pornography have always been wrong, but in His patience, God has let us connect the dots that He laid out in the Scriptures and that He has been communicating to society over generations. Note that, apart from any new commandment, the apostle Paul was led by the Holy Spirit to connect the dots of the Old Testament and to communicate to the church, "You know what? Polygamy has never been okay." More recently, the church and society have had similar moments in regard to the issues of slavery, sexism, and racism, and they rejected these sins not because someone clearly called them "sins" but because the love of God continued to be poured out on the world, and His ways began to be absorbed even by those who still rejected Him. In this Renaissance Era, we are all going to grow significantly in our knowledge of the nuances of God's character and of the ways in which He thinks and reasons. Every one of us has a role in properly revealing the beauty of who He is and how He is. But first, we have to begin by really seeing Him ourselves.

Find Your Place in God's Hope-filled Storyline

There is no greater pursuit than to see and know our God in a more intimate way. I encourage you to discover Him and champion Him! May this book serve as a personal catalyst to help you become further enraptured by who He is and what He's about to do. Be convinced of His hope-filled storyline and run to find your place in it. Heaven on earth awaits your participation. God thought of you in eternity and caused you to be born on earth in this generation for such a time as this. Again, no matter what your color, age, gender, level of education, amount of wealth, or status in life, God has given you something with which you can shine in a reflection of His glory. Moses had a stick. David had a stone. You've been given something specific that can be used to bring fame to God on earth and to display the truth about how good He is. There is some nuanced knowledge of who He is and how He is that you were designed to carry—the Isaiah 60 aspect of God's glory that He's given you to arise and shine with. May you discover that glory and rise like the noonday sun.

> *Heaven on earth awaits your participation.*

ABOUT JOHNNY AND ELIZABETH ENLOW

Johnny and Elizabeth Enlow have been married for twenty-nine years. They live in California and have four daughters: Promise, Justice, Grace, and Glory. Both Johnny and Elizabeth come from a rich spiritual heritage and grew up in Christian homes. Johnny was born and raised in Peru, South America, where his parents were missionaries for over fifty years. Elizabeth was born in Birmingham, Alabama, and lived most of her life in Atlanta. Before Johnny and Elizabeth married, he promised her that there were two things they would never do—become missionaries or become pastors. Of course, they ended up not only traveling all over the world speaking in churches, but also founding a church in Atlanta and serving as pastors there for over fourteen years.

In their early years of taking their friends and family members on short-term mission trips, Johnny and Elizabeth saw God use very ordinary people like themselves to heal many people—in body, mind, and spirit. But a frustration surfaced in Johnny that caused him to begin asking God questions about the cities and nations they were investing their time in. Even while they witnessed countless salvations and supernatural healings, nothing seemed to change the problems in the overall culture, which was often the reason so many people needed miracles to begin with. The more Johnny sought God's heart, the more God showed him how much He cares not only about individuals but also about all the influences that affect their lives. He discovered that the same God who wants to heal our bodies, minds, and spirits also desires to heal our cities and nations through transforming our culture. He began to understand that no matter where we live, the primary areas of our nation's culture—government, media, religion, family, education, economy, and arts/celebration—help to shape what we believe about ourselves and about God.

From those times of questioning came Johnny's first three books, *Who Me?!*, *The Seven Mountain Prophecy*, and *The Seven Mountain Mantle*. The more Johnny studied, wrote, and taught about the need to transform culture, the more he and Elizabeth realized their role was not only to awaken Christians to this new way of thinking but also to help those who may not feel close to God change their perspective of who they think He is and discover His true heart toward them. Johnny and Elizabeth coauthored the book *Rainbow God: The Seven Colors of Love* as an expression of their renewed understanding of God as Love, and all the ways He desires to show up in culture through those who are willing to believe that He cares and has the best way of solving our present problems in all areas of culture. Johnny's most recent book prior to *The Seven Mountain Renaissance* was *Becoming a Superhero: A Pocket Guide to a Life Like David*, a short but deep teaching about how David overcame issues familiar to every human—feelings of rejection and insignificance—which enabled him to access the supernatural destiny for his life.

The Enlows relocated from Atlanta to Los Angeles in 2013 in order to position themselves and their family for mentoring and impacting those with influence in the seven mountains. Some have asked, "Why California?" The Enlows believe that, for good or ill, California is the leading state in all areas of culture; therefore, they felt it was important to obey God's direction for them and geographically align themselves with the front edge of the exciting things God is doing there now and will be doing in the coming years. They know that it's more critical than ever to release a hopeful prophetic perspective from the West coast, and they consider it a privilege to align themselves with those who are contending for reformation there.

The Enlows sum up their vision and purpose in this way: to communicate in every way possible the profound yet simple reason we're all here on earth—to know the real God, to make the real God known, and to learn to love and be loved.

For more information, please go to www.johnnyandelizabeth.com.